GOD, GIVE US WINGS

Felicia Prekeris Brown

Hope is the thing with feathers
That perches in the soul,
And sings the tune—without the words,
And never stops at all

Emily Dickinson

Table of Contents

Dedication

This is a record of our family's experiences during the confusion and terrors of World War II in Europe. Our small nation, Lithuania, found itself a pawn between Hitler and Stalin. Survival was precarious. In 1944, the threat of deportation and death in Siberia thrust Father and Mother on a long road to self-exile, hoping to find a refuge that would offer a chance of a decent life to my sister Milda and me.

The events of those years are engraved in my memory because, throughout their lives, my parents and Milda would often talk to me about our journey, recalling the hardships and the miracles we experienced. While their memories were still fresh and powerful, I asked Mother and Father to set down in writing the core events during our flight from home. I tape-recorded their reflections about our lives from 1939 to 1952. I hoarded the letters, photographs, and documents that survived our long journey to a new and bountiful land. The oral and written stories of my parents and sister serve as the framework for this book.

Remembering our many miraculous escapes, Father and Mother often mused, "Why were we saved when so many perished? We did nothing outstanding in our lives to deserve it." As we aged, Milda and I also asked the same question. Did we survive so that, down the generations, some special person might be born? That is my belief. Thus, with hope, love and faith, I pass the torch to Father's and Mother's grandchildren: Ray Lietuvninkas, Milda Leonard, and Algis Brown; and to their great-grandsons: Mitchell and Theodore Leonard, and Ugnius Byron Braun.

And to the great-granddaughter for whose existence I continue to hope: my dolls await her.

Acknowledgment

The first thing Americans notice about me is my unusual accent. "Where do you come from?" they ask. And soon I'm sharing bits and pieces of our family story. I have always had the intention of writing it down—someday. Time rolled on. Memories began to fade.

One day, our son-in-law, Bill Van Doorn, pointed out that I owed it to the family to record those searing events of long ago. I promised I would, but the task seemed overwhelming.

Then I met a friend who writes as effortlessly as others breathe: Evelyn Cole Turrill. "You must write it down," she said. "It's a piece of history that should not be lost." Not so easy for me! It took her months of prodding to get me going, and bribes of delicious home-cooked meals to keep me staying on task. This book owes much to her enthusiasm, affection and persistent encouragement.

My parents and sister had left writings, tapes, and documents, but still many details of time and place were missing and needed research. I also wanted to verify how factual were the memories of our years in the displaced person camps, and Mother and Milda's work conditions in England. I am deeply obliged to Dieter Zoremba, city recorder and archivist in Blomberg, Germany, for making available to me documents from the years 1945–1949, which greatly enriched my understanding. Many thanks also to my fellow DPs from Blomberg, Judita Matulionis Čuplinskas, Mrs. Tamulaitis, and Mr. Mažeika, whose recollections added an extra dimension to the story. I am especially grateful to Hilda Simanavičius for her vivid, personal memories of Mother and Milda at work in England.

A big thank-you also to friends from the Lifelong Learners of the Central Coast, Carol Fulmer and Asta Hamann, who read the initial manuscript and offered reassurance and guidance: their confidence in me meant a great deal.

Special thanks to Todd Abel of the Arizona Southwest Incident Management Team for permission to use his wildfire cloud photograph for the cover. And I am profoundly grateful to my friend Marilyn Palermo, who used her keen artistic eye and professional skills to restore and enhance old photographs, and who overcame a mountain of obstacles to create the front cover of this book. I am in awe of her persistence, dedication, and generosity.

To my husband Lew Brown, I give a medal of merit for long-suffering patience, and unflagging emotional support plus a gold star for endless technology rescues.

To our son Algis—my heartfelt gratitude for undertaking the comprehensive editing of the manuscript, and for pushing me to relive and write down details of events I preferred to forget. Thanks, son, for your invaluable help. You inspired me to go the distance.

Felicia Prekeris Brown

CHAPTER 1:

The Troubles Begin

Mother had mettle and Mother had motive, but she was not in shape for running. Heart thumping like a jazz drum, gasping for air, she ignored the broken heel on her left shoe and rushed on, determined to reach her husband. *Does he know yet? What's going to happen? Dear God, what now?*

Minutes before, she had been trying on a new bra in her friend Lena's boutique for ladies' garments, notions, and accessories. Finding something that fit was not an easy task: Mother was endowed. She and Lena were cheerfully chattering about dresses and hats and hairstyles they would show off at Easter, less than three weeks away. Suddenly, the entrance door flew open and a woman rushed in, shouting in German, "*Frau Kondrat, wir sind noch einmal Deutsch!*" She kissed Lena heartily and flung herself out again. Lena looked stricken.

"What did she say?" asked Mother, who did not speak German. Instead of answering, Lena quickly turned on the radio. The announcer, his voice cracking with emotion, was reporting that Hitler had sailed into the Lithuanian port of Klaipėda, called *Memel* in German, and had declared that as of this day, March 23, 1939, "*Memelland*" was returned to Germany, and that all Lithuanians who had settled in the territory since 1923 would have to leave.

"What she said is that we're once again Germans," said Lena. "I sense trouble; we've got to warn our husbands. Hurry, your Felicius should know so he can prepare the other teachers."

Father was the principal of the Lithuanian elementary school in the small but lively town of Smalininkai, located in a region inhabited primarily by two ethnic groups. For Lithuanians, the area was known as "Lithuania Minor;" for Germans, as "Memelland." For centuries, it had been ruled by the kings of Prussia, then by German administrators. When, at the end of World War I, the Treaty of Versailles imposed severe punishment on Germany, this territory ended up annexed to Lithuania. Most of the inhabitants were ethnic Germans but Lithuanians constituted a large minority.

Mother's headlong rush to find Father ran into a human barrier. Strutting up the street toward her were several German infantry soldiers, rifles held high, shooting off volleys into the air. A flood of excited supporters waving the flags of Hitler's Third Reich, red with a black swastika, were pouring into the street, shouting *"Heil Hitler"* and whooping with joy to honor their great leader, the *Führer.* They enveloped Mother in their midst. By the time she managed to extricate herself, she saw down the street children and teachers running out of Father's school, some towards the celebrating crowd, others, silently, away.

She found Father in his office, listening to the radio. "Well, Stase," he said, "our days in paradise are over."

Place names significant to our family are shown in bold.

THE PREKERIS FAMILY, 1939

I, DALIA

In early 1939, I was two years old, a coddled, spoiled, stubborn toddler. My official birth date and birthplace are noted as February 7, 1937, Smalininkai, Lithuania. At the time of my birth, Lithuania was at peace with the world, and though the political situation in Europe was fraught with danger, for an elementary school principal and his wife the future looked rosy.

I came into the world on an icy cold, brilliantly sunny Sunday morning. I'm told that my first cry coincided with the ringing of church bells calling parishioners to Mass. The previous thirty hours had been a tough labor for my mother and a huge worry for my father. The relief was immense when I finally emerged, fat as a butterball, expressing strong lungs in a piercing soprano.

Father was so moved by the sun sparkling on the snow, the bells, and the call to church services, that he predicted I would lead a sunny, happy life, blessed with the proverbial luck of the "Sunday's Child." For insurance, my parents quickly agreed to name me Felicia (happy) and Dalia (destiny). Since my father's name was Felicijonas (Felicius for short), I was dedicated as primarily his to raise. However, the name "Felicia" was uncommon in 1937 Lithuania, so everyone called me Dalia.

I was born a mimic with an excellent auditory memory. In 1939, at age two, I was an unstoppable chatterbox and an irrepressible singer. I was also precociously self-aware with a tender ego. I could not stand to be criticized, especially not by my beloved father. I did not trust strangers and would hide under the floor-length tablecloth if someone I had not met before came to visit. I was a torment to my sister Milda, who had been told never to scold me. I was sure of my own importance because my father always called me his "Beloved Sunshine," and my grandmother Ona treated me like a princess.

There was just one sorrow in my life: I did not have a lifelike baby-faced doll, and I longed for one obsessively.

MY SISTER, MILDA

In April of 1939, Milda turned ten years old. She was a gorgeous child with curly blond hair, a freckled snub nose, and eyes the color of blueberries. She was a very affectionate little girl with a smile that could melt your heart. She is the one who caused our family to come into being.

Some years previously, as Milda started first grade, she could not say enough good things to her mother about her teacher, Felicius Prekeris, a big teddy bear of a man who, once lessons were done, could be persuaded to stay and tell the children stories while the girls tried to braid his hair and the boys climbed all over him as if he were a tree. He was kind and generous. If the class had studied hard and behaved well, he would reward everyone with treats.

Milda at age six, 1935.

Milda was totally smitten by him and clung to him like a burr. She had not been lucky in the biological father that the fates had given her. One day she confided to her teacher, "I don't have a daddy anymore; would you be my new daddy?" Thanks to her persistent matchmaking, Felicius married her mother, Stasė, in 1936, and Milda's wish was granted.

Milda was born with an unquenchable talent for finding joy no matter where she was, even if Mother was severe with her and often unfair, even if I was a demanding brat and an annoyance to her. She was gregarious and genuinely interested in what everyone was doing. Mother called it being nosy.

From a very early age Milda would often disappear, "gone visiting" an entire day at the cost of getting spanked by Mother when she returned. As a child, she was completely unselfconscious and criticism did not stick or hurt her pride. "Scolding her is like throwing peas against a wall," Mother would complain. Milda's sunny and trusting nature did not make it easy for her to deal with the nightmarish war that was brewing in Europe.

MY MOTHER, STASĖ

In 1939, Mother was thirty-three years old. She was five feet four inches tall, with pleasing features, light brown hair, dark blue eyes, and a curvaceous figure. Men found her attractive, but she mistrusted them. Until she married Father, her life had been largely a depressing struggle. She had learned to always expect the worst, to make few long-range plans because life would overturn them, to cling to the few accepted truths she believed she could trust. She thought in black and white and in stereotypes. She disdained certain groups, such as the traditional enemies of Lithuania, Poles and Russians, but she appreciated many individuals who belonged to them.

She was sociable and generous but choosy in her friendships. She never forgot or forgave a slight. She clung to pride but could give it up when the survival of her family required it. She was a pragmatist. In the struggles to come, without her energy and practicality we would have perished, even though many of our tribulations were due to her stubborn refusal to accept those facts which did not conform to her wishes, beliefs, or opinions.

Mother was born in the small village of Jūžintai, in northeast Lithuania, on July 10, 1906. Her parents, Jonas and Ona Vaikutis, were both fine singers, and Jonas served as the organist in the big parish church. They had some land, which they farmed for essentials, they raised a few animals for food, and Ona, a much-admired weaver, earned extra income producing fine linen cloth for the rich landowners in the area.

Life in rural Lithuania, which until the end of World War I suffered under the rule of Tsarist Russia, was bitterly hard. When Mother was a toddler, three of her sisters died within hours of each other from diphtheria. There were no doctors for miles; the nearest one was some twenty miles away. When his little ones developed the characteristic, strangling cough of diphtheria, Jonas harnessed a horse and wagon and hurried as fast as he could over the rutted country lanes to find the doctor, hoping to get help in time to save them.

He found the doctor ready to leave his house, a gun slung over the shoulder. Jonas begged him, literally on bended knee, to come save his children, but the doctor refused. He was on his way to a hunting party. "I'm not going to disappoint my friends for some peasant's spawn," he sneered—words engraved on my grandfather's memory and, from him, on Mother's. Of the ten or twelve children that Ona bore, only three survived to adulthood: the eldest daughter, a son, and my mother.

My grandmother Ona was not a warm, affectionate mother, though she was a most tender grandmother to Milda and me. Mother reminisced that she could not remember being hugged or allowed to sit on her mother's lap. She recalled Ona saying that it was no use getting attached to your children because you suffered too much when they died. Lacking the example in her own life, Mother was not openly affectionate with Milda or me except when we were sick or in danger. Much later, like her own mother Ona, she was a kind and loving grandmother.

From Mother's reminiscences, it is clear that she adored Ona. She courted her love the best she knew how, which was to take up as many jobs as she could to lighten her burdens, including many that should have been done by her older brother Jurgis. Mother thought him selfish and lazy, and she blamed him for the miseries of her childhood.

Mother, aged 13, and Jurgis, both wearing clothing woven and hand sewn by their mother Ona.

When Jurgis was about eleven or twelve, an unusually fierce wind caught him outside in the field, lifted him from the ground, and carried him some distance before dumping him into a bush, shocked but otherwise unhurt. From then on, his parents considered him a miracle child who had survived abduction by dark forces. Jurgis could do no wrong and very little was required of him. From his boyhood, Jurgis spent much time with his father in the village pub, sharing in the pastime of singing and storytelling at which both excelled, learning to gamble and "drink like a man."

Grandpa Jonas died in early 1919, at fifty-five years of age, probably from lingering effects of the Spanish flu. At his death, Mother was twelve. Jurgis, who was twenty-one, proceeded to drink and gamble away house, land and animals. Through a relative, he managed to get a job as signalman and station keeper for the Lithuanian railways. He married, and Mother and Ona went to live with the young couple.

That was the end of Mother's formal schooling. She was the unpaid servant in the household and nanny to the first-born, Vytas. Later, Jurgis decided that Mother would learn to transmit and receive Morse code signals for the railroad telegraph. In 1923, when she was seventeen and old enough to get a work permit, Jurgis sent her away to make it on her own at the west end of the country, the area known as "Lithuania Minor." This territory had just come into possession of Lithuania, and had many jobs available. The little town of Pagėgiai became her home.

When she was nineteen, Mother was coerced into marrying Jonas Balčiūnas, a fellow employee at the railroad station. He was a bully, one of those men who enjoy making others suffer. He frightened and repelled her. He blackmailed her into marriage by threatening that he would ruin her reputation: he would tell everyone at work and in town that she was sleeping with him for money, that she was no better than a whore. Mother could not imagine what to do. If he made good his threat and others believed him, she would become the butt of everyone's derision, she would lose her job and her future would be hopeless. She thought her only choices were suicide or marriage to Jonas. She was not ready to die.

Mother did not have a champion to stand up to this brute. Deprived of options, she married Jonas. He enjoyed having a slave whom he could control and abuse. Some years later, much against her will, he got her pregnant, and Milda, my sister, was born on April 24, 1929, when Mother was twenty-two. Jonas became even more unbearable, demanding all of Mother's attention, a rival to his own child. Mother was concerned he would hurt Milda, which finally gave her the courage to leave him.

Everyone at work knew what a nasty character he had and how he enjoyed inventing gossip and making trouble for others. Nobody openly opposed him, fearing his vicious tongue, but they helped Mother on the sly. She easily received a transfer to another railroad station in Kaišiadorys, located in the center of Lithuania proper. It was not an easy life for her, because the narrow-minded housewives in town ostracized those who did not toe the strict line of traditional and religious marriage. How dared she live apart from her husband? They put up with theirs, didn't they?

Then, in 1935, Mother met Milda's teacher and her life changed completely.

MY FATHER, FELICIUS

In 1939, my father was thirty-one years old. Everyone looked up to him and wanted to have him as a friend. Perhaps the attraction flowed from an inborn font of charisma, or perhaps it was because, at six feet four inches and a solid two hundred pounds, he stood out like a Goliath among a crowd of Davids who felt compelled to check him out. He had brown wavy hair and merry blue-gray eyes, and women found him irresistible, though he was always the gentleman with them.

Father was sociable, fun loving, perpetually optimistic, easygoing, tolerant, and forgiving. He was also committed to an old-fashioned, romantic idealism that kept him from looking out for his own interests— or those of his family. He loved all the arts, especially poetry. Although he was intellectually extremely bright, with a photographic memory, he did not have the personality to do well in times of conflict and want. He did not think in practical terms and could not take advantage of others. It was his charm and friendliness that contributed to our survival during the war.

Father was born on May 18, 1908, in Šeduva, a well-established little town in central Lithuania. He was the youngest of the seven surviving children, four sons and three daughters, of Boleslovas and Aleksandra Prekeris. The Prekerises were "boyars," old nobility who maintained their special privileges even though, over the generations, they had lost their landholdings. The title of "boyar" had its uses while Lithuania remained under the rule of Tsarist Russia. Until the overthrow of the Tsar by the Bolshevik revolution of 1917, Father and his siblings gleefully enjoyed immunity from punishment in school.

At the time of Father's birth, grandmother Aleksandra was forty-six years old and tired of motherhood, so in many ways he was left to raise himself, and could have developed into a little hellion. His older sisters spoiled him. There was something in his nature, however, that always chose the "higher" path: he was religious and idealistic and for some years contemplated becoming a priest.

The majority of the boyars in Lithuania considered themselves ethnically Polish, but grandfather Boleslovas instilled in his seven children that they were pure Lithuanians. At home among themselves, the family spoke Polish, but used Lithuanian with the town residents. Until 1917, school was taught both in Russian and Lithuanian, so my father was trilingual before he was ten years old. Then, in late adolescence, he fell under the spell of a young female German teacher who transmitted to him her love of romantic poetry. "By the time I was in my teens, I was responsible for plowing our fields and mowing hay," reminisced Father. "The hours of work flew by more quickly while I recited to myself poems by Schiller, Goethe, and Heine in the original German. So I never forgot them."

Grandfather had a modest farm, raised animals to feed the family, and worked as the manager of a lumber mill in the area. World War I and Poland's attack on Lithuania in 1920 created chaos for the family. The three older sons were drafted to perform military service for the Russians during the war, and then later were conscripted to fight for the newly independent Lithuania against the invasion from Poland.

At the age of fourteen, Father was the only male still at home to help his father, by then already sixty-four years old, with all of the work on the farm. His formal schooling ended, but not his lust for knowledge. He continued to study on his own, with encouragement from his former teachers. He passed the national high school equivalency examination and was accepted at the Teacher's College of Šiauliai.

In 1930, on graduation, Father's first assignment was to establish an elementary school in a tiny village near Papilė in northern Lithuania. Classes for all four grades were held in a spare room offered by a local farmer. Father reminisced how bored he was there, with no one around who read literature or wanted to discuss ideas. However, he was young and energetic and liked children. He had joined the Lithuanian scouting movement while in college, and threw himself into organizing scouting groups in the village and surrounding hamlets. The little peasant children responded eagerly to all he did. The only criticism of his work that the school inspector noted was, "He is too lenient with his pupils."

Apparently, Father's superiors approved of his performance because two years later, in 1932, he was promoted to a much bigger elementary school in Kaišiadorys, a good-sized town where opportunities for cultural life were available. He was jubilant. His salary allowed him to rent decent rooms, buy decent clothes, and buy books—a lifelong passion.

In 1935, in his first-grade class, there was a sparkly little imp of a girl named Milda, who followed him around like his shadow. One day she confided, "I don't have a daddy any more; would you be my new daddy?"

What a proposition to make to a tenderhearted, romantic, poetry-quoting young fellow of twenty-seven! He met Mother, and her sad life story moved him deeply. He felt such pity for her, an attractive, shy, vulnerable woman forced to earn a living for herself and her child, subjected to disapproving gossip and pressure to go back to a vicious man. He felt himself called to be her protector, her knight in shining armor. True, the two didn't have much in common. To begin with, Mother had not even finished junior high school, which in those class-conscious days put her far beneath him. However, he noted that she read voraciously and did everything she could to improve herself.

What Father and Mother did have in common was a love of singing and acting, both activities abundantly available in those years in every town in Lithuania. People had to make their own fun in the days before television. So their contacts were frequent, and soon Father proposed and Mother accepted. But they faced a major difficulty: Mother already had a husband, and there was no divorce in Catholic-dominated Lithuania.

Because of the vagaries of history, resulting in changing borders and uneven legal systems, a solution presented itself. The section of Lithuania called "Lithuania Minor" had been ruled from Prussia and was predominantly Lutheran. It retained many of its old laws and continued to grant divorces under certain conditions. Having worked in Pagėgiai, a town in the region, Mother was somewhat familiar with the civil rights there. To become a "resident" of Lithuania Minor again, she would have to live in the region for six months. But not in Pagėgiai: her husband still lived there. She decided to stay with friends in Smalininkai, a charming little town on the banks of the Nemunas River.

By a lucky coincidence, Father was assigned to run the Lithuanian elementary school in Smalininkai. No sooner was the divorce granted than my parents were married at a civil registry in town, despite the hysterical objections of Father's very traditional family. His proud parents were planning a much more suitable match for him with a well-to-do young woman from his town. That the youngest son of the noble Prekeris family would marry a divorcée with a ready-made child—a divorcée who grew up a barely literate peasant of an insignificant family in some godforsaken backward village—was a terrible shock to them. So who could have predicted that within a year, Mother would be their favorite daughter-in-law?

Mother and Father in 1936, shortly after their wedding.

For over a century, Smalininkai, known as "Schmalleningken" to the local majority, had been a part of German Memelland, ruled from East Prussia, but a large proportion of its residents came from Lithuanian ancestry. In 1923, when this area, renamed "Lithuania Minor," was annexed to Lithuania proper, it was granted significant autonomy. Its German residents, who were in the majority, prevented the use of the Lithuanian language in the territory's public schools. In 1930, Smalininkai had opened a private school funded by donors interested in renewing Lithuanian patriotism among the "*Lietuvninkai*," the name given to German citizens of Lithuanian ancestry. By 1937, there were five teachers at this private school, and Father was to be the school principal.

From the stories told by my parents, the happiest days of their life together were in Smalininkai. It is clear from the reminiscences of his fellow teachers and his pupils that Father loved his work and was honored and cherished not only by everyone in the school, both teachers and pupils, but by the parents and the residents of the town as well, both Lithuanian and German. The school became the social and cultural center of the village, hosting dances and concerts, plays and lectures. Father often included visiting German speakers and choirs in an effort to maintain good relations.

Father and Mother enjoyed acting and helping arrange theatrical performances, but above all, they loved music. Mother was a fabulous singer. Father could play just about any instrument he touched except for wind instruments. In his younger years, he favored the violin above all others. I never fell asleep without a lullaby.

Smalininkai was an ideal place in which to live and raise children. It was a small town of about 2,000 residents, located on the imposing Nemunas River which formed the border between the German territory of East Prussia and Lithuania Minor. Smalininkai was always crowded with visitors, because all river traffic had to stop there for border control and payment of customs duties. The hotels, restaurants, shops, schools, and government offices that lined the principal street parallel to the river were of substantial brick construction, but winding up the slope were charming wooden houses with proud, white lace curtains, almost hidden among apple and plum trees, and covered in lilacs. One of these was our home.

Outdoor activities proliferated—the river was a source of much sport, and the surrounding pine and birch forests welcomed picnickers and mushrooming expeditions. A narrow-gauge train from Smalininkai made it easy to get to the bustling city of Tilsit (now Sovetsk) when the mood called for bright lights and fancier shopping.

It was never easy for Lithuania to survive between its pushy neighbors, Germany and Russia. In 1938, threatening rumbles multiplied from both sides, but my parents paid scant attention. They lived cocooned in happiness. Father and Mother remembered that life was perfect for our family for two joyful years, but by the end of 1938, they and everyone in Lithuania had to admit that something nasty was imminent. Hitler had annexed Austria and the Sudetenland, and the Soviet Union was arming itself heavily.

In January of 1939, realizing that a nation of three million did not stand a chance against Germany (which, with its annexations, had 79.5 million inhabitants), and even less of a chance against the Soviet Union (whose population numbered more than 170 million), the Lithuanian Parliament passed a law that would allow it to declare its neutrality, hoping to be left alone like Switzerland. But Switzerland held the world's money, and Lithuania? It had farm products. It should have known that nobody would pay any attention to its decrees.

On March 23, 1939, Hitler invaded. Smalininkai changed back to "Schmalleningken," and Lithuanians were ordered to get out. "*Raus!*" We were cast out of Eden.

CHAPTER 2:

The Red Dragon
Takes Over

Wn hen Hitler re-annexed Memelland to the expanding territories of the Third Reich, he openly broke the terms of the Treaty of Versailles which had ended World War I. By March of 1939, he was confident that nobody would object strongly enough to cause him concern. Nobody did. Hitler's orders were for all Lithuanians, except spouses of German citizens, to leave the area forthwith. Father's school was shuttered.

People do not cope well when given only a few days to uproot their lives. Mother and Father passed through disbelief, denial, depression, and ended in anger. At least anger gave them energy to act. Milda, who was almost ten, was in mourning because she had to leave her friends.

The order to move out affected thousands. Chaos ensued. Mother and Father joined the frantic crowds looking for transport to get us, and our possessions, out of Smalininkai. Local friends helped. The accumulated household goods were taken by cart across the Memelland–Lithuanian border, to be stored in a barn on a farm in Jurbarkas.

Father found transportation for the four of us on an overloaded steamboat churning up the Nemunas to the city of Kaunas. I have a vivid memory of the noisy, throbbing paddlewheels, which scared me silly and gave me nightmares for weeks. My anxious parents wondered what would happen to us once we reached Kaunas.

Because Poland had seized our capital city, Vilnius, and its territories in 1920, in 1939 Kaunas was the seat of Lithuania's government and the central clearing point for civil service jobs—including teaching. Governmental agencies were swamped with refugees from Memelland needing food and shelter, and civil servants whose assignments had disappeared with Hitler's takeover. Father had to go to Kaunas to present a final report to the Ministry of Education concerning the accomplishments and the fate of his school in Smalininkai and to hand over its records. He hoped the authorities would quickly assign him to another school.

The flood of people who lost their homes to Hitler and streamed into Kaunas meant that it was almost impossible to find any space to rent. Father was counting on his two older brothers, Benediktas and Karolis, to shelter us until he was posted elsewhere. They lived in Kaunas, and were both well off by our standards. But both had difficult wives who bristled like threatened hedgehogs at the prospect of sharing their space with the four of us.

The Ministry of Education placed Father in an administrative job in Kaunas while it worked to find new postings for all the teachers exiled from Lithuania Minor. In those days, a teacher's salary was sufficient to provide a decent living for a small family. Mother did not have to work. Remembering that period, she told me, "Our biggest worry was to find a room or two to live in. You were two years old and a real obstacle. Every rentable space had waiting lines, and landlords didn't want children whose noise would disturb others."

Fortunately, my "Sunday's Child" luck came to the rescue. One potential landlady seemed to be wavering whether to refuse or accept us. "What if her crying and yelling annoy my other renters?" she asked, looking at me dubiously.

Mother began to reassure her about my quiet ways, so I boldly intervened with, "I am a quiet little girl, I know Our Father and Hail Mary, I don't scream or run indoors, and I only sing when asked."

This unexpected, long narrative from a two-year-old so flustered the landlady that she blurted out, "So sing something!" I did, and won her over. Mother said that after three ditties sung in perfect tune, the landlady was too amused

Milda at age 10, and I at age 2, summer of 1939.

to see me as a problem for the others in her house. In fact, I soon became everyone's pet, as did my sociable sister.

Summer was passing. While Mother and Father worried about his next teaching assignment, in August 1939, Stalin and Hitler negotiated the Molotov–Ribbentrop Pact, officially presented to the world as a German–Soviet Friendship Treaty, a typical non-aggression pact. However, it also contained a "Secret Additional Protocol" dividing Eastern and Central Europe into so-called "spheres of influence." By spheres of influence, Hitler and Stalin both intended outright annexation, but between themselves they coyly termed the plan a "territorial and political rearrangement." Initially, Hitler wanted to keep Lithuania because of its ties with Memelland. Subsequent amendments to the Secret Protocol re-assigned it to the Soviets.

For the time being, Stalin wished to dissemble his real aims, so for the sake of good propaganda home and abroad, in October of 1939, his envoys forced Lithuania to sign a Soviet–Lithuanian Mutual Assistance Treaty. It allowed the Soviets to bring in about 20,000 heavily armed troops to be stationed at several bases in Lithuania—not a popular move among the populace. To lessen the general objection to the arrival of Russian soldiers and tanks on its territory, the Soviets proclaimed their good-will and generosity by taking Vilnius and part of its region away from Poland and returning it to Lithuania.

Many Lithuanians were not fooled. They did not trust the Soviets. The cost of regaining Vilnius was too high. Their opinion of the proceedings was, *Vilnius mūsų, o mes rusų*—Vilnius belongs to us; we belong to the Russians. People foresaw that 20,000 troops were just the first installment.

Stalin delayed occupying the country because his first goal was to conquer Finland. In the meantime, the Lithuanian government continued to work under the illusion of independence. It urged celebrations to welcome Vilnius back into our land, and quickly set up administrative oversight to promote its rapid reintegration into Lithuania. High near the top of its priority list, the government placed the re-establishment in Vilnius of Lithuanian language schools, which were suppressed under Polish occupation.

When assignments were handed out, my idealistic father volunteered to run a school for the retarded, a posting that did not carry much distinction. Mother was not well pleased. Like many in Lithuania, she thought retardation was in some way an infectious disease. Was it his lucky star that prompted Father's choice? Because when the Soviets did make their move and occupied Lithuania, his relative lack of prestige working with the developmentally disabled helped Father survive.

In autumn of 1939, we moved to Vilnius, and rented three small rooms in an old rickety wooden house near the Church of the Bonifratres. We lived upstairs, and another family, the Gudliauskases, downstairs. They had a baby boy and a little girl my age who shared my name, Dalia. She was my First Best Friend. The grown-ups had to worry about the political situation—we two were happy to play all day. There was an airy gazebo in the back yard that became our very own fairy castle. To me, life was wonderful because my friend Dalia shared her doll with me. And Milda was happy once again, delighting in her new school, which had so many more students for her to turn into friends.

The year 1940 began with Lithuania still officially free. The Soviets still had battalions stationed on Lithuanian territory, but had been too preoccupied to complete the ultimate takeover. They were not having an easy time fighting the Winter War in Finland. The winter of 1939–1940 was one of the coldest recorded in northern Europe. The Soviets suffered heavy losses because they had not amassed enough warm clothing for their troops, who were freezing to death by the thousands. At the end of March 1940, Finland and the USSR signed a peace treaty.

Now the Soviets could concentrate on implementing the Molotov–Ribbentrop agreement. Their goal was to add the three Baltic countries, Estonia, Latvia, and Lithuania, to the Union of Soviet Socialist Republics. These three countries, facing the Baltic Sea, had ice-free harbors that the Soviets craved for their Navy. Stalin held off for some months, waiting for the perfect time when France and England would be too distracted to pay attention to his activities. Those powers were frantic about Hitler's *Wehrmacht*—armed forces, who were rampaging closer to home. In April 1940, Hitler had invaded Denmark and Norway; on May 10th, Nazi troops entered Holland, Luxembourg and Belgium; and on May 12th they were in France.

The first step Stalin's minions took in Lithuania was to wave their fists at our envoys in protest against the supposed kidnapping and killing by Lithuanians of soldiers from the five Soviet bases. *You have broken the Soviet–Lithuanian Mutual Assistance Treaty! You will pay for this treachery!* There actually were no kidnappings. Some soldiers had indulged in too much alcohol and got into fatal accidents. Others had deserted their posts for a more prosperous life integrated into Lithuanian society.

One of our relatives harbored such a soldier, whose origins were from the Ukraine, a country that Stalin had abused beyond all bounds. He did not want to serve the communists. One day he disappeared, tracked down by his Soviet mates and executed as a deserter. They blamed his death on Lithuanians.

Against the Soviet accusations, explanations by the Lithuanian government were futile. The Soviet military gave an ultimatum to surrender or fight. What could be done against an overwhelming foe? Wipe out the entire nation? Our government surrendered.

Mother and Father spoke often about the tragic day of June 15, 1940, making sure that Milda and I would always remember the end of the Lithuania they knew.

As mentioned, Vilnius had been forcibly torn from Lithuania twenty years previously, and held under Polish rule. Now that it was again a part of Lithuania, everyone who could do so made a pilgrimage to the beloved city that our revered Grand Duke Gediminas had established as the capital of our country in 1323.

At the start of summer vacation in June 1940, when schools in the city stood empty and available as shelter, a joyous influx of students from all corners of Lithuania, especially from the villages, invaded Vilnius. To those born after World War I, Vilnius was a magical, legendary place that everyone wanted to experience.

One village teacher who brought his students for this purpose was Adomas Kaulius, Father's colleague from Smalininkai, who now taught at a small school in Žilinai. The trip had been planned long in advance. In mid-morning of Saturday, June 15, Adomas appeared at our apartment to announce that his group of boys was waiting for further directions at the Vilnius railroad station.

Father had arranged for a couple of classrooms in his school to serve as dormitories for visitors. The weather was perfect, so Mother and Milda volunteered to go with Adomas to the station, to show him and the boys the way to the school. I had been left for the day with the neighbors. Father stayed home temporarily—the political situation with the Soviets was at the breaking point, our Minister of Foreign

Affairs was in Moscow on Stalin's orders, and Father wanted to listen to the news on the radio before he joined the group to begin a tour of the city.

Mother remembered how thrilled the village boys were to be in Vilnius. They lined up two by two, and, singing marching songs which they had learned during scouting activities, strode off in formation—Milda, beaming, leading in front. Their heads turned constantly to absorb all the sights.

Adomas asked Milda to lead them on a short detour to pay their respects at the revered, miraculous icon of the Virgin Mary hanging above the one remaining sixteenth-century entry gate to the city. The Chapel of Our Lady of the Gate of Dawn is a place of worship both for Lithuanians and Poles; pilgrims kneel in the street to pray before the gold-encrusted painting. The boys knelt in awe for a minute, and then were ready to go. As they walked on, they were amazed at the number of churches and the variety of their architecture. "Can we go see that one? Can we go inside it?" they kept asking Adomas.

Arrived at their designated dorm, they filled the air with happy noise and commotion. They chose their spots on the floor for sleeping, ate a snack from the supplies they had brought with them, disposed of their backpacks on the benches, and then gathered, excited and eager for more adventures.

"Suddenly the door swung open," said Mother. "There stood Father, almost unrecognizable. His eyes dilated, his white face a mask of tragedy. The boys gasped in surprise and concern. Father got control of his voice. 'Goodbye Freedom. The Russian army has invaded; they are approaching Vilnius.'"

Adomas was aghast: what if the Soviets stopped train service? How would he get the boys home? How could a group of young boys walk forty-three miles to Žilinai? They did not have enough food, or the equipment for sleeping outdoors. What to do? Communications were primitive, there were few telephones and they worked only randomly. To find out if there was hope for a train they had to go back to the train station.

The boys, dismayed and bewildered, silently scooped up their belongings and ran with Adomas in a mad rush to the station. Mother said, "Eventually we learned that they did make it home, thanks to good-hearted people along the way, but it took them days. I hate to think what the parents of the boys went through, not knowing what had become of their sons."

"We also had to act fast," said Father. "Mother, Milda, and I ran to the dairy store and butcher shop and grocery to buy food. Mother and I had lived through waves of invasions during World War I, so we knew that the stores would be emptied."

News of the imminent arrival of the Soviets had spread like a cloud of noxious gas: everywhere people were rushing to buy up whatever was still available, but shop owners did not want to sell because they feared that the Lithuanian currency, the litas, would have no value once the Soviets took over. Storekeepers hid everything that was non-perishable.

Mother continued, "Most stores were closing as we got there. Fortunately, we had made friends in the shops we frequented. Some owners drew us into the back storage room and let us buy a few supplies like flour and barley. For the next two weeks, there was no food to be bought anywhere in the city. The staples we had saw us through, but we could not get any vegetables, nor milk for our girls."

Father said, "It sounds strange that in an agricultural country like Lithuania, people did not just drive out of town and buy food directly from the farmers. But in 1940, private ownership of cars was extremely rare and there was no bus service. The Soviets took every motorized vehicle for their own use. There were trains, but only between the bigger towns. Travel was slow and unreliable, and the Soviet military forces brought everything to a standstill.

"The communists wanted total control of all supplies, so they forbade farmers to bring food to the city in their horse-drawn wagons, as had been the custom for centuries. The only way for ordinary citizens to get out of the city to nearby farms was by bicycle, and we didn't own one."

In the afternoon of June 15, 1940, the Soviet army poured into Vilnius. Communist sympathizers turned out in droves to greet the invaders as if they were precious guests, perhaps even saviors. Oh yes, at first there were many sympathizers, primarily old Marxists and young liberal intellectuals, and the large population of Jews who then lived in Vilnius. Many supported the Soviets because they feared, correctly, that Lithuania was in an untenable political position, and if the choice came to occupation by the Nazis or the Soviets, they preferred the latter.

Thousands of Jews had fled Germany for safety in Vilnius, and were well aware of the misery Hitler was inflicting on their friends and relatives in the territories he ruled. Thus, on June 15, the streets were filled with people throwing flowers and wreaths at the arriving tanks, trucks, officers' cars, and foot soldiers.

The Soviets had pre-planned every detail of the takeover. Immediately, there were changes in every governmental agency and ministry. Party members quickly replaced the incumbents. Every day, the Soviet-run Ministry of Education churned out new decrees to re-form the curriculum according to communist principles. A whole new level of oversight was added, run by trusted party-members.

There was to be absolutely no more teaching of religion and all re-ligious books were to be destroyed. In schools and libraries, all history books had to be reviewed and certain sections, especially those that described the 1917 Russian Bolshevik revolution in unflattering terms, were to be excised. Photographs of past Lithuanian presidents had to be cut out.

Word spread that if you were smart, and wanted to please your new masters, you would immediately, without waiting for a directive, take down the Lithuanian flag, the national emblem and the post-er with the words of the Lithuanian National Anthem, and ask your new Communist Party bosses for framed pictures of Marx, Lenin and Stalin.

Although the occupation took place during summer vacation, the Commissar of Education issued orders to recall students back to school. The teachers had to make sure their charges learned com-munist slogans, formed choirs, put on skits, and participated in well-rehearsed "spontaneous" demonstrations expressing joy at the arrival of the Soviets. Such activities were photographed and print-ed at home and abroad to "prove" how popular the Soviet takeover had been.

Teachers also had to persuade their students to join the Young Pioneers, but all other associations, such as the boy and girl scouts, were to cease forthwith. Moreover, teachers were to organize the older students for work camps in the countryside to help farmers harvest their crops. Because Father's school served those the administration considered as slow-witted, his students were excused from most of these activities.

"Most of my students, already in their late teens, were not born retarded," said Father. "In those days of no antibiotics and little medical care, children with congenital problems like Down syndrome seldom survived childhood. My school served mostly Polish orphans raised in Catholic orphanages. Back then, few people knew about the need of babies to bond to a parent figure, or that language development had to happen early in life or be forfeited.

"There were not enough nuns to mother the children. In a typical orphanage, twenty to thirty cribs would be lined up in one room. The sisters barely had time to feed and clean the babies, but the only language they heard was their own babbling. Without language, mental development is severely delayed. Some of my students turned out to be good at math, many were talented in music and art, but their use of language was minimal, and attempts to teach them Lithuanian were, for the most part, a waste of time."

Because his charges were considered unsuitable for summer assignments, Father had to accept some other service. The Soviets ordered him to serve in the Electoral Commission. They planned a highly advertised election to show the world their "respect" for democracy. Of course, only one slate of candidates was listed on the ballot, only those selected from communist ranks—or puppets approved by the party.

Why then bother with elections at all? Stalin was no fool: he knew the value of propaganda. As far as the rest of the world was concerned, it had to appear that Lithuania, as well as Latvia and Estonia, had freely and legitimately elected to join the Soviet Union.

The Commission's first job was to register all inhabitants as voters, including the thousands of Jews who had escaped from German-ruled territories into Vilnius. In addition, the Commission had to flood the city with voting literature ahead of the elections, and after the election, to count the votes and certify the results. It was up to the Commission to ensure that the results would be overwhelmingly in favor of the communist regime.

The problem was how to make everyone vote. The Soviets devised an effective ploy. They issued a proclamation that to buy any goods, ride trains, or obtain any services or permits, people would have to show that their internal passport—the universal identification document—had been stamped at the polling place. A small purple stamp showing the letters LS for "*Liaudies Seimas*—People's Parliament" within an oval cartouche was affixed after voting. No exemption from voting was available: old, disabled or sick, you had to come and support the new regime.

And yet in spite of all these measures, the first day of the election, July 14, 1940, was a disappointment. The expected crowds of voters did not materialize. Voting was extended one extra day. Radio announcements made it clear that punishment awaited the enemies of the people who failed "to perform their patriotic duty." Reluctantly, more voters came, though nowhere near the "95% turnout" claimed by the Soviets.

In reality, the election was a complete fraud. Instead of voting for the official candidates, great numbers of voters cast blank ballots, or wrote in the names of deceased national

Father's internal passport, stamped "LS" to prove he voted.

heroes, or daringly penned curses and anti-communist slogans. The underground resistance, at tremendous risk, soon created fake "LS" stamps for the passports.

"This will never do!" raged the chief of the Electoral Commission when the ballots had all been tallied and he saw the abysmal results. Committee members in every polling place were made to work through the night replacing every bad ballot with one naming the listed party candidates. Before the fixing of the votes and the final counts were even completed, the Soviets broadcast to the world that 99% of the voters had approved the candidates.

A month later, in August, it was announced that Lithuanians had voted to join the Soviet Union. This was an outright lie. Lithuanians as a nation had no say in it: the falsely elected candidates alone, all of them communists, had made the unanimous decision to become part of the USSR.

My own memories of the year under Soviet occupation are mere shadowy sketches and feelings. I was too young to understand facts, but old enough to feel that almost overnight, everything had changed. One immediate result was that my parents no longer spoke openly before my sister or me. I had always been very curious. I loved listening to my parents' talk, even about subjects that I did not understand. Their voices were the soothing background noise of my life.

Before the Soviets came, our home was full of friends, talk, and laughter. I remember people listening to the news on the radio and having spirited discussions. BBC was a source of fun, because to Lithuanian ears, English speech sounded like rolling a hot potato in one's mouth. Because living space was limited, we would all be in the same room, parents, guests, and neighbors; voices discussing this and that, Milda, alone or with a friend in one area doing homework, me with some plaything, or hiding under the table, soaking in all I could.

With the communists in power, all talk ceased. There were no more gatherings, the radio disappeared, and our parents often went into another room to talk behind a closed door, keeping Milda and me away. The communists instituted a system of spying which promoted questioning children about their parents' conversations.

The little innocents could be tricked into revealing all sorts of information. *Do your parents have a typewriter?* If so, they may be distributing clandestine anti-Soviet literature. *Do they listen to programs on the radio?* If so, they are probably absorbing Hitler's propaganda, or—heaven forbid—they are getting their news from the BBC. Mother and Father had to be extremely vigilant with chatty, guileless Milda, and with me, a little parrot, to keep us from unknowingly saying something to someone which could be interpreted in an unfavorable light and reported to the authorities.

One day, my sharp little ears overheard Mother say to Father, "The Red Dragon will devour us all." I was horrified and shrieked, "Where's the Red Dragon? Where can we hide?" What consternation for my poor parents. They admonished me, more severely than I had ever heard from them, never, ever to say the words "Red Dragon" out loud. They gave me no explanation, knowing how dangerous it could be if I talked. I had nothing but fairytales to guide me, so I thought that saying the words out loud would make the monster appear. I believed the Red Dragon was a real creature, a huge bloodthirsty menace.

How was I to know that *"Raudonasis Slibinas"* was a metaphor for communism, similar to "the Red Tide" or "the Russian Bear" in English? I did not understand metaphorical dragons. My imagination enlarged and embellished it; I had repeated nightmares of running away from a fearsome red monster, but it always gained on me. I would awake screaming as it opened its maw and I saw its sharp teeth closing down on me.

But I was obedient to my parents' command. They ordered me never to talk about it, so I could not share my terror even with my father. What if Daddy got angry with me? Nightmares were more bearable than losing his approval.

CHAPTER 3:

Life in the Worker's Paradise

How does one adjust to living as a virtual slave? Because under Big Brother, Comrade Stalin, the majority of Lithuanians felt enslaved, having no choice in where or how to live, having to silence their very thoughts. Fear of offending our new masters spread like scabies. Of course, communist supporters and poor farmers who were promised the moon to join in the coming collective prosperity were pleased to finally be in power.

For some such as Mother, it was simply a question of avoiding anyone's notice. The Communists required that all able-bodied women work. They assigned her to the central railroad administration as an expert sender and receiver of Morse code—in those days, the only reliable means of communication for the management of railroad traffic. It was not a politically sensitive assignment, and as long as she attended the required indoctrination meetings and kept her mouth shut about any topic that could be interpreted as anti-communist, she was left alone.

It was not so easy for Father. For him, living and working under the new regime became a constant psychological battle. He was a dreamer, a lover of music, art, and literature, with a head full of poems and stories, and not a practical bone in his body. He had never been active in any political parties. He was, however, very social, had numerous friends, and was dedicated to scouting, which, he believed, enhanced the idealism of youth. His motto was "noblesse oblige," which to him meant that anyone who enjoyed wealth, knowledge, ability, or power should use these gifts for the benefit of others. Above all, it was unthinkable for Father to harm the innocent.

Father avoided the limelight as much as he could, but the Communist Party had him in its sights. It did not help that he was taller than most Lithuanians or Russians. At six feet four inches he stood out like a beacon. Everyone gravitated to him. The good and the bad wanted him on their side. Almost immediately he became the focus of the NKVD ("Narodnyy Komissariat Vnutrennikh Del," later renamed the KGB). Although the innocent-sounding words stood for "People's Commissariat for Internal Affairs," the agency acted as the secret police organization of the Soviet Union, with unlimited power to enforce Communist Party directives. The operatives of the NKVD decided that because everyone, especially fellow teachers, trusted him, Father would be an ideal spy.

The inducements to spy started in August with an attractive job offer. The administrator of the school district summoned Father for a chat, and softened him up with tea and cookies. He told Father that the Communist Party approved his lack of prior political commitments: "There are no black marks against you. We need loyal workers. So how would you like a job as a school inspector?" The administrator explained that Father would be in charge of ensuring teacher standards and enforcing compliance with regulations.

"I knew what this offer meant," Father said. "I would be expected to unearth and report all political gossip about every teacher. I respectfully declined, regretting that I was just a low-level instructor for the retarded, not trained for such an important position. The administrator insisted. I invented every argument I could to avoid the assignment. I must have convinced him I was an idiot, because for a little while, they left me alone."

Not long after the school year started, the new government ordered all teachers to attend an obligatory meeting. The purpose was to form a teachers union and elect the governing board. Polish teachers proposed their candidates; Jewish schools named theirs. The Lithuanian contingent nominated Father. He almost had a heart attack. "I knew if I accepted, I would be forced to climb higher up the party ladder. And each rung meant finding someone to report for engaging in anti-communist activities. I had to refuse, though I suspected it would cost me dearly."

Once the nominations closed, the next step was for each candidate to tell the assembly why he or she would make a good board member. When it was Father's turn, he said he was sorry to disappoint those who had put forward his name, but that he had no background in management, and his only group activities had been with the scouts, now a banned organization. "I really put my foot in it," he recalled, "but I could never have lived with myself if I'd had to file reports knowing they would send fellow teachers to prison, or worse." He was allowed to withdraw his candidacy, but saw that he had angered many. He caught colleagues glaring threats at him.

Lithuania's Soviet masters promulgated new orders every day. One of these required teachers and older students to "volunteer" for extra work assignments. Father and a few of his more capable students were given the task of inventorying the contents of a warehouse. There were great numbers of warehouses in Vilnius, owned predominantly by Jewish merchants who, before war broke out, had used the city as the depot from which to ship goods to retail outlets throughout Poland, Belarus, and the Baltics.

Father's warehouse was full of dishes, cutlery, pots and pans—everything to do with preparing and serving food at home and in restaurants, much of it consisting of fine porcelain and heavy German silverware. After Father had made his second report, which covered perhaps 20% of the contents, he was told to stop and forget the rest. The communist government simply "nationalized" everything, including businesses and buildings. The owners of the warehouses were considered too well off to be tractable under the Soviet regime, and were exiled to Siberia. The Central Committee in Moscow issued an official regulation authorizing the NKVD to "confiscate" all property belonging to subversives and "enemies of the people." The communists in power, especially those in the NKVD, soon lived like princes. Trainloads of goods left Vilnius heading to Russia's interior.

There were a few relatively quiet weeks in November and early December of 1940. Father's students were a compliant group. Many loved music and singing, and excelled in art, though expressing themselves verbally was mostly a lost cause. They were housed predominantly in group residences. Nonetheless, because the communists ordered every teacher in every school to interrogate students to learn how their parents or caregivers felt about living under the new Soviet regime, such questioning had to be pursued even among the disabled at Father's school.

"Not much could be gleaned from them, thank God," said Father. To run his school, he earned food and fuel allocations by having the students draw and color posters glorifying the values of hard work. All in all, the school did not particularly interest the new authorities, which meant that Father was not under constant observation—or so he thought.

As Christmas approached, the Ministry of Education decreed that there would be no time off given to celebrate such religious nonsense. In 1940, Christmas fell on a Wednesday. It was to be just another ordinary workday. In addition, knowing that Christmas Eve is the heart of the traditional celebration for both Poles and Lithuanians, the Ministry commanded that on Tuesday, December 24, at the end of the school day, all teachers had to meet and decide on the programs and schedules for the coming year.

The teachers in Father's school surreptitiously decided to combine the meeting with a modest celebration. They did not expect Mrs. Mahler, a Jewish school inspector, to show up snooping in their insignificant school. She arrived early, and was pleased that classes were being held, but not at all pleased that the teachers seemed to be dressed for a special occasion. She announced severely that she was going to report it to the authorities.

"But Mrs. Mahler," said Father in his most sincere voice, "now that we are all equals under communism, we always wear nice clothing!" Did he mean it as a compliment or was this subversive irony? Perhaps she could not decide, because nobody heard anything more about it.

After classes ended, and the teachers were setting up chairs and desks for the meeting, the school guard rushed in to summon Father. "There's a man waiting for you in the principal's office." *Oh-oh*, Father thought, *who could he be?* He was greeted by a well-dressed civilian smoking a good cigarette, not the smelly version available to "the masses." Speaking in Russian, the man asked Father to sit in front of his desk, which had a number of documents on it. No time wasted on chitchat.

"We have been observing you," the man said, "are you aware of that?"

"No," said Father, "I don't consider myself that important."

Dark eyes bore into him. "We'll decide that. You were praised for the excellent work you did with the Electoral Commission. You seem to be a good man who keeps his nose clean and you appear to have no enemies. Reports confirm that you are respected and well-liked. I think we will soon reach a mutually beneficial agreement."

"About what?" asked Father, though he guessed it was another bid to force him to spy.

"About this," said the man, turning one of the forms around so that Father could read it.

Written in Russian, the top line was already filled in: "I, Felicijonas Boleslovich Prekeris, promise to do the following:" and then, set out in neat numerical order, were a dozen or so statements with a blank space next to each for Father's signature. Signing on the line committed him to carry out the task that was listed.

It was in fact a contract to do what Father was least able to accept: to spy on his friends, his fellow teachers, the parents of his students, my mother's friends—in short, anyone who crossed his path. Periodically, he was to file a report detailing any overt—or merely suspicious—words and actions made in his presence or reported to him by others. He was to drop off the reports, signed under an alias, at an address to be specified later.

"I was in a panic," Father said. "I blurted out, 'Who are you?' The man didn't like that. He glared and shot back, 'If anyone asks, I am a friend (*tovarich*) from the Commissariat of Education.' Then he left the room. I craned my head to better see the cover of a small, red leather notebook in which the man had made notations. On the cover in gold letters it read NKVD. The dreaded secret police. I feared I was lost."

The Russian's absence, though short, gave Father a chance to send a prayer to God and to compose himself. The man returned and for the next four hours, while outside deep night descended and snow started to fall, he cajoled, threatened, argued, shouted, wheedled, and never stopped smoking.

"If you want to have a career, you must report the activities of all your contacts. We in the government must know what people think. Not everyone is in favor of our rules, we have enemies, there's danger of sabotage. So what if you have never been a Communist Party member: you can be a non-affiliated Bolshevik! You will not see your home again if you don't agree. Your family will live so much better: all you have to do is file written reports under an alias—is that so hard?"

And so it went for four long hours, while Father kept pointing out that he didn't have the personality to be a spy, that he had a habit of speaking out impulsively, without thinking, that he stood out too much, and finally—a lucky thrust—that even though, in elementary school, he had learned to speak Russian, reading in the Cyrillic alphabet was difficult for him, and he had not mastered writing it. This was a bald-faced lie, but apparently this detail had slipped through the NKVD's background checks.

"So you don't want to help us?" shouted the Russian.

"It is not that I don't want to, it's that I'm not capable," insisted Father. Some minutes of silence ensued while the man wrote out a note.

"Here, sign this." In the note, Father swore to never reveal to anyone the subject of their conversation. Father signed.

Finally, the man stood, stretched, and gathered up his paperwork. He looked at Father with venom in his eyes. "We will continue this discussion at 9 a.m. tomorrow." He gave Father the address of the NKVD building, the room number to report to, and stalked out.

"I sat there in the dark for a good half hour, waiting for my heart to return to its normal rhythm," said Father. "The room was very cold. I must have been in a sweat of fear, because my shirt felt wet, and I was shivering uncontrollably. What was I going to tell Stasė when I got home? Would I get home at all?"

Father's delayed return, hours after the expected time, had Mother trembling with dread. She was sure something bad had happened. Her silent alarm infected Milda and me. We clung to each other, Milda repeating under her breath that this was the worst Christmas Eve of her life. We did not understand why we did not have a Christmas tree. There were no traditional Christmas Eve foods.

Our parents had to fear everyone. What if a neighbor or friend dropped in and saw us celebrating the birth of Christ and reported us as "reactionaries?" The communists had succeeded in spreading massive distrust. Even if there was nothing to report, those who disliked you could make up any tale to show your disloyalty. You were automatically guilty unless you could prove your innocence. Sociable folks like Mother and Father learned quickly to isolate themselves. What if a good friend turned out to be a spy?

When at last Father arrived home, Milda and I shrieked with joy. Now that he was safe, we let ourselves be put to bed. His news was not for our ears.

Neither Mother nor Father believed he would come home from the next morning's meeting. During the previous months, people had started to simply "disappear," hundreds gone never to be heard from again, as Father knew from experience. At one of the weekly communist indoctrination sessions, one of Father's acquaintances had dared to ask an intelligent question: "How could two such incompatible systems as Nazism and Communism agree to sign the 1939 German–Soviet Friendship Treaty?" A day later, he vanished without a trace. The Soviets had no tolerance for thinkers or discussion. They only wanted dumb submission.

My parents spent Christmas night discussing what Mother should do if Father did not return. Where could she go? Her salary at the Railroad Ministry was insufficient to provide for her and Milda and me. If Father were imprisoned or deported, what innocent-looking words could they use as a code to tell each other what was really happening, presuming that some form of communication would be available at all? How much should Milda be told? What lies would work? Milda was eleven, too naïve and trusting not to blurt out something to the wrong person. And what about Dalia, almost four years old, who heard everything and might repeat it?

Christmas morning was an ordinary workday. Mother had to report for work at 8 a.m., as usual. Father put on double layers of warm clothing, knowing that prisons were not heated, and this winter was again one of the coldest in people's memory. Into his briefcase, Mother packed underwear and warm socks, bread, dried cheese and smoked bacon. They made the sign of the cross over each other before parting, thinking this might be a final farewell.

"Walking to work," Mother said, "I was bawling like cow who'd lost its calf. By the time I reached the office, my tears had turned to ice. I was a mess. My boss asked me what was happening. I was too upset to even lie, so I said that my husband had been summoned by the NKVD. She was no fool; she knew what that might mean. She had a kind heart, for all she was a member of the Communist Party. 'Go home,' she said, 'I'll mark on your record that you came in feverish and I feared you'd infect us all.' So I left. And I still cannot find words to express my shock when Felicius came through the door less than an hour later. I thought, *Surely I'm hallucinating!* But there he was."

So what did happen? "I got to the guard post early," Father recalled. "I gave my name and said I was reporting as instructed to room such-and-so. I was told to wait while one of the guards went to let them know I was there. A few minutes later, the guard came back and sneered at me, 'Nobody in that room wants you.'

I could not believe I'd heard right, so I just stood there. 'Go back to your teaching, we know where to find you if we want you.' Believe me, I got home in record time. Kissed my Stasė, changed clothes, and went to teach as though it were indeed just an ordinary day instead of a miracle."

Postscript: a week or so later, Father ran into the Russian NKVD operative passing on the street. Father raised his hat to greet him courteously. "*Durak!*—Idiot!" hissed the man, "we have never met!"

CHAPTER 4:

We Will Never Forgive or Forget

As 1941 began, Hitler was continuing his blitzkrieg bombing of England and making plans to invade it, and Stalin was making secret plans of his own—to attack the territories taken by the Nazis in 1939. Stalin's military advisers thought that Hitler would be too preoccupied with his nefarious plans for England to react with sufficient speed against a surprise Soviet attack.

Soviet military officers were learning German and studying detailed maps of Germany and Nazi-occupied Poland. Stalin's military services accumulated huge stockpiles of war materiel and equipment close to the borders of what had been Poland before the Nazis overran it, especially in the Soviet territories of Byelorussia (now called Belarus) and the Ukraine.

In Lithuania, the Soviets erected a large warehouse to hold explosives of every kind in Kalvarija, near the East Prussian border. The Soviet governing body, the Council of People's Commissars, demanded the complete cooperation of every Soviet resident for this endeavor. There are documents that show Stalin was planning to attack sometime in July 1941.

Before this offensive was launched, Stalin ordered his underlings to completely remove all "reactionary elements" from the newly acquired Soviet Socialist Republics of Estonia, Latvia, and Lithuania. Time was running short. Orders from the Politburo required party members and supporters to vigorously root out nationalist patriots, dissenters, and potential troublemakers. Especially suspect were those who, in free Lithuania, worked as teachers, policemen, soldiers, administrators, businessmen, or merchants.

Equally despised by the communists were those with a higher education (the "intelligentsia"), the successful middle class (the "bourgeois"), all who belonged to the old nobility, and the owners of successful farms who would object to collectivization. To ensure the success of his invasion plans, Stalin would tolerate absolutely no resistance of any kind to any of the party's objectives.

Of course, it was a perfect opportunity for the greedy and the envious to accuse innocent people who would then be liquidated, or sent away to prison, or to the work camps in Siberia. Soviets rewarded the informers who turned in their neighbors and colleagues. Snitches prospered.

To the Communist Party, Father presented a triple threat: he was educated, a teacher, and came from the old nobility. And he had refused to spy! He was constantly followed. He recalled, "Everywhere I went, alone or with friends or family, there was a grey presence I could see out of the corner of my eye. He didn't really try to fade into the background. I knew he made a note of my every move, every place I set my foot in, and every person who spoke with me."

Many of Father's friends and colleagues had vanished. Lithuania's occupiers saw treason in the most innocent situations. But there was also passive resistance. Sometimes Father would find a note slipped under our apartment door or inserted among the books and papers on his desk warning him to beware of a particular neighbor, or a school colleague assigned to report on him.

Father said, "I had a feeling that several of these notes came from the 'spies' themselves: I recognized their handwriting. The warnings suggested to me that these people had been coerced to report on others. One day, my communist supervisor whispered to me, 'Don't ever discuss politics in my presence.' Spying had become so pervasive that spies were spied on by spies who were themselves under observation. Nobody trusted anybody."

The first half of 1941 had been enormously stressful, and life was lived in constant fear. In June, school was over for the summer, Mother was due a vacation, and we hoped for the chance to relax a little. Fate willed otherwise.

Almost a year had gone by since the Soviets had absorbed the Baltic countries, but apparently in Moscow, the Soviet Supreme Council was dissatisfied with the Balts' level of participation in the establishment of the "workers' paradise." They planned to teach these recalcitrant natives a lesson they would remember. First they would experience complete terror at home, and then life in Siberia.

Not ever discussed but clearly understood by Moscow was that these three small countries were prime real estate in which to resettle valued party members from frozen East Russia. A nicely balanced exchange: Balts go to Siberia, Siberians come to the Baltics. The Deputy Commissar of the NKVD, Ivan Serov, the man responsible for starving to death literally millions of Ukrainian peasants, delivered to those in charge a series of detailed instructions on how the Baltic deportations were to be carried out.

Those who deal in drama know that to enhance the horror of a terrifying situation, stage it in the dark. Between two and three in the morning on June 14, throughout Lithuania, Latvia, and Estonia, co-ordinated pounding on doors roused almost every inhabitant. Party members stood in assigned locations with lists of those condemned to deportation. Others accompanied soldiers to designated addresses. The shocked victims were given at most twenty minutes to prepare for exile to Siberia. Men were told to pack their stuff separately, but not told why. Who can make a wise choice of what to bring when thrown into panic?

Soldiers, with bayonets attached to their rifles, marched or drove whole families—children, babies, and old folks—to the nearest railroad stations. There, ignoring the shrieks and wails of women and children, the military separated the men from their families. Their fate was to be worked to death in the *gulags* (forced labor camps) mining or felling trees. Women and children were to work in lumber mills or on collective farms in Siberia. Soldiers then crowded everyone into the boxcars and freight cars waiting in readiness at each station.

The conditions in the wagons were unendurable. There was no room to sit, let alone lie down. There were no toilets, only a hole in the floor. Doors were bolted. Some lucky ones were in wagons that had a small high window for air. Who had remembered to bring water to drink? No matter how people shouted and begged for food or water, none was given, and bystanders were forbidden to come near on pain of death.

Some wagons stood at the sidings for days until an engine arrived to collect them. Hundreds of the weak died before the trains moved. The living piled the dead near the doors and survived as best they could. It was mid-June, and some days were hot. For the confined, it was literally—hell.

The roundups were repeated for days. There is not one person in the Baltic countries who did not lose a relative, a friend or a neighbor.

Mother lost two cousins who owned substantial farms, together with their families. Father lost a fellow teacher from his school in Vilnius, and several from his days in Kaišiadorys. Miraculously, Father's two rich brothers managed to avoid deportation, and his eldest brother, Boleslovas—having married a woman from a left-leaning family—was untouched in Šeduva, as were his three sisters.

This infamy will never be forgotten. Although exact numbers are hard to fix, most historians and examiners agree that starting on June 14, in a single week, about 60,000 were deported from tiny Estonia, 34,000 from Latvia, and 38,000 from Lithuania. Fewer than 10% of these survived eventually to return home.

Those who witnessed the events did not learn to love communism. Rather, they learned to hate all those who had contributed to this tragedy. The names and faces of the traitors were seared into the collective memories of every village and town; the identities of the executioners who made up the lists and helped send totally innocent people to their deaths.

What about our small family—how did we escape exile to Siberia when Father had openly refused to cooperate? Truly, a guardian angel watched over us. When school vacation started in early June, Mother, Milda, and I took a train to a station near the village of Žilinai, to spend some time in the country under the care of our good friend Adomas Kaulius. Father's vacation did not start until July, so he remained in Vilnius.

Early on Friday, June 13, the day before the deportations began, Father went to his school to take care of some administrative work. He expected a quiet morning: no students, no lectures. Instead, as he approached the building, he was confronted with a hair-raising sight: the streets near the school were congested with military trucks and soldiers milling about, cleaning their weapons, fussing with bayonets. At first he thought he would just turn around and go home. But he had a report due the following week and he needed to gather statistics.

He went into the building unobtrusively, by a side entrance. Inside, he found a fellow teacher known to be a Communist Party member. Father deliberated whether to ask her if she knew what all the commotion was about. Would that be a dangerous question politically? He worked on materials for his report, then noticed she was getting ready to leave. He gave her a smile.

"I guess she felt some kindness toward me," said Father. "She came over to shake my hand. She looked at me with an expression that I could not interpret. Fear? Sorrow? She whispered, 'Felicius, after midnight tonight, the deportations will start. You are in grave danger. Save yourself if you can. Goodbye.' Thank God I ran into her!"

What to do? Father grabbed the materials he had at hand in case some officious NKVD policeman, or nosy soldier, asked him to justify his presence. He left quietly by the door he had come in ("I even remembered to lock it"), and hurried to the train station. Not far away, visible in the sorting yard, he could see endless rows of old green boxcars and dark red freight cars, patrolled by guards. Pretending to have noticed nothing, Father asked at the ticket window if there was a train that day running to Valkininkai, the closest station to Žilinai. Father was desperate to rejoin Mother, Milda, and me and somehow find a way to hide us. He knew he could trust Adomas, if only he could reach him.

"Yes," said the ticket master, "there's a train scheduled this afternoon around two, though who knows if it will be running."

The train was late, but it did come. Father put on double layers of warm clothing and filled two suitcases for the three of us already in Žilinai. He took whatever non-perishable food was on hand. If our fate decreed exile to Siberia, at least we would have some clothes for the coming winter. "I tried to think of everything, but forgot shoes," Father said later. "Shows what happens to the brain when fear rides it."

Although he had no warning of Father's coming, Adomas happily welcomed him to his residence, located in the same building as the elementary school of which he was the principal. The school, a large building that once belonged to a wealthy landowner, stood isolated near a forest and did not have close neighbors. Mother, Milda, and I had spent many days there already, and did not expect Father until July. The three of us, and Adomas, were burning with curiosity to know why he had suddenly appeared, loaded with suitcases full of winter clothing. But Father evaded answering, and Mother, intuiting that something was amiss, told Milda and me to stop prying. She promised to tell us what we needed to know later. The adults had to make sure we knew nothing that we could reveal to the curious ears of strangers.

"June days are very long. Adomas suggested we go for a twilight walk," said Mother. "While you girls ran around, Father had a chance to warn Adomas and me of the deportations starting that very night, and the danger facing all of us.

"Adomas immediately assured us of his help. He was still a bachelor, which made it easier for him. He had no family whose lives would be placed at risk if he were found aiding us 'enemies of the people.' Besides, he thought it prudent to be absent from the schoolhouse himself. Maybe his name was on the deportation list too."

As soon as it turned dark, which was close to midnight in Lithuania's northern latitude, Adomas led us all (Father carrying my sleeping dead weight) to a woodcutter's shack a good distance away, deep in the nearby forest. The moon was still partly visible and the shimmering ribbon of the Milky Way allowed Adomas to lead us safely to our destination. "Adomas was a brilliant planner," Father said. "He even brought along his cow so there would be milk, and his dog to bark a warning if anyone approached."

That night, June 14, before dawn, Adomas walked to Valkininkai to get news from people he knew and trusted. We girls were not privy to the report he gave at the time, but Father said later, "He came back devastated by what he had seen—the confining box cars, the hysterical mothers, the ruthless soldiers who used their bayonets to prod trembling old people who were unable to climb into the train wagons on their own. It was the way he sobbed that stays with me, because Adomas, though the most kind-hearted of men, was never one to show much emotion."

We settled in. The shack stood on the edge of a marshy clearing in a forest made almost impenetrable by thick undergrowth. Astounding numbers of mosquitoes visited my body, finding me more delicious than any of the others. Frogs croaked everywhere. Long-legged storks, back from overwintering in Africa, and now busy raising hungry chicks, gorged on them. Everyone in Lithuania loves storks, but I felt sorry for the frogs.

The shack consisted of one small room. You could see the sky through holes in the roof, and a breeze blew through the large gaps between the boards. The furniture consisted of a couple of rickety log benches. Pulled together, they made a bed platform for us females, but the men slept under the stars. Cooking was camping-style, outside.

My city-child's soul was appalled: how could we eat without a table? How was I to go to the bathroom? There was not even an outside privy.

Father dug a hole some distance from the shack. I wondered what my parents were talking about as they murmured to each other, "Here, for now, we'll be safe." Safe from what? But I knew better than to ask. The adults never answered my questions.

Some days later, Adomas stole away again to get news from Valkininkai. On his return, he said that the previous day, the last of the crowded wagons had pulled away from the station. Most of the soldiers were gone. The Communist Party "informers," however, were still active and to be feared.

"Despite the risk," Mother said, "we decided to return back to Adomas' rooms in the schoolhouse, because it had rained hard and the shack leaked, and it was too small to shelter all of us. At the schoolhouse, we were constantly on guard, nervously expecting soldiers to burst in and arrest us. Every time the dog barked, we grabbed our suitcases, ready to run out the back into the forest again. Milda badgered us to tell her what was going on. But we could not risk telling you girls anything for fear that somehow you would blab the wrong thing to the wrong person."

A couple of days later, on Sunday, June 22, 1941, a booming noise like thunder made all of us jittery. Could not be thunder: the sky was clear, barely a wisp or two of cloud. Adomas went to investigate. He found the village in an uproar. A man had ridden down from Valkininkai with the news, "Hitler has invaded the Soviet territories. The communists are retreating."

What a relief! *No more cattle cars full of dying children, no more Siberia*—that was the hope. Most Lithuanians welcomed the arrival of the Nazis, seeing them as our saviors from communist brutality. Poor Lithuania: out of the frying pan, into the fire.

CHAPTER 5:

Everything for the Reich

News of the Germans' approach threw Lithuania into turmoil. In the tiny village of Žilinai, anyone known to have spied for the communists was run out of town. The thick forest nearby became a refuge not only for the civilian "traitors" who had helped the Soviet government persecute their fellow Lithuanians, but also for the numerous Russian soldiers who had been unwillingly separated from their regiments—and those who did not want to rejoin them.

Villagers had to go about armed and in groups, as robberies and burglaries became the norm. Russian soldiers wanted civilian clothing so they could escape the notice of the coming German troops. And of course, everyone needed food.

Hitler's *Operation Barbarossa* had begun with a lightning-fast strike—a *blitzkrieg*—along the entire eastern border of the German Reich, wherever it touched the lands held by the Soviet Union. German armed forces, the Wehrmacht, quickly overran vast territories, but it takes time and civilian personnel to impose administrative order. There were some weeks of instability in Lithuania, and hopeful dreamers thought the country could be free again. In fact, from day one of the German incursion, Lithuanians rose up against the occupying Soviets, secured such strategic locations as railroads, bridges, and communication centers, and declared a Provisional Government to re-establish Lithuanian independence.

Father was anxious to return to Vilnius at once, both to consult on his assignment from the restored Lithuanian Ministry of Education, and to check on our apartment. It was a dangerous journey. Trains were not running, so it took him days of walking and hitching rides on farmers' carts. Our friend Adomas stayed put for a week, but he needed news of his own status as well. He rode off on his bicycle, covering the forty-three miles to Vilnius through a countryside wracked with lawlessness.

We three, Mother, Milda, and I, remained in that isolated school building, much too close to the forest for safety. One woman and two youngsters: we were ideal targets. There were no curtains and no locks. Anyone standing outside the building and pressing his nose against the windows could see there were no men inside. It was not so bad during the day, but Mother did not dare light a lamp at night, because we would be visible as if on stage.

Thank God the nights in June and July are extremely short, with long twilights and early dawns, and less than five hours of darkness. Mother said we huddled at night in a windowless supply area, ears open to the warning barks of Adomas' vigilant dog. When men came in the daytime, the dog would hold them at bay. Mother would ask what they wanted, then pretend to go inside to ask "the teacher" what to do. Usually, they asked for food, and Mother would bring out bread and cheese and milk. "In those weeks, I aged ten years from fear and worry," Mother said.

At the Ministry of Education, the upheaval caused by a year of Soviet rule was immense. It took days before Father learned that the Lithuanian administration had a new assignment for him as School Inspector for elementary grades in Vilnius. This promotion came in recognition of his refusal to cooperate with the Soviets and the risk he had taken in declining to spy on his fellow teachers. We were also approved to move into much bigger quarters, containing four tall-ceilinged rooms, plus kitchen and bathroom, on the third floor of a four-story apartment house at 19 Basanavičiaus Street.

The appointment by the Lithuanian Ministry of Education to the post of Inspector was short-lived. By the end of July, a scant four weeks later, the Nazis had made it clear that the only government in Lithuania would be theirs, the Third Reich's. Nonetheless, because they lacked the manpower to fill every governmental post with a capable German, many positions remained in Lithuanian hands. The German administration in charge of education confirmed Father's assignment as "Schulrat," Inspector of Schools. His lack of political involvement and his ability to speak and write German were probably in his favor. They also confirmed the allocation of the bigger apartment.

By the end of July, we were reunited. The small house we shared with the Gudliauskas family in Vilnius had escaped looting. We moved our furniture into our new quarters on Basanavičiaus Street. Mother was delighted, because the Ministry of Railroads where she worked was just a short downhill walk. Mother still had her job sending and receiving Morse code messages: the Germans needed her expertise as much as had the Soviets. And we needed her salary.

The first wave of invading German soldiers had impressed Lithuanian citizens with their polite demeanor and helpfulness. No raping, no looting. There was food in the stores again. People spoke freely, thrilled to be rid of the menacing Soviets. This favorable opinion lasted through the summer, indirectly encouraged by reports in the press and on the radio focusing on the atrocities perpetrated by the Soviets, not only during the mass deportations, but also during their withdrawal into Russia. People were appalled at the needless massacres of "political" prisoners whom the police forces of the NKVD had held incarcerated in Vilnius, Kaunas, and elsewhere.

In one case, the NKVD, fleeing the advancing Nazis, had crammed Lithuanian and Polish prisoners into trucks to take them along to Moscow. At a nighttime stop in Minsk, Belarus, as the German air force was pulverizing the city, the NKVD policemen apparently received orders from Moscow to "take care of the prisoners where you are." Near the village of Cherven, they ordered everyone out of the trucks and told to walk. As the sun rose on June 26, the Soviets bellowed two orders: "Run! Fire!" As the prisoners ran, the NKVD hunted down the hundreds of weakened victims like so many helpless deer. The handful of survivors who made it back to Lithuania inflamed its citizens against these "butchers." Compared to them, the Germans seemed civilized and cultivated, and in the beginning, before they showed their true intentions, the natives of Estonia, Latvia, and Lithuania hoped that this might be a humane occupation.

The polite conduct of the Nazi occupying force did not last long. By mid-August, all three Baltic countries were swarming with German civil-service personnel, intent on fulfilling Hitler's long-term organizational goals. For Hitler, the only purpose of the occupied lands was to provide soldiers, food, and raw materials for the Nazi war effort. The plan was to replace the natives with Germans within a given number of years, to be determined later, after the expected victory over Russia.

Although most Lithuanians, Latvians and Estonians met the physical characteristics of the so-called "Aryan race," Hitler's special forces from the SS (*Schutzstaffel*—the shield squadron) organization treated the Balts with contempt. Just as Poles and Slavs were considered inferior *Untermenschen*—sub-humans, so were the Balts, unless they were of German ancestry going back several generations.

Because many government departments and agencies remained in Lithuanian hands for a long time, passive resistance to German orders was possible. The field of education was, until 1943, an island of relative safety. Teachers were not persecuted, they were not systematically forced to spy on one another, and until the war started going badly for Hitler, they were not forcibly drafted into the armed services. They were allowed to travel if there was an educational excuse, one that in some way promoted German interests. Naturally, all travel had to be officially pre-approved.

"We led double lives," said Father, "the persona acceptable to the Germans, versus who we were among people we trusted." Everyone was smart enough to practice the lesson learned from the Soviets: any kind of overt resistance to the Germans would lead to extermination.

Nazis would not tolerate any public criticism of the Führer or his policies, so Lithuanians organized underground resistance groups. Mimeographed publications seemed to appear like mushrooms after the rain. The underground press disseminated pamphlets and bulletins offering news translated from broadcasts heard on the BBC. Respected elders offered practical advice and urged non-cooperation with the Nazis, emboldening young men not to join the SS legions. Because schools had access to paper and printing capabilities, no matter how primitive, they tried to help the resistance, but such help was supremely dangerous, as school supplies were closely monitored.

Once German civilians arrived in force, our lives under the Nazis went from bad to worse. "Our biggest problem," said Mother, "was how to provide for our daily needs. Father's salary, like those of all Lithuanians paid by the Third Reich, was tiny, and mine, at the Railroad Ministry, was even smaller. Rations for us were half those allotted to the German citizens in our midst, who had their own exclusive shops. Father and I didn't have jewelry or shoes or furs to barter for food or clothing on the black market. Before 1944, there were supplies available in stores, but they were extremely expensive, and you needed to have rationing coupons for everything. Father asked for a job transfer to a village where food was easier to obtain, but was denied."

Our little family had one advantage: nobody smoked. Coupons for cigarettes were highly prized and could be exchanged for food. Food rations became more and more restricted as the war dragged on. All production was poured into the Nazi war effort. As before, under the Soviets, farmers were our hope and salvation.

City dwellers looked hungrily at the farms which covered Lithuania, but so did the Germans. The fewer supplies were used by Lithuanians, the more there would be for the military. Baltic farmers had enormous quotas to deliver so that German soldiers could eat while conquering Russia. If they exceeded the prescribed quotas, they would get special "points" to buy shoes and clothing, sugar and alcohol. The government forbade farmers to sell certain products, such as meat, or face severe penalties. Of course, cheating was rife, but farmers wanted valuable goods for taking risks. Nobody trusted the *Reichsmarks*, Hitler's money. Barter was the only solution.

Nazi governmental officials banned civilian travel to the countryside unless the applicant could provide justification. As mentioned, an educational goal was acceptable, as was visiting sick close relatives, especially old parents. The teachers under Father's jurisdiction kept his creative imagination busy inventing pretexts that would pass scrutiny by the commissioners who were authorized to issue travel permits. He understood what Nazi officials wanted, and besides, his ability to write in German was better than that of most of his colleagues. The usual cover story was that the trip aimed to deliver lectures to villagers about German culture.

Fortunately, train service was good until 1944, even though many tracks had been sabotaged or blown up by those who objected to the Nazi occupation. The teachers for whom Father obtained travel permits invariably shared with us a little of the food they brought back.

One such family of teachers, Ona Zailskas and her husband, were truly generous friends. Ona was unusually successful during her forays into the countryside. Lithuanians said, "*Ji turi geras akis*— she has good eyes," meaning that she was hard to embarrass. She could take rejection and not let it bother her. She would buy cheap costume jewelry made of tin and glass, and wooden toys carved by Russian prisoners in Vilnius, and then exchange them for food in hamlets and villages. She would persist in her bargaining until the farmers found something they could spare, even a single egg. "Spiders made of glass and tin were her best sellers," remembered her son Arūnas, "because in some Lithuanian legends, spiders bring good fortune."

Every couple of weeks, Ona would send Arūnas to visit us, carrying a basket of food like Little Red Riding Hood visiting her grandmother. In 1942, he was about nine years old, and even more shy than I was. I loved him with all my heart. I was four years younger, but he did not disdain to play with me and even allowed me to choose our activities.

My favorite was "going for a train ride." We would set out chairs to serve as train carriages, and take turns acting as the engineer, blowing the whistle and deciding when to stop. The "station" at each stop had a supply of food, but only of one kind, so we had to travel from one station to another to another in search of supplies. The game lasted until we decided our baskets were full.

Arūnas could remember foods I had never tasted. He and Milda would talk of marmalade and almonds, and remind each other of the taste of oranges and bananas. Just legendary names to me.

Father's mother, his brother Boleslovas, and his three unmarried sisters continued to live and farm in Šeduva. They too had heavy food quotas to deliver to the Germans, but barely enough land to produce enough for themselves, especially after Boleslovas married and my cousin Zenonas was born. Nonetheless, once the snows melted, Mother or Father would take me to stay with "the aunties," and Milda also would come for some part of the summer holidays. We could roam the fields bare-footed, pick sorrel leaves for soup, find mushrooms in the woods, and gather blackberries growing wild.

Every Lithuanian child knew how to forage. Sometimes the aunties would catch fish in nearby ponds, or cook a chicken that had "escaped" the notice of German requisitions. For the first few years, some fruits and vegetables were not placed on the requisitions list. I remember that Milda and I often gorged on cherries and raspberries, strawberries and hazel nuts. By the end of the summer vacation, our white anemic faces would turn rosy again from nature's bounty.

War is never kind to children. Milda, who was almost eight years older than me, had a good resistance to illness, but I was, it seems, always sick. Poor and meager food for most of the year meant that my immune system was unable to fight off germs. Mother and Father protected me as best they could, but between 1941 and 1944, childhood maladies kept me all-too-often confined to bed.

At first, some medicines were available, but by 1942, as German battle losses mounted, they were hoarded for the military, and if any were on hand, they were reserved for German citizens, not the undesirable native populations. Colds were a constant in my life, as were recurring tonsillitis, strep throat, and ear infections. Occasionally, I went to play outside with other children—who passed on to me chickenpox, measles, rubella, scarlatina (a milder form of scarlet fever), and dysentery. My poor parents had no respite from worry.

The only remedy was bed rest and herbal infusions from supplies gathered by the aunties: raspberry, chamomile, and my favorite—linden flower tea. I would lie with my eyes closed and make up stories for myself, combining my favorite pieces from the fairy tales I had heard. When I was allowed to sit, I drew. I had a facility for copying what I saw. Father would bring me books on loan from the schools he supervised, and I would copy all the pictures. Some illustrations were so appealing I wanted to hear the stories they portrayed, but Mother, who worked the night shift, needed to sleep, and seldom had the time to read to me. Lithuanian is a phonetic language and much easier to read and spell than English, so before age five, I figured out the words for myself. There's no better friend than a book for an ailing, solitary child. I had company!

In 1942, I almost died from diphtheria, a disease as dreaded as plague in old Lithuania. At that time, although the German forces invading Russia had not succeeded in taking Moscow, Hitler's prime target, he still had complete confidence in an ultimate victory. He was sure that the battle of Leningrad, which had been raging for months, would be won at any moment. As a propaganda gesture, our German rulers in Vilnius offered a two-week residence camp for the Lithuanian and Polish children of governmental employees.

My parents were happy to read that I would be in fresh air and enjoy ample good food. I was not convinced. I was only five, and had never been left on my own with strangers. Mother and Father promised that one or the other would come to visit me every two or three days. Nonetheless, I was dreading it.

The reality of camp life did not match the glowing promises made to our parents. The food served to us children was barely edible. The better supplies disappeared to feed the cooks and favored staff. Visiting dignitaries were, of course, abundantly feasted. I still recall the fury of the older campers at this injustice, how they banged their plates on the tables and shouted complaints about the "pig-swill" we were being served.

We were housed in some sort of barracks. The girl's dormitory was crammed wall-to-wall; there was barely enough room to move between beds. I could not sleep. I was not used to the noise of children all around me, coughing and crying and shouting out in their nightmares, and wetting their beds because the outhouse was too far to walk to in the dark.

Sanitation was practically non-existent. Some children arrived with fleas and lice, which soon spread to everyone. Bedbugs chewed us at night. Many of us became infected with pinworms. My parents were contacted. Mother arrived to find me listless, my neck swollen, feverish, with a deep cough. "I knew that pinworms will give you a fever," she later remembered, "but not a cough. And yours did not sound right for an ordinary cold." Before she took me home, Mother insisted that I be checked out at the infirmary. "It was our great good luck that the nurse on duty was both competent and caring," said Mother. "She examined your throat, and immediately called a doctor."

At that stage of the war, there were not many doctors left to care for civilians. The vast majority of them were patching up soldiers on the Russian front, but luckily, the nurse located one. Mother guessed, "I think he was willing to come out to the camp because I overheard her say the dreaded word diphtheria. If you had it, they would be facing a flood of contagion."

The hours waiting for the doctor to arrive were torture for Mother. She remembered, "I was not able to call your father; they would not give me permission to use their phone. Keep in mind that when I was eight or nine, I lost three sisters in one night to diphtheria. The pain my own parents went through is seared into my soul. It was the most dreaded of all childhood diseases. To me, your hacking cough sounded worse by the minute. What parents can bear to hear their child choke to death?"

When the doctor arrived, he brought a supply of diphtheria antitoxin with him. He was disgusted to confirm that I had diphtheria because now he would have to inoculate everyone in the camp. He gave me the injection and told Mother to get me out of there at once.

We all spent a difficult night. "It was a nightmarish time for us as we listened to you trying to catch your breath," Mother said. "It was touch-and-go, but you made it. Of course, we had another worry: what if Milda caught it from you?"

I escaped death that time, but then almost died from another bout a couple of months later. As soon as I had recovered from my "vacation" in the government camp, Father took me to spend the warm months in Šeduva. Because of the fear associated with the word "diphtheria," he did not tell anyone that I had just survived an attack. A few weeks after arriving, I developed a deep hacking cough and ran a high fever.

There was no doctor available in town, but the aunties found a veterinarian to examine me. What did the poor man know? He guessed that I had diphtheria, and from some dusty corner of the town pharmacy, he unearthed a dose of antitoxin with which to inject me. It turned out to be a very bad decision. To begin with, I had pneumonia, which was serious enough because there were no antibiotics available to cure it. But giving me the shot against diphtheria made matters enormously more dangerous.

"In those days," explained Father, "diphtheria antitoxins were obtained either from horse or from sheep blood. It was very dangerous to administer both kinds to the same person without waiting for at least a year because there would invariably ensue an allergic reaction. Sure enough, the injections you had, one in May of 1942 and then again in August, must have come from two incompatible sources. You spiked fevers so severe you were either incoherent or catatonic. My poor sisters and my old mother could not imagine what I would do if you died. They finally sent me a telegram to tell me how very ill you were. It took about fourteen hours on slow trains to get from Vilnius to Šeduva. And those Nazi devils would not give Mother permission to leave her job! They said one parent to visit was enough. Imagine how she felt."

Father became emotional at the memory. "When I saw you, I thought you were dead. You lay so still. Your lips were full of sores, your eyes closed and crusted. I picked you up, your little body burning with fever. I pressed you close in my arms. '*Saulute Mylimiausia*—my Dearest Sunshine,' I kept murmuring, rocking you as I used to when you were a baby. Then I felt you move. Barely audible, a whisper: 'Daddy, you've come at last,' and then you went limp again. I can't tell you what I went through. I've never prayed so hard. Toward morning the fever broke. All of us wept with relief, sure that God had given us a miracle."

CHAPTER 6:

Life Under the *Führer*

F or us Lithuanians, the quality of life deteriorated in tandem with the battle losses suffered by our new masters. In 1941, Hitler and his generals started their attacks on Soviet territories with total contempt for the abilities of the "primitive" Russians, failing to grasp the unyielding persistence of the natives against any and all invaders. They also ignored the deadly lesson learned by a former would-be conqueror, Napoleon: it is impossible to overcome Russia's climate.

First, Hitler started the Siege of Leningrad, which lasted over two bitter winters, from September 1941 to January 1943. Then came the battle for Stalingrad, from August 1942 to February 1943.

As fate would have it, the Eastern European winters of the early 1940's broke records for their severity. Hitler's military lacked enough warm clothing and footwear, and thousands froze. When the rains poured in spring and autumn, transportation floundered in a sea of mud. During the long winters, because of impassable deep snows, supplies of ammunition, fuel, and food for the troops were catastrophically inadequate. The loss of lives was astounding, as German soldiers fell to exposure, starvation, disease, and combat.

Of course, the German media spoke only of success, but their propaganda did not persuade us. Over the course of 1942, the Lithuanian underground spread news of the continued impasse in Leningrad and the huge losses the Wehrmacht was sustaining in Stalingrad. Hitler's one bright spot had been Rommel's successes in North Africa, but then the military forces of the United States joined their British allies, and by November, Rommel had to retreat. As 1942 came to an end, Lithuanians were convinced that Hitler would eventually lose all his occupied territories. He had overextended himself. The only question was how soon it would all be over.

We did not need news reports to tell us of Hitler's troubles—we could tell just by looking at the empty stores. Ordinary household goods disappeared off the shelves. "Can you imagine?" Mother said. "There were no toothbrushes, though we could still get some sort of compacted powder in a round tin container supposedly made for brushing teeth. Good soap disappeared. The kind we Lithuanians could get in our grocery stores was an evil smelling, abrasive grey slab. I can't imagine what it was made of: cement powder?"

"Remember the head lice?" Milda said. "Kids didn't want to wash with that horrible soap! If it got into your eyes, it almost blinded you. I was always catching the pests in school. Mother would get so angry! Then she'd sit me down and drag a scratchy lice comb through my curls. The tines would break and pull horribly—each session would tear out handfuls of hair!"

"That's why we finally had to cut off your braids," said Mother to Milda. "Dalia's hair was too thin and short, so she caught lice only once, but you were a prime carrier!"

"How about toilet paper? There was none," Father said. "We saved every scrap of newspaper and tore up outdated school books for that purpose. And remember the large, old hanging wall maps we had in schools? Desperate for cloth, we soaked them for days to get the paper off the backing, which was made of light cotton. Perfect material for making underwear."

Every month, we could find fewer essentials. Until 1944, the Germans, whether at home or abroad in conquered territories, had no such troubles. The Nazis had openly instituted a dual system of pay, of shops, and of justice, favoring German nationals working in Lithuania and other occupied lands. Germans could get clothing: they wore nice shoes and their soap was fragrant and mild.

Lithuanians had to make do with shoes made with wooden soles and canvas tops, and sandals from discarded, torn-up tires. The most valued tradesmen were the shoemakers. The skillful ones collected old footgear and, from the usable pieces, cobbled up something wearable. All shoes had little iron moons nailed to the bottom of the heels to extend their usefulness.

The relief that many had felt at the arrival of the Germans in June, 1941, when we viewed them as our saviors from the Soviet atrocities, turned to resistance. Hitler desperately needed more soldiers and more workers. His attempt to mobilize Lithuanian men to fight for the Third Reich was unsuccessful. Lithuanians were not anxious to go freeze in Soviet Russia. Why should our men risk their lives for a nation that considered us "sub-humans" useful only as cannon fodder?

In the winter of 1942–1943, as losses soared, the Nazis tried to entice the youths of the Baltic States to form SS Legions. Underground resistance organizations in Lithuania urged the young not to join. There were no illusions: we knew our men would not be assigned any easy jobs, like guarding the regime's top officials, but would be designated as "storm troopers"—the first to be thrown into battle. Although in the other two Baltic countries, such recruitment resulted in the formation of the Estonian and the Latvian SS Legions, in Lithuania the campaign was an abysmal failure.

Just like Stalin before him, Hitler blamed the "intellectuals" for discouraging cooperation. In reprisal, his administrators shuttered universities and curtailed higher education. In their stead, they established "trade schools." Students had little time to study books in a trade school. Instead, they were trained to manufacture for the war machine.

As Hitler's military disappointments mounted, his administrators in Lithuania ordered all males between the ages of eighteen and forty-five to fulfill "work duties." This meant a transfer to Germany, to live in squalid, crowded conditions, working at least ten hours a day, six days a week, with minimal rations.

In 1943, Father was thirty-five years old. "I lived in fear," he said, "that I would be taken away to spend my days in a factory producing parts for the Wehrmacht's tanks or guns. Once again, I had a suitcase ready, into which I could throw clothing and food saved for such an emergency. I had survived the Soviets, but now I was expecting the Nazis to come knocking on the door."

Food. It became our obsession. Nazi administrators tightened the rationing rules. Because both Mother and Father worked, it was Milda's job after school to stand in line to buy whatever was available at the store to which we were assigned. Hungry people forced to stand in long lines are not inclined to be fair or kind, and pushy people often elbowed her away to the back. She soon learned to use the full force of her smile and perky chatter to keep others amused—and herself in her spot. But it was not easy.

"For me, being responsible for buying our food was a horrible nightmare," said Milda. "First, I had to somehow get to the counter. Not only did people try to push in front, but there were men who would try to pinch me or get their hands into my blouse. A couple of times, guys tried to slobber all over my face, offering, 'I'll let you go first if you give me a big kiss.' I tried to get between two women, but sometimes the old biddies were really nasty. When I did manage to buy whatever was available from Mother's list, my next challenge was to get it home. I was mugged several times, my groceries wrested out of my hands. I learned to always walk close to a family with kids going in my direction, pretending I was one of them."

We lived mostly on buckwheat porridge, or *košė*, and barley groats, and on lucky days we had potatoes. Many were the days when *košė* was on the menu morning, noon and night. There was always a bread ration available, but people swore it was made with sawdust. It was so dry it crumbled in your hand; it tasted awful, and made the intestines bloat. Mother said, "It was a day to celebrate when we had something to put on the bread. Occasionally, we could find preserves made from sugar beets. You girls were in heaven on the rare occasions when we had a bit of sugar to sprinkle on a slice moistened with water."

The most worrisome deficit was fat. Never mind that cereals, potatoes, and bread, eaten bare-naked, lacked taste. Without fat in the diet, people had constant diarrhea. Butter was pretty much unobtainable. It was a feast day when we got some fatback pork, salted or smoked. To obtain meat in Vilnius was a rare event. Once in a while, Mother's nephew Vytas, who worked as a train conductor, brought us a sausage or some eggs which he had received from a grateful passenger for not examining the required travel documents too closely. Milda and I thought of him as our wonderful older brother. Occasionally, Father succeeded in exchanging cigarette coupons, or homemade brandy he had received as a gift, for a bit of pork or hamburger meat. My memories of those years revolve around food: would Mother manage to make something for us?

In the summer of 1943, I missed seeing the tapestry that had always hung above the sofa. It depicted a proud stag in the forest, antlers raised, and a group of does in the foreground drinking from a stream. In those days with no television, it had served as my window into an imaginary green world of calm and beauty. We traded it to a farmer for three sacks of potatoes. Other possessions followed. Father grieved to give up the beautifully carved bookcase with glass-fronted doors, which housed his personal collection of antique books, some in old gothic script. The bookcase was the first valuable piece of furniture that Father had acquired on being promoted to teach in Kaišiadorys in 1932. Of course, it went in exchange for food.

Milda taught me to play a few elementary exercises.

In the spring of 1944, our beautiful grand piano disappeared. The loss was heartbreaking for my talented sister. It went to a well-to-do German farmer in Smalininkai, in exchange for flour, potatoes, smoked bacon, dried sausage, and a big tin of *schmalz* (rendered pig fat, or lard). Oh, the heavenly taste of bread spread with lard and sprinkled with salt!

Father took a chunk of smoked bacon with him in early 1944, when he was chosen to accompany his superiors on a cultural tour of Dresden, the beautiful city of art and architecture which the British and Americans annihilated a year later.

"You had been sick with strep throat all winter," Father said to me, "to the point that a doctor cut off a third of each tonsil. He believed that tonsils served some useful purpose, so he refused to simply remove them. We thought you'd never stop bleeding. You seemed to lose all interest in life. For me, going to Dresden was a treat—such collections of priceless art! But my main purpose was to find you a doll. You had yearned for one for so long, but no dolls were to be found in Vilnius—whoever had a nice doll hung on to it. A pound of smoked bacon got me your heart's desire. I swear you sprang back to life when you saw it."

At last, my greatest wish had been granted: Father brought back a perfect little girl doll. I named her "*Laimutė*"—Little Luck. She was made of a very light, hard material, which I later learned was celluloid. Molded on her head, she had short, wavy, light-brown hair, and her blue eyes seemed to look at me expectantly, as if asking, "What next?"

She wore a white dress with pink rosebuds protected by a lace-edged white apron. White ankle-socks and black-patent Mary Jane shoes completed her outfit. I made sure my hands were immaculate before I picked her up, and then I spent hours holding her, singing to her, and telling her stories.

Most of the stories featured tables that would produce an abundance of food if I, the heroine, said the right magic word. I elaborated a story of trees from which hung sausages, hams, roasted chickens... I had heard similar fairy tales and I feasted on imaginary banquets when hunger gnawed. Laimutė understood me perfectly and shared all my dreams. Each night, I put her to sleep in her original box, hidden under the big wardrobe in the bedroom because I thought this made her safe from bombs.

Vilnius was receiving its share of bombing, mostly in the late evening and at night, usually targeting the train yards and supply warehouses. Our apartment building was not near a military target, but aiming was an inexact art and many bombs went astray. For a while, when the sirens warned of approaching enemy planes, and the sky lit up with searchlights, we four hurried to the air-raid shelter prepared in the basement of the building in front of ours. The place would get choked with people.

After the door slammed shut, we felt that the oxygen supply was gone. Father and Milda were especially subject to panicky claustrophobia. The basement had a musty smell to start with; add to that the smell of tightly packed people, sweating in fear, and an open pail that was the only toilet. The stench would simply overcome us. After a few weeks, my parents decided that it would be better to be killed outright in our own beds than die choking in that filthy hole.

In September of 1943, I started first grade. It was my first experience of enduring the noise, the pushing and shoving of about thirty other children in a room. The year before, I had missed kindergarten. German public health rules mandated that, after surviving diphtheria, a year must pass before a child was allowed to attend school. This limit could be shortened if some laboratory test could be passed, but no such test was then available for non-Germans in Vilnius.

To walk to class, I had but to cross the courtyard separating our apartment building from the one in front, in which the school, and the dreaded air-raid shelter below it, were located. I did well in school: my report card shows a neat row of "fives," the highest grade in those years.

Getting good grades was easy, but life in school was not. I was downright miserable. My talents for singing, drawing, and reciting poetry did not impress my classmates. I was mercilessly teased because I was timid as a wild hare and had no social skills with children who were strangers. Boys pulled my hair, and yanked out the white ribbon that I insisted on wearing everywhere. It was my one bit of vanity. They would pass it on to other girls, who would refuse to give it back until I complained to the teacher, at which point I'd hear a chorus of "Tattle-tale!"

It did not help that my "Sunday Child" luck had forgotten to include a dose of charisma, or just more attractive looks. I was about the plainest child imaginable—skinny, pasty-faced (poor diet did not help), with straight mouse-colored hair. I had unusual blueberry colored irises, exactly like Mother's and Milda's, but while their eyes were large, mine were small. I did have nice teeth and my parents said I had an appealing smile, but in school I never found anything to smile about. At times, I was glad to be sick, just so I could skip the misery of what awaited me when I crossed the yard.

One drizzly autumn day in 1943, I was at home, feeling unwell, when there was a timid knocking at the front door. Neither Milda nor Father was home. Unexpected knocking on the door usually meant trouble, so I rushed to cling to Mother for protection.

Before us stood a gaunt, ill-dressed child about my age. She held out a small empty bag, the size of a child's pillowcase, and said, in Polish, that she was very hungry, and could we spare a little bread? Mother asked her something in Lithuanian, but the child shook her head, indicating that she could not understand. Because, in recent history, the Poles had treated Lithuanians very badly, at first Mother was going to turn her away—but I pleaded, "Give her my portion." Mother had a kind heart, but the privations under years of occupation had made her abrupt and impatient.

My words must have shamed Mother, because she went off to the kitchen, leaving the two of us to stare at each other. Her enormous brown eyes stared back at me anxiously. She wore a dark headscarf wrapped tightly against the cold. Her cheekbones stood out in her small face. She had outgrown her coat, and her bony wrists stuck out from the frayed sleeves. I looked at the bird-like legs, the knee joints red and swollen. Her canvas shoes were wet and muddy and I thought, *She'll catch a cold if she does not dry her feet soon.*

I gave her a shy smile, and her face relaxed. It hurt me to see such a thin child. I was often hungry too, but at least I did not have to beg. Mother came back with a generous portion of bread and some dried Lithuanian cheese. The little girl's eyes lit up; she tried to kiss mother's hand, then put her arms around mother's thighs, which was as high as she could reach.

Every time Mother remembered the incident, she burst into tears. She said, "I bowed down to return the hug. Under her thin coat, all I felt were bones. She clung to me for dear life. She whispered, 'Lady, dear angel, please, can you save me?' I suddenly realized that this little child was not a Polish waif, but from the Jewish Ghetto! How had she managed to avoid the Nazi patrols and get out of that heavily guarded place? To risk all in search of food, perhaps for a chance at life! It hit me how desperate the plight of the Jews must be, to send their little ones out into the cold and danger, hoping for goodwill from strangers. What eats at my conscience still is that I had to refuse her in order to protect my own."

After the little girl left, Mother and I sat together and bawled. I felt so sorry for this little girl whom I had liked on sight. I cried in sympathy with Mother, who was sobbing her heart out. Many years later, Mother said: "Like most Lithuanians, I had been furious at the Jews who aided the Soviets to terrorize and deport us. I had closed my ears to stories of Jewish massacres when the Nazis invaded. We knew that Jews were shut up in ghettoes, but we were told that they were basically like forced labor camps, no different from those in Germany where our own men had to work. But to see this little girl, so like my Dalia, pleading for her life—I had to conclude that something unspeakable must be happening in the ghettoes."

I don't know what my parents would have done had this little girl returned, or had some other Jewish child come to our door. Harboring Jews was high treason in the eyes of the Nazis, punishable by death or removal to a camp together with the Jews. I do not believe that Father could have turned a child away, even if the four of us would have been in mortal danger. Could Mother have done it a second time? She had a practical, realistic nature. Would she have chosen, once again, to protect the lives of her family? But no child ever came again.

CHAPTER 7:

Never to See My Home Again

In the spring of 1944, the German military was retreating from Russia. The previous year, when the battle of Stalingrad was lost, Hitler had commented, "The god of war has gone over to the other side." Presumably Hitler thought he was important enough to win without the god's help. His armies were spread too thin, but he believed in his own superior strategy.

He still trusted commander Göring's vaunted air force, the *Luftwaffe*, and he was sure that his secret, deadly weapons would be ready in time to turn events back in his favor and destroy the allied forces. However, his civil-service administrators were more realistic and very worried, and worry made most of them imperious and cruel. They wanted more from Lithuania than it had to give. Most of all, they wanted soldiers for their armed forces and free labor for their factories. Father and Mother tried to make themselves invisible.

The Soviet air force intensified its bombing of Vilnius. Its army was pushing the retreating Germans ever closer to Lithuania's borders. How long could the Germans hold out? For my parents, the situation was too confusing: smuggled news reports from England were drowned out by Nazi propaganda. One decision was firm: for summer vacation, Father wanted us out of the city. Mother suggested that we go to Šeduva, as usual. Food had become nearly impossible to obtain in Vilnius, but in Šeduva we could manage.

And yet, if the Soviets advanced more rapidly than expected, what would we do? They would invade from Latvia, to the northeast, and along Lithuania's eastern border with Belarus. Šeduva lies north of Vilnius—closer to the probable point of invasion. For us to avoid the Soviets, the only direction for escape would have to be to the south and west, toward Prussia and the German-occupied territory of Poland. My parents knew one thing for sure: to be caught by the Soviets would mean death for us. We would not avoid deportation to Siberia a second time.

If we could not go to Šeduva, where could we go? Father's brother Benediktas offered a solution for Mother, Milda, and me. He had some good friends, the Varnakas family, who had a big farm near Kybartai, located on the border of East Prussia. Before the war started, Mr. Varnakas had borrowed a large sum of money from Benediktas to construct a water mill.

Uncle Benediktas did not want to be repaid in worthless German Reichsmarks. He asked Mr. Varnakas, as partial payment, to let Mother, Milda, and me stay at his farm for the summer, and to provide us with food. By the grace of good management, or well-chosen friends, the Varnakases had managed to fulfill the requisition quotas demanded by the Germans, and still had food to spare.

Father had to stay in Vilnius to organize school children for mandatory work details to help the Third Reich. Why allow those energetic young students to loaf on vacation when they could be scouring fields and forests for medicinal herbs and leaves and wild berries to help the military? Of course, most children had disappeared into the countryside from the first day of vacation. Still, Father had to cooperate, or else…

Mother, Milda and I left as soon as school ended, at the start of June. Our good clothes remained in Vilnius; we three packed one Sunday outfit each, and then only our oldest clothing and worn sandals for the stay in the country. I saw Milda put two photograph albums into her bundle and wondered whether I should tattle. But I was mad at Mother because she was making me leave my doll, Laimutė, in Vilnius, and I was grief-stricken to be separated from her. "It's dirty in the country," Mother said. "Besides, there will be peasant children around. They're rough. They will tear her to pieces." I hated adult logic.

Father and Mother thought that we were going as guests. Apparently, the Varnakases understood the agreement very differently. To her dying day, Mother spoke of them with venom. "They treated us exactly the same as the two Russian prisoner families whom the Germans had assigned to slave for them. Milda and I were just additional unpaid labor. Varnakas put us in an uncomfortable little room in a storage building. We had to weed the gardens and rake hay, churn butter, make cheeses, and help in the kitchen, exactly as if we were country maids. In the meantime, Benediktas' wife and her friend, Mrs.

Šimkus, stayed in the main house and pretended not to know us. Those scum! They never invited us to eat with them. We were relegated to the kitchen with the servants. I swear they resented every slice of bread we ate, may they rot in hell!"

I was seven, and had to earn my keep. I helped pull weeds, which was boring, but I enjoyed my next assignment: to protect goslings from the predations of the hungry hawks. Someone would release the baby birds from their night quarters and they would follow me, peeping anxiously and flapping their little wing stubs, down to the brook below the dam. I loved the feeling of morning dew under my bare feet.

As long as I was with the goslings, the hawks stayed away and my charges were safe. They'd splash and upend themselves in the water: I envied them their fun. The first week or two, they tired rapidly. It was the sweetest feeling in the world to sit in a meadow surrounded by downy yellow fluff-balls, all trying to get into my lap and sleepily peeping their soft gosling lullaby. But they grew fast, and soon it was a challenge to keep them close, because they wanted to forage further down the stream.

I spent many hours exploring the shallow brook, which burbled merrily over stones and rocks. Under the rocks hid delicious crayfish. While my goslings enjoyed themselves close by, I often searched out a few, even though they could give my fingers a nasty pinch. I liked the praise Mother gave me when I came home with an apron full of crayfish, but I had to watch out for enemies: the two Varnakas sons were the worst. They would take my catch and throw it back into the stream, laughing uproariously. But the little Russian children were more wily. They would ambush me on the way home and run off with my haul. I hated them all.

I was lonely, and kept whining about missing my doll. In a few spots near the stream grew stands of cattails. Mother showed me a trick from her own childhood, when there were no toys to be bought in her village. The first step was to pull a cattail gently out of the marshy ground. The bottom of the stalk ended in a white bulb, with many thin white roots. The bulb and the roots represented the face and hair of a primitive doll. With some thread, I attached a twig to the stalk, crosswise, for arms, and wound another V-shaped twig to the bottom, for legs. My doll wore leaves and dandelions for clothing, which tore and fell off. It was not satisfactory at all. I wanted something realistic, with a pretty face. I wanted Laimutė.

While Mother and Milda worked all day, I was often left to cope on my own. I enjoyed the fields and the stream, and the nearby woods, full of wild strawberries in early summer. Their smell was intoxicating. I imagined that heaven smelled of wild strawberries.

Away from the tormenting boys, I could have been happy, but Mother was grouchy, and especially mean to Milda. When Mother was upset over something and Father wasn't around, she tended to slap Milda, calling her lazy and stupid, or worse. It was only many years later that I understood why: Mother expected Milda, her first child, to be just like her: practical, responsible, punctual and ultra-neat. She took it as a direct affront to herself when Milda was late returning from an outing, or left her things lying about. But Milda was born more of a *vėjo vaikas*—child of the wind, living for the moment, consumed by the good or the fearful of each day.

Mother behaved better when Father was around. Although Mother did not mistreat me, she had little time or patience for me. I missed Father bitterly. If he were with us, I thought, the Varnakases would treat us much better, and Mother would be nicer to Milda and me, and the thieving boys would leave me alone for fear of a beating.

Our hosts seemed to have some access to news other than German propaganda. In early June 1944, when we first arrived, they told Mother that the war would end soon; Rome was in the hands of the Allies, and the British and the Americans had landed on the beaches in Normandy, France. Then, at the end of June, the rumor was that the Red Army was harassing and pushing the Germans out of Belarus.

The Varnakases were intelligent enough to know that if the Soviets returned to Lithuania and found them enjoying their unusually prosperous farm, they would be doomed to a terrible fate in Siberia. It was time to go. They threw all hands into a tornado of activity to prepare for departure.

Like most Lithuanians, they expected the war to end soon. The Varnakases were sure that by the terms of the Atlantic Charter, the three Baltic countries would regain their freedom as soon as the war ended and the Americans and British restored their Independence. They did not expect to be gone from home very long. In the meantime, they planned to bury on their property large supplies of seed grain and food products, securely sealed up in the large milk cans, made of galvanized metal, which were universally used to deliver milk quotas to the German collection centers.

They ordered their workers to slaughter the pigs. Everyone sweltered, singeing the carcasses, making sausages and drying them, smoking hams and slabs of fatback bacon, and salting pork. Mother and the other servants baked dozens of rye loaves, sliced them, and then dried them. Such bread is light to carry, does not spoil, and can be reconstituted with any liquid. I loved sucking on a dry rusk until it got soft again.

Milda had to work in the overheated kitchen, rendering pig fat into drippings, which were then put through a sieve to remove the solid bits. At room temperature, the resulting liquid hardened to the consistency of soft butter. This was the famous "*schmalz*," so delicious to me when spread on a potato or a flavorful piece of rye bread and sprinkled with salt. In a cooked state, pig fat lasts for months.

Mother's mood worsened day by day. Stress overwhelmed her. She had no news of Father and no way to contact him. Telephones worked only intermittently, and our hosts would not countenance her sitting by their phone all day trying to reach Father. We had no telephone at home in Vilnius, and his work took him to a number of schools. Where to call? Mail continued to arrive through June, but then deliveries stopped. She heard that Minsk, the capital of Belarus, was re-occupied by the Soviets on July 3. Minsk is only 105 miles from Vilnius. With the vaunted German Wehrmacht in flight, how soon would Vilnius be back in Soviet hands? Would Father have time to escape?

Then came the day which forced me up the ladder to adulthood. For months, perhaps beginning with the visit of the little Jewish girl, I had been aware that something was seriously wrong—something more threatening than the disappearing furniture or the lack of food. Why were my parents so worried? Questioning them resulted in few answers. Under the Nazis, as under the Soviets, it was better if your children knew as little as possible, so they would not say anything politically objectionable to the wrong person.

It was mid-July. The weather was warm, and raspberries were ripening. Mother, Milda, and I loved raspberries almost as much as wild strawberries. Mother found a small basket for me, told me to be careful, and sent me off into the nearby woods, where raspberry bushes rambled in abundance. I prayed to my favorite saint, St. Theresa, to protect me from my tormentors. "Please, Little Flower, don't let the bullies find me!" They were not the only ones I feared. I had overheard the grown-ups whispering among themselves that the woodlands harbored desperate men, "German deserters," "partisans," "guerillas," and "communists," all of them looking for a way to survive. What would they do to me if I disturbed them?

Saint Theresa took good care of me that day. Nobody around the berry bushes in the coppice but the birds. Raspberry canes scratched me till I bled, but my little basket was brim-full of fragrant berries. Mother and Milda could have them all. I had eaten so many my stomach was beginning to cramp. I was thirsty. It was time to return.

The quickest way back to the farm, I knew, was by the cart track just beyond a stand of beech trees. Still, I was not going to risk losing all my work to those thieving boys, so I crept out of the trees as stealthily as a mouse—and almost dropped my precious basket. A short distance away, on a stump at the border of the path, his back toward me, sat a giant man. To get home, I would have to pass him. Just then he was bent over, doing something at his feet. Panicked, I wriggled under the low branches of the nearest tree.

What was he doing? Removing his shoes? Putting his shoes on? Slowly, slowly, the giant man picked up his bundle and briefcase, rose, stretched to full height, and started to limp down the road. Should I follow behind? I studied him as he moved. But wait! That familiar head—*That's no giant that's—that's—oh God, it's Dad!*

"Dad, Daddy, Daddy, it's me, Dalia!" I screamed, scrambling, running full tilt, flinging myself at his legs, nearly laying him out flat. It had been too many weeks since I had seen him. Inside his bear hug, I was in heaven.

Father was the parent to whom my little heart was glued. Certainly, I loved Mama, what would we do without her? But she was so unpredictable. I never knew when she'd stroke my hair or push me away, praise me or scold for no reason I could detect. The love I felt from Father and for Father was total, unconditional, and all encompassing. He was my teacher, my forever friend, my protector, the one who encouraged rather than yelled, who found little surprises to cheer us all, the one I could always trust to make everything better. Now that I felt his familiar, long arms tight about me, kisses in my hair and on my forehead, my joy was total. *Everything will be fine now*, I thought.

I felt a drop of wetness. Not rain, clearly. Tears? Was Father crying? Why? Had someone died? I wriggled free.

"Daddy?" Like an echo, my eyes started brimming over. "Daddy? What's happened? Why are you crying?"

Father fished around for a handkerchief. "My Little Sunshine," he murmured. "Mama and I have tried to shelter you, to let you live a normal life despite the war. But what shelter is there for you now? Bombs have destroyed our home and all we own. The Soviets are back. If they catch us we'll be sent to Siberia. And I don't know where to go."

I looked at him, puzzled. I understood the words, but not the meaning. "We can't go home? Never? Forever?" It took a while to sink in. "Can't we go to Šeduva?" I asked, watching him hungrily eat the raspberries.

"That's impossible now, the Soviets have barred the way," said Father sorrowfully. He picked up his things and gazed up into the blue, blue sky, following with his eyes the effortless darting of barn swallows. "Look at them," he said to me. "Look how free they are. Safe above the dangers here on the ground. Ah, freedom, freedom. They travel for thousands of miles. When they want to settle, they build a snug little nest. If only we could fly. Our feet are slow, they hurt, they bleed. And where in this wide world will we find a safe site to build our nest again?"

Slowly, we made our way to the farm. Father's feet were a mass of blisters. While he soaked them, he told Mother what had happened. Much of what Father said went over my head, but I grasped the fact that we were now homeless, and that nothing of ours was left: no clothes, no food, no bedding—and no precious doll. It hurt to think I could never go back to our warm kitchen, or to feel the soft comforter on my face before I went to sleep. But knowing that I would never again see Laimutė simply broke my heart. I cried for hours, remembering her sweet expression, and the stories we used to share.

Father described that more than a week before, when the air raid sirens sounded unusually early in the morning, he had a premonition. For once, he decided not to remain in the apartment. He grabbed the briefcase that held all our documents, and was inspired to throw his warm winter coat over his arm.

He ran as fast as he could up the hilly Basanavičiaus Street, away from the buildings and toward an area that had already been bombed. "I crouched among the wrecked brick walls and felt bombs falling nearby, heard buildings exploding, saw clouds of dust and smoke. When the planes were gone and the dust settled, I saw that our apartment building lay in ruins. I went to look, but there was nothing left to rescue: it was a pile of smoking, charred rubble. I didn't know what to do, so I went to the Regional Administration office to see what they would advise. The place was empty."

It took Father about ten days to get to us. There were no trains running; Soviet bombs and the artillery of the retreating Germans had wrecked bridges and railroad tracks. He went on foot, and sometimes succeeded in hitching a ride on a passing military truck. He asked farmers driving by in carts if he could ride along. There was no food he could buy. Stores were closed; farmers did not want German money. He zigzagged his way to us, stopping here and there at the homes of friends and relatives to recover for a day or two. The town shoes he wore were not meant for a hike of a hundred miles.

Father's news upset Mother terribly: our losses were irreparable. She kept moaning, "God, oh God, oh God, what's to become of us?" She lamented bitterly that Father did not have so much as a change of underwear, and the three of us had left all our better clothes and shoes in Vilnius.

Mother and Father said they needed to talk privately. Milda and I went out and sat under a shady birch. Milda absentmindedly played with some pebbles scattered on the ground. She looked stricken, her mind far away. I needed her to explain to me what was going on. I had but vague memories of the year under the Soviets. Why was Father afraid of them? What was Siberia? Milda was fifteen, an adult in my eyes. But would she talk to me? Or would she shoo me away as she usually did, saying I was too young to know?

Milda did her best to make me understand the situation. Although our parents had tried to shield her from the most bestial examples of Soviet and Nazi conduct, she had picked up information from friends whose parents were less reticent. In addition, these past weeks she had been listening to the farmhands and the maids in the kitchen, and had heard horror tales about both sides. She feared the Nazis, but was terrified of the Soviets. She described to me what she had heard about life in work camps and in prisons in the snowy wastes of Siberia. She said if a child had nobody to protect it, the Soviets considered it useless and left it up to someone to take it in or let it starve or freeze to death.

"You know the worst part, sis?" she said. "They take the men away to logging camps and mines, and they leave the women and children on their own. And sometimes they take away the women too. The healthy ones, the prettier girls. I can't face what they do to them. Sis, I am scared to death. Remember, Dad said the Red Army is just having a rest. When the Red Dragon advances, we'd better be gone. God, I'm scared."

The Red Dragon! I gasped, remembering my old nightmares. Now I understood that there was no such animal, that the Red Dragon was a name for our communist, Bolshevik, Soviet enemies, by whatever label you named them. I shivered. Suddenly an appalling possibility hit home. What would happen if the communists grabbed all of us, but then took both Mama and Dad away? It could happen! Hadn't Milda said so?

And what was that bit about *the prettier girls*: Milda in my eyes was more than merely pretty! What if she were also taken away? Who would look after me? For the first time I realized that I could be left alone in a world that seemed bent on destroying all of us. I would be like the little Jewish girl who had come begging at our door, and we did not take her in. I had to grow up. I had to learn how to survive.

I had no idea where to start.

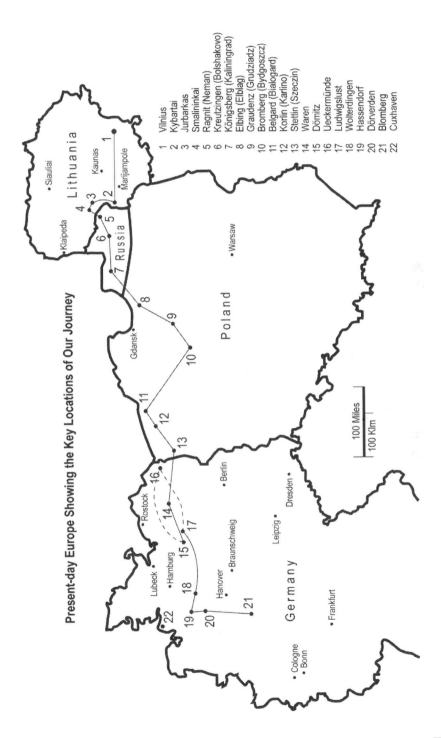

Present-day Europe Showing the Key Locations of Our Journey

1 Vilnius
2 Kybartai
3 Jurbarkas
4 Smalininkai
5 Ragnit (Neman)
6 Kreutzingen (Bolshakovo)
7 Königsberg (Kaliningrad)
8 Elbing (Elbląg)
9 Graudenz (Grudziadz)
10 Bromberg (Bydgoszcz)
11 Belgard (Bialogard)
12 Korlin (Karlino)
13 Stettin (Szeczin)
14 Waren
15 Dömitz
16 Ueckermünde
17 Ludwigslust
18 Wolterdingen
19 Hassendorf
20 Dörverden
21 Blomberg
22 Cuxhaven

CHAPTER 8:

Departure Delayed

Shortly after Father's arrival, on July 13, 1944, news came that the Soviets were back in Vilnius. The Varnakas family began loading wagons with food, bedding and portable treasures such as their jewels, crystal and silver. They were planning to wait out the war in Eastern Germany. The food products and seeds stored in the galvanized milk cans were to await their return, safely buried in the garden or under the floors of various farm structures. Milda overheard two of the maids giggling in the kitchen. "The Varnakases will not have gone ten kilometers before we dig up all their hidden food supplies. Do they think we'll go hungry so they can gorge when they return?" Milda felt no desire to tattle on them.

The next weeks are a blur in my memory: too many impressions, too much to absorb, and what a commotion at the farm! I stayed out of the way and watched keenly. I was trying to learn how grown-ups went about living. How did they know what to do? But all I saw was confusion.

As soon as his feet healed enough to put on his shoes, Father borrowed a horse and rode to the German administrative center for the area, to talk to the *Gebietskommissar*—the regional commissioner whose job included issuing travel documents and permits for rationing cards and food coupons. We needed official documents if we were to escape westward, into German-controlled territories. Father was not sure of his reception: would it be a curt refusal? Would the commissioner even be available, or already gone on his way to a safer location?

Father's luck held out. "I greeted him politely in German, the old-fashioned way," he said. "I would not shoot my arm out and shout *Heil Hitler* for anyone, ever. I told the commissioner I was from Vilnius, which was now overrun by Soviet Russians. I said I wanted to go work in Germany, and asked him for the documents and ration cards I would need for all of us." Father shook his head at the memory. "The commissioner asked for my identification. I handed it to him, together with the certificate of my assignment as *Schulrat der Stadt Vilna*—School Inspector of the city of Vilnius. The commissioner practically jumped to attention!

"He called an aide to bring us tea. Not only did he issue the permits and the coupons, but he also wrote out, in beautiful calligraphic penmanship, a certificate stating that the holder was an honored member of the Ministry of Education who had done important service to the Third Reich as Inspector of Schools in Vilnius. He added an instruction that agencies and individuals were to render all possible aid to my family and me. He signed the certificate with a flourish, then decorated it with a seal and two very impressive-looking stamps. That certificate was a lifesaver in days to come.

"Afterwards, we sat, drank tea, and discussed the wonderful influence that Schiller had had upon Goethe, and vice-versa, and the pleasure of friendship in general. The man was hungry for talk about subjects other than the war. An innate respect for culture and education was typical of the ordinary German, as I was to experience months later under dire circumstances. Of course, that sort of respect did not exist among Nazi fanatics."

The tired Soviet troops had stopped for a breather in Vilnius. There was a short period of blessed calm. Some trains were running, though not regularly, from the nearby border town of Kybartai into East Prussia. With an important-looking document in his possession, Father thought we could get tickets and ride away from the Soviet danger. Mother would not consent. She did not believe that the soldiers of the Wehrmacht would honor any piece of paper presented by a non-German, no matter how many official-looking seals and stamps it had. Besides, she had learned very little German. What if we were separated from Father?

Moreover, she had heard rumors that famine was raging in Germany. If she could have found a supply of dried bread and rendered fat to take with us, she might have been more rational. But Mr. Varnakas would not part with a crumb or a drop, and there was none to buy. And when Mother made up her mind, no amount of reasoning would move her. Our parents could not agree on the next step. Milda was distraught at Mother's refusal to leave immediately, while it was relatively easy.

We were at an impasse when a bit of luck drove in. The husband of Mrs. Šimkus, who, with her children, was also a guest at the farm, held a high position in German-occupied Lithuania. He sent a truck to take her and the children to Jurbarkas, a town my parents knew well from their years in nearby Smalininkai. On the truck, there was room to spare, and Mrs. Šimkus liked having a big man like Father along for protection.

The truck did not run on gasoline, which by then was used only for important official cars and essential military vehicles. This truck had a tall round tank, in which small pieces of wood were burned. From the tank, pipes went here and there, and somehow, mysteriously, made the motor run—but it was noisy, belched smoke, and needed a supply of wood on hand at all times.

There were no seats. Mrs. Šimkus rode in the cab with the driver; her two children and the four of us with our small bundle of possessions climbed into the open truck bed. Most of the trip we spent standing, clinging to the railings. Sitting on the floor rattled our bones because the unpaved track was nothing but potholes. The truck wobbled and bounced "like a drunken Bolshevik," said Father.

The journey was very slow. We stopped near a forest for a rest. I was not used to wearing shoes: weeks spent running barefoot had raised calluses on my soles as tough as leather, and I was much more comfortable without the confining sandals. I had probably outgrown them. I took them off and put them on a stump where I could see them. The adults went to search out suitable branches to fuel the truck's boiler. I wandered off a little ways and found a small stream. Lively little fishes were darting about, inviting me to put my feet in the water to see if they would explore my toes. I lost track of time. When I heard hollering for me to return to the truck, I flew back, someone lifted me up, and off we went.

When we reached Jurbarkas, an outlying section of it was in flames. Apparently, there had been a sneak artillery attack by the Soviets, who planned a beachhead from Jurbarkas into East Prussia. Although the Soviets had re-taken most of Lithuania, Hitler's Army Group North still held the area starting at the border of Memelland (the former "Lithuania Minor") and going north all the way into Latvia. The Red Army, however, was slowly descending from north to south along the Baltic Sea. They meant to encircle Army Group North from all sides. The Germans were determined to hold on and fight back.

The truck dropped us off in the center of Jurbarkas. We had a long walk ahead of us to reach the home of the Piročkinas family, whom

Father had known from the time he had taught school in Smalininkai. As Father was helping me off the truck, he noticed my bare feet and asked, "Where are your sandals?"

Oh, my Lord. I burst into tears of rage and embarrassment. *Stupid, irresponsible idiot.* I called myself every bad thing I knew. Was this how I would act if I had to survive on my own? Mother, of course, scolded me unmercifully, but I did not even hear her. I despaired at my own uselessness; I could not even be trusted to remember my only pair of shoes. My self-confidence fell to zero. How was I to endure the coming winter with bare feet?

Fortunately for me, one of the Piročkinases' daughters worked at a regional co-op store, normally available only to Germans. By this time, late July, most German civilians had left Lithuania and gone back to safety—to their homes in Germany. There remained on the shelves a small supply of shoes and clothing available for sale, and because it was a government-run store, it accepted Reichsmarks. She found a pair of lace-up ankle-high shoes that were a little big for me, but would be perfect with thick socks for winter. She also found a winter coat for mother.

The Piročkinases were the souls of generosity. From people they knew, they obtained for us two used, but sturdy suitcases. They gave us towels, a couple of pillows, sheets, and a cooking pot. They baked loaves of delicious rye bread, cut them into thick slices and then slowly baked them again until completely dry. The resulting light rusks do not spoil. We had enough to fill a pillowcase. They gave us a bag of flour, and a whole dried Lithuanian cheese that stays edible for months.

Almost every day there was a Russian artillery attack on the east side of Jurbarkas. Who knew when they'd launch a serious offensive? Now that we had some food, Father persuaded Mother to get on a train toward Germany. There was a train connection from Smalininkai to Tilsit and from there to Königsberg (now called Kaliningrad). Father thought we could manage to walk from the Piročkinas home to Smalininkai.

I remember the summer morning we started the walk. It was a "sauna" day, so hot and humid it was hard to breathe. Father, Mother, and Milda were laden with suitcases and bundles containing all we had in the world. Arnoldas, the youngest of the Piročkinas family, walked with us, helping Milda—who had been his schoolmate in Smalininkai—with her load. I was having a miserable time because my new shoes made my feet sweat, I had no socks, and blisters soon covered my heels and toes. I was fighting not to whine, but lost the battle.

Suddenly, in the distance, we heard a duet of heavy artillery, probably Germans repulsing a Soviet attack. It sounded like non-stop thunder. Above the trees we saw a ribbon of smoke rising from the direction of Jurbarkas. Father urged Arnoldas to run home.

We covered perhaps five miles, then simply gave up, worn out by the heat. We could have abandoned some of the heavier things we carried. Father could have let me ride on his back from time to time, and we might have made it to Smalininkai. But no. Mother would not part with any of our possessions—especially not the food. "Everyone said Germans were starving because all they had went to feed their military," she explained. This was not true, but that was the gossip she chose to believe.

We sat down on the verge of the road, leaning on our bundles. We must have looked like a sorry lot of vagabonds. I had taken off the new shoes, but was careful to hang them by the laces around my neck. I was determined not to cause more trouble for my parents.

Sounds of heavy artillery fire continued from the direction of Jurbarkas. Mother fidgeted anxiously, wondering what to do. We could not go back. Father urged us all to be patient. Undoubtedly some farmer would drive by eventually on his horse-drawn cart. He was right. One did come. "Could you take us to Smalininkai?" Father asked, but the man said no.

"Could you take us to the nearest hamlet? To a farm?" said Father.

"What'll you give me?" answered the grizzled peasant, in a dialect I could barely understand. For 150 Reichsmarks, the cost of a bottle of vodka at the German co-op, he let us clamber on.

He was not much of a talker. A couple of miles later, he turned north. Mother asked, "Where are you taking us?"

"Don't know yet, but most farmers hereabouts need help with the harvest. Can you work? You act like lazy city folk and talk like judges," the old man laughed. Mother was insulted. "Don't get upset, Ma'am," he continued, "I do have someone in mind. The Ulėnases recently lost their son. They are hurting for help. I'll see what the man says about taking you in."

The first thing Mr. Ulėnas said to our driver was, "*Kažin ar jie neturi ilgų rankų*—maybe they have long arms," implying that we might be thieves. Mother's pride was cut to the quick. She burst into tears. Later, she said, "To think we had fallen so low! We looked like homeless beggars, which of course we were, but I was not used to thinking of us that way. Having to face the truth was like a knife in my heart. I was completely undone. Were insults to be our future?"

It was a rough start, but it changed into a deep friendship. Antanas and Ulijona Ulėnas were wonderful to us. They were simple Lithuanian peasants, smart but without book learning, unable to speak any language but their own. They led us to a good-sized room in the granary which already held a couple of primitive narrow beds, previously used by farm help whom the Germans had taken away to dig anti-tank trenches.

Mr. Ulėnas nailed together a bed to fit Father's long frame. They brought fresh straw and helped us make ourselves three "*čiužiniai*", the typical Lithuanian farmer's mattresses: straw stuffed into bags woven from rough linen. Mother and I shared a bed, but on hot nights she left to sleep in the open. Of course, we had many insect guests who were especially fond of my young body. Mother spent hours scouring the beds and walls to get rid of bedbugs, but complete victory eluded her.

When our new hosts learned of Father's background and ability to communicate freely in German and Russian, they were ecstatic. Mother and Milda took on the typical farm jobs, but Father's duty was the most important of all: to protect the farm and everyone and everything in it. It was a dangerous assignment. His only weapon was a sharp rake.

The dense forest, which brooded across the dusty road from the farm, sheltered groups of men who would not hesitate to kill to get what they wanted. All of these, during the weeks we were there, came to the farm at one time or another demanding food or clothing or medicine. All of them were armed with knives, some had pistols, many had rifles. It was Father's job to negotiate with them so they would do the least damage.

Some of the men were able-bodied Lithuanians, hiding from conscription into the German Wehrmacht. A few of them were pro-communist, waiting for the Soviets to arrive. But most just wanted to go home as soon as the Nazis left. There were also German deserters, tired of the conflict, hoping that the war would end in the western part of Europe and they could return home alive and whole. There were also Soviet military spies and their sympathizers, spying on the strength and movements of the German troops in the area. It was nerve-wracking for Father to placate them all.

Fortunately, the Ulėnases had managed to conceal from German requisitions a good supply of sausages, hams, smoked bacon, and dried white cheese—the typical staples of the country. There was plenty of milk, even after the daily quota was given over to the German collector. Mrs. Ulėnas had medicinal herbs, and honey to care for wounds. Father's polite greetings and conversation seemed to calm those who might have become aggressive because they were afraid. He would call me to fetch one of the Ulėnases so they could decide what to give to these dangerous extortioners. They always gave something, and usually received a "thank-you" in return.

Although the farm was not on a main road, German military units often used the track as a shortcut toward Tauragė and from there to Memel, an essential port in Hitler's estimation. At least once a day, someone in uniform would stop and demand to know who was working there, or would try to requisition a cow or a sheep. Father's magnificent stamped and sealed certificate from the Gebietskommissar provided good protection. A chunk of smoked bacon or a bottle of homemade whiskey was an even surer argument.

Milda's duties were to help feed the pigs and cows, clean out the sty and the barn, and then help in harvesting. My job was to feed the rabbits and watch over the poultry, to scare away weasels and hawks. Physically, it was hardest on Mother.

Harvesting had returned to primitive methods: machinery was not available, or there was no fuel to run what remained. In August, she sweltered and burned in the hot fields of ripe, spiky rye. Then came the flax cutting, and in September the backbreaking potato harvest. One person would go down the rows digging up the plants, while another gathered the potatoes into pails. Rains began. Nothing could be wasted, so mother and the Ulėnases grubbed in the mud to find every last tuber. It was a terrible job. "Oh, my back," Mother would groan, "I'll never be able to stand straight again." Her sciatic nerve became inflamed, and for a few days, she could barely walk.

September brought anxious nights. The low bass notes of distant artillery seemed much closer after dark. The night sky would suddenly turn white: either the Germans, or most likely the Russians, dropped magnesium parachute flares which lit up the landscape, allowing the military to see enemy positions and to reconnoiter future march routes, or select places for concealment or bivouac. Mother said of the flares, "*Iškabino lempas*—they've hung up the lamps." I thought they were beautiful, like celestial beings descending slowly to the ground. They made my sister frantic.

Milda was desperate for us to leave before fighting broke out on top of us, but our parents seemed unable to come to grips. Mother's excuse was the coming winter. She said we did not have the right clothes to endure the cold, and she was right.

She and Mrs. Ulėnas went through every discarded rag and clothing scrap in the house to see what could be salvaged. They found a couple of threadbare jackets left by the deceased son, and patched together a winter coat for me. A torn blanket had just enough usable parts to make Milda a short jacket, but what she needed was a coat. Mrs. Ulėnas gave me an old woolen cardigan to unravel. From its yarn, Mother knitted mittens for all of us. They gave us some metal soup bowls and a frying pan.

"I knew we would be forced to go soon," said Father. "I went to the local Gebietskommissar and showed him the impressive certificate penned by his colleague to the south. They knew each other. This man wrote out a document stating that I was assigned to a temporary job teaching in Pašventys, about a mile or so from Smalininkai. I needed an official residence permit so we could register at a specific store where we could use our food coupons. That was the system: you could not buy anything unless you were registered by someone in authority at a specific store. I was making preparations to leave. I just could not make your mother come until she felt ready."

It was October, 1944, and we were still at the Ulėnas farm. Early one morning, a rumbling and a roaring came pouring down the road in front of the farmstead. Soon a stream of tanks, armored vehicles, light artillery, trucks, military cars, a cavalry unit, motorcycles, horse-drawn wagons, and a long line of dust-covered Wehrmacht infantry seemed to occupy even the air we breathed. An official in the sidecar of a motorcycle pulled out of the flow and into the farmyard to smoke a cigarette. Father approached him, and in his most courteous manner, asked what was happening. "We're on our way to defend Memel," said he. "I don't know how long you people here will remain under our orders. We can no longer protect Jurbarkas; it'll fall to the Soviets very soon."

The decision to leave or not to leave was taken out of our parents' hands. No more delay was possible now. Father turned into a dictator and ordered Mother to pack, or he, Milda, and I would leave without her. Mother knew that the inevitable moment had come. The Ulėnases cried, but understood that we had to go. They had made up their minds to stay, hoping that the Soviets would leave them, insignificant farmers, alone. They brought out a handcart for us to take. It was soon filled with our two suitcases and the bundles of bedding, our cooking pot and frying pan, and a few dishes.

In farewell, they handed us a bag of food, which included a supply of dried bread, some smoked bacon, and a bottle of homemade moonshine. With Mother and Father pulling the handcart, we started down the verge of the road in the opposite direction from the military, heading once more toward Smalininkai.

We watched the military column dwindling down to tired soldiers on foot, some horse-drawn carts carrying supplies, a few men on horseback. Father noticed a small group of cavalry riders leading three horses. A couple of the horses looked lame and worn out, but one, "a huge Swedish mare," though swollen at the hindquarters down to her hocks, seemed otherwise healthy. Father had spent his first twenty years on a farm, and knew horses pretty well. "I ran up to the men and asked if they would let me have the mare in return for a bottle of booze. The one in charge said, 'Let me taste it.' He must have been pleased with it because he said, 'Here, she's yours.' They handed me the lead and rode off. That mare was our salvation. Mr. Ulėnas' *schnapps* saved our skins."

I had been around many farm horses, but this mare was the biggest I had ever seen. Father was able to attach some of our bundles to the mare's back, so now I could ride in the handcart when I got too tired. However, Mother and the horse did not like each other. If Mother came close, it tried to bite her or kick her. Milda and I stayed far away from it, well out of reach.

By noon we had made it to Smalininkai without any trouble. It was October 9, 1944. The last train from Smalininkai to Tilsit had left a couple of days before. We had delayed too long.

CHAPTER 9:

Goodbye, Native Land

Missing the train from Smalininkai to East Prussia was a big blow. How would we get out now? Father had planned to sell the horse in Smalininkai for some extra food or warm blankets, and then we would ride the trains. He was counting on old friends who had farms locally to purchase the big animal. But now, with the last train gone, we would have to rely on the mare to get us away from the approaching Soviet army.

Mother and Father agreed that if we could make it to Tilsit, and if trains were still running from there to Königsberg, we might have a chance to escape to safety. However, Tilsit, on the East Prussian side of the Nemunas River, was thirty miles away, an impossibly long and tiring walk if all we could use was the handcart. We needed a proper cart that the mare could pull, plus all the equipment to harness her. When the soldiers gave her to us, all she had was a halter and lead.

In Smalininkai, Father and Mother were relieved to re-connect with a couple that they had known from 1937–1939. The Navickas family still ran a restaurant-pub, and told us we could spend the night there after the early closing hours. They had a suggestion for Father concerning a cart. They said that mutual friends, the prosperous Karvelis farming family, had departed into Prussia just days earlier. Perhaps they had left something on their property that we could use.

Father immediately went to investigate, taking the mare with him. It was not far, less than two miles away. He found the farmstead in good order, in the care of an amiable Russian prisoner of war whom the Germans had placed with the Karvelis family a year or two previously. The man was thrilled to meet someone who could speak Russian with him. "Let me show you around, and take whatever you want!" he said to Father. "I expect to be with my countrymen within days. I don't need any of this."

Left behind, near the barn, was a small, two-wheeled pleasure cart. Although it could hold only two persons, it was a great improvement over the handcart. Inside the storage area of the stable, Father and the Russian found a pile of worn harness parts, including a beat-up old horse collar. The two men picked through the tangle of discarded gear and cobbled together the required equipment.

Together they managed to harness the mare to the little cart, but when the moment came to pull it, she refused to cooperate. She was a German cavalry horse, unused to dragging something behind her. "She snorted and bucked and tried to rear—I didn't know what to do," said Father. "I stroked her and whispered sweet sounds in German. Finally, it occurred to me to bribe her. The Karvelises had left behind an ample supply of oats. I didn't think the mare had had any for a while. I filled a nose bag I found there and let her have some. Then I took it off, and asked the Russian to walk in front, holding it out in front of her while I led her forward, still harnessed to the cart. Every few steps, when she began to spook, we'd give her some more oats. She was a very clever animal: she figured out the work-to-reward ratio very quickly, and decided the oats were worth the pulling. I suspected I'd need to bribe her again and took a big bag of oats along with me."

By the time Father was done, it was late afternoon. He was astonished to see that during the time he had spent at the Karvelis farm, the main road leading toward the bridge across the Nemunas river had become thronged with military vehicles, horses and carts of every description, and pedestrians with bundles on their backs, or dragging loaded wheel barrows, hand carts, even baby carriages, all forced to move at a slow crawl.

The nearest crossing over the Nemunas into East Prussia was a few miles downriver from Smalininkai by way of a temporary bridge that the German military had erected near Ragnit (now Neman) when it became clear they might have to withdraw. Rumor circulated that when the Soviets got close, this bridge would be blown up to prevent them from using it.

It took Father and the skittish mare a long time to get back to the pub where he had left us. As he struggled out of the main road to the street where the pub was located, a couple standing by the side of the road barred his way. A pile of possessions surrounded them; suitcases and shapeless bundles wrapped up in sheets or stuffed into pillowcases. A little girl sat on top of the suitcases, wide-eyed with fear. Seeing Father alone with an empty cart, the two adults threw themselves at him, pleading with him to take them to the Prussian side of the river. They said they were the Pranskas family from Kaunas. They must have noticed that Father looked concerned for the child, because they started to beg, "Have a heart, save our poor little girl!"

Father explained that he had his own family, and that the cart was too small. "Mrs. Pranskas said she'd pay us with jewelry or clothing or shoes or bedding—whatever we wanted, only please take them with us. Leaving them to wait, I led the mare toward the pub and consulted Mother, who was suspicious. She wanted to check them out herself. She told them what we needed most and asked what they could offer. When Mrs. Pranskas mentioned that she had an extra wool coat, the deal was made."

Mother said, "Milda needed one desperately. They gave it to her on the spot. It was really ugly, with wide vertical stripes of burgundy, dark greens and browns, but it was made of excellent wool and would be warm, and it was only slightly too large for Milda."

Father felt anxious about staying overnight at the pub. He went to find out what was happening on the main road to the bridge. It was mobbed. He heard that the town of Jurbarkas had fallen to the Russians. All who could, including large numbers of German military, were fleeing the approaching Soviet forces. If the Soviets were in Jurbarkas, it would not take long for them to arrive in Smalininkai, only nine miles away. Father returned breathless: "The Soviets are on the offensive—the road is choked, barely moving at all. We have to leave right now."

Remembering that day, Milda asked me, "Do you recall how I had grabbed two photograph albums as we were leaving our home in Vilnius for the summer? I don't know what inspired me to do it. I had nothing but some photographs to remember our lives, but now that we had the Pranskases to take along, Mother said to leave the albums— they were too heavy and bulky, we had to be practical. But how could I live without my past? The coat I received from Mrs. Pranskas had two deep pockets. When Mother wasn't looking, I quickly yanked out as many pictures as I could and stuffed them in. So thank me for my quick thinking, or you would have no images at all from the first seven years of your life!"

While Milda was saving glimpses of our past, the Pranskases stuffed all their belongings into the cart, my parents laid ours over theirs, and their little girl Lina and I were placed on top of the heap. The big challenge was the mare. Father had made the mistake of taking off her harness, because he had thought we would spend the night sleeping in the pub. To get her harnessed between the shafts again was close to impossible. She actively resisted.

The Pranskases were deathly afraid of the mare, and drew back out of the angry animal's reach. Mother had to drop everything she was doing to help Father. But the mare had decided Mother was an enemy and as she walked by, caught the top of her head between its huge yellow teeth. It bit hard, drawing blood. Mother was furious. "She'll be the death of us!" she cried, and wondered aloud if horses carried rabies. She got some iodine from the pub owner's wife and escaped infection, but the bite left some interesting, permanent scars.

It took Father almost an hour to calm down the mare. He had to stroke her and murmur horse endearments and repeat the oat bribe before she reluctantly consented to get going. The Pranskases were muttering to each other. I overheard the wife hiss, "Did the devil make us ask this useless oaf for help?" Of course, I told Mother and Father what I had heard, which really upset them.

When we reached the main road, we were astounded at the chaos. We managed to get into the flow, which moved at snail's pace. It was dark, clouds hiding the waning moon. We had traveled on for perhaps an hour when "Oh God, stop!" yelled Mother, panicked. "I left all our documents by the pub!" In the commotion of dealing with the angry mare and searching for iodine to clean the painful bite on her head, she had placed her handbag, which contained all our documents and remaining Reichsmarks, next to a fence by the stable. Without documents, we would not be allowed into Prussia.

Father immediately started to pull out of the throng onto the verge of the road, but Mr. Pranskas objected loudly. "Let your wife run back and get it, but let's walk on. She knows where it is. She'll catch up with us because the going is so slow."

Father could hardly believe his ears! We were trying to help them out, and in return they were urging us, a drop in a river of fleeing humanity, in the dark, to separate from Mother. Of course, Father ignored them. He tethered the horse to a tree and rushed off back to Smalininkai, urging us all to pray he would find the handbag.

The Pranskases were furious at the delay. Had they not been so afraid of the mare, they might have forced us to keep going. Father's absence could not have lasted long, but our anxiety made it seem like hours before we saw him appear, worn out but triumphant. He had the handbag. "I did not think for a minute that it would be there for me to find," he confessed, "but there it was, right where Mother had left it, untouched. One of us has a powerful Guardian Angel." He gave Mother a big, reassuring hug.

I could tell that the adults were agitated about the slow pace of our progress. Milda kept rushing forward as though her haste could make everything move faster. She would speed ahead, then stop and wait until we caught up. Mother kept yelling at her to stay close, that we could lose her in the dark. Once she did get lost for some minutes, and even Father lost patience. She was so scared of the Soviets and the sickening stories she had heard about them that she could not wait to get to the other side of the Nemunas River, which their tanks could not cross.

German military trucks and light artillery were trying to get past the fleeing crowds, which made the congestion worse. We heard the thunder of artillery coming closer, then retreating again. It started to drizzle. My parents and Milda had no protection. The Pranskases had umbrellas for themselves, but all the contents in the cart, the bundles wrapped in sheets, pillowcases and tablecloths, were getting wet. Mrs. Pranskas found a length of water-repellent parachute material in one of her parcels to spread over Lina and me and the pile of belongings. The temperature was dropping. Lina and I held on to each other for warmth. She loved to cuddle. The problem was that both of us had to go to the bathroom, but our parents grumbled at any delay.

We were creeping in a traffic bottleneck less than half a mile from the bridge when suddenly, a thunderous volley of artillery fire burst close by, to the north. Voices in German and Lithuanian screamed, "The Reds! The Soviets! They have broken through! Hurry! Run!" Over the noise of the explosions, you could hear screaming.

At first, everything was chaos, a dead stop, and then the pace of the fleeing masses picked up. Officious German military personnel had been checking everyone's documents before allowing them on the bridge, but the terrorized crowd overwhelmed them and pushed them out of the way. The bridge was unguarded, and everyone rushed and shoved their way to the Prussian side. Our mare must have been used to front-line action, because the dark, the crowd, and the noise did not bother her at all.

We were in Prussia! We were across the river: we were safe! Milda was grinning ear-to-ear. Safe at least for a while, thought my parents. Everyone had heard Hitler stamp and roar that never ever—"*nun und nimmer!*"—would he give up this territory to the Soviets. "We wanted to believe Hitler's guarantee to protect Prussia at all costs," said Father.

Once over the bridge, Father pulled the mare away from the pandemonium on the main road toward the nearby outline of a forest of young pines, planted not long before in regimented rows. The long, damp trek, plus the stress and anxiety of the last hour, had exhausted everyone. "Our legs had turned to jelly," said Father. "We had to sit a while."

As we stood under the dripping trees chewing on rusks of dried rye bread, we could clearly see the explosion of artillery on the far side of the bridge, and soon we heard responding fire from the Prussian side, quite close to us. Then—CRASH! A heavy mortar shell exploded almost at our feet, fired from across the Nemunas. "Let's get away from the river!" yelled Father. He grabbed the mare's lead and guided her deeper into the pines.

The flash of explosions was our only light. We zigzagged between the trees, unsure of finding an opening wide enough to allow passage to the little cart. For what felt to us like hours, shells whistled above and around us, shaking the earth as they exploded, hurling trees and branches and clods of earth. All of us thought this was to be our end. Lina and I sobbed and held on to each other tight. Only the mare seemed untroubled by the explosions.

Unbelievably, we made it safely out of range of the heavy artillery. Late in the evening of October 9, 1944, we left our homeland, still believing that our exile would be temporary.

When the adults felt it safe to stop, they held a discussion. Father and Mother's plan to get to Tilsit, and from there to catch a train to Königsberg, now seemed too dangerous to pursue. There was no way to find out if Tilsit, located right on the border, was also under Soviet attack and if trains from there were still running. The adults agreed that train service was likely continuing into Germany from Königsberg, a key city for the defense of East Prussia.

But where would they go from Königsberg? Father's dream was to reach neutral Switzerland, but Mother still wanted to wait out the war near our homeland. She continued to argue that when the fighting was over, the Allies would once again recognize Lithuania's right to exist as an independent country, as they had done after World War I. In fact, nobody in Lithuania foresaw that the entire area, including East Prussia, would fall permanently to the Soviets.

The Pranskases wanted to get to Berlin, to the center of Germany, far from the battle lines. Prussia was too dangerous, they thought. My parents disliked them heartily. We had brought them across the river to the Prussian side; the agreement was completed. Mother and Father wanted to leave them at the nearest village, but once again were assailed by pleas and promises. They offered to pay us with a piece of valuable jewelry if only we helped them reach Königsberg and a train. My parents gave in.

A day or so after leaving the bridge, we stopped in the small village of Kreuzingen (now called Bolshakovo). For centuries, this area had been inhabited by "Lietuvninkai"—Germanized Lithuanians of Lutheran faith. I had come down with some sort of intestinal infection: I was feverish, my skin and the whites of my eyes had turned yellow. Mother called it *geltligė*, the yellow sickness. It was probably some sort of liver malfunction from contaminated water or food. It took me many days to recover.

We asked around for lodging, but the locals, overwhelmed by demand from the fleeing crowds, wanted valuables instead of Reichsmarks. Finally we came to a small house where we were welcomed. Reassured that we would stay put, the Pranskases negotiated better accommodations close by. They did not want to share our diseases.

Our hosts, the Vitkūnases, were a very poor, devout, elderly couple who still spoke the old dialect of Lithuania Minor. They were moved to tears when Mother and Father sang for them in their tongue old Lutheran church hymns which they had learned in Smalininkai six years previously.

The old people were completely selfless: whatever they had, they shared with us, but our parents saw that they barely had enough for themselves. Whenever Father and Mother spoke of them in the years to come, they became quite emotional about "those saintly people" and their boundless charity.

Obtaining food was our biggest problem. We still had a supply of official ration coupons to buy food, but they were useless because, as non-residents, we could not register at a store that would honor them. We had a little flour left, and two pillowcases of dried rye bread. We had consumed almost every crust from one of the bags, but Mother insisted we keep the other as our ultimate safety net, to be used when all else failed.

"There was no way to avoid it," said Mother. "I had to swallow my pride and go begging. Oh, how I hated it! To be an "*ubagas*"—a beggar—was to fall below the lowest rung of society. But you do what you must. Milda had to come with me. She spoke pretty good German, and her sweet personality got us an egg here, a few potatoes there, a slice or two of bread. Every bite was a victory for survival."

One day, a severely disabled veteran, a neighbor of the Vitkūnases, stopped by to see how they were, and to make sure that we, the *Flüchtlinge*—refugees, were not taking advantage of them. The man had lost a foot and part of a hand in the battle of Leningrad. He asked about our escape, about the little two-wheeled cart we had parked by the stable, and about Father's background. On learning that Father was a school inspector, he became very friendly: he had wanted to be a teacher, he told us. "I know of a more useful cart that you can have," he said. "A German supply platoon was bivouacked over by the forest and left it there. It's a small, one-horse, Russian-type wagon. It might work for your family."

Father found it, a sturdy little cart about six feet in length, the top portion sitting like an open rectangular box between the wheels, with a board nailed across its width in front for the driver. At first, our choosy mare did not approve of it, flinging her head and capering from side to side, unwilling to go between the shafts. However, she seemed to have accepted Father as a friend, so that persuaded by his sweet words and some oats, she was harnessed. Father noted that the shafts were a bit too short for our big mare, and the wagon came too close to her hocks—it had been built for a smaller breed. But there was no way to fix the problem, so Father could only hope for the best.

With the autumn weather upon us, we needed a cover over the cart. There was nothing to be bought. Mrs. Vitkūnas gave us two sturdy linen sheets, saying, "We had saved these for guests, and here you came. Take them and may they protect you."

Mother sewed them together at the long seams. Then Father, with help from Mr. Vitkūnas, fashioned a triangular wooden frame over the cart, draped the sheets over it, and nailed them to the sides, creating a tent. The sheets gave us some shelter from rain—at least until they soaked through.

One morning, the disabled veteran arrived looking very agitated. He had learned that the Soviets had infiltrated deep into the southeastern territory of Prussia, across the border from Poland. It looked as though the Red Army planned to encircle the German forces in Prussia and then destroy them from all sides at once. I was not allowed to listen, but I watched from a distance, and saw my sister get extremely disturbed and upset. Much later, I learned that Soviet soldiers had brutalized, raped, and massacred civilians at a place called Nemmersdorf.

The veteran recommended we hurry west, toward Königsberg and the Baltic Sea. He had heard that Hitler was planning to send ships to evacuate Prussian civilians from areas threatened by the Soviets.

Königsberg was the proud capital of Prussia and the biggest city in the region. It lay about fifty miles west of Kreuzingen. It was a beautiful place of parks and churches, its famous Albertina University the host of professors like the philosopher Immanuel Kant, its museums offering access not only to great collections of art but also to prehistoric antiquities and anthropological collections. It had been a showplace, but two months previously, in August 1944, the British air force had bombed it repeatedly, razing the historic downtown area, and now in October, the Soviets continued to attack it daily by air. We started toward it and tried to hurry, but progress was slow, because we had to go at a walking pace. Father still had to lead the mare when she was in a difficult mood, and walking mile after mile in his one pair of city shoes gave him painful blisters. The other adults and Milda could take turns riding in the cart, but there was no one except Father who could deal with the foul-tempered horse.

And always there was the problem of food. The Pranskases only looked out for themselves, and grumbled that if we did not move faster, no trains would be left running. We would have gone on without them, but their promise of valuable jewelry made my parents patient.

We knew that something like gold earrings would come in very useful if we had to roam much longer.

Unlike the Pranskases, we had nothing with which to bribe our way, or barter for food or shelter, and competition for both was fierce: thousands were on the roads. Father and Mother would start seeking a place for the night in mid-afternoon. Days were getting shorter, night came early, and sometimes it took hours to find proprietors willing to let us stay in their barn or stable. Often, Father had to sleep curled up uncomfortably in the cart, where he could watch over the horse and protect our belongings. Morality had fallen to the survival of the wiliest: thievery and robberies by refugees from each other were all too common.

Meanwhile, Mother would try to find food, or a means to take a bath, if only a quick rubdown using a rag, a piece of abrasive soap, and a bucket of water. The straw and hay in the haylofts, barns, and stables, which sheltered fugitives, were full of bedbugs and fleas, and soon we also had lice to torment us. Mother was always desperate to wash our clothes, but an even bigger challenge was how to dry them. The weather had turned cold and rainy, and laundry did not dry properly. Damp clothes mildewed and smelled.

The German authorities maintained as much order as they could during this chaotic time. Usually, in the smaller towns and villages, it was up to the mayor to assign the fugitives to a specific local residence, but more often than not, the mayor had already fled.

As more and more residents left their homes in East Prussia for more secure locations deeper in Germany, the refugees were often able to camp out in the vacant buildings. Sometimes, we were lucky and found some abandoned items we could use: a blanket, a pillow, a sheet. There was almost always hay available, so our mare never went hungry.

There were times when we would pull into a homestead and find refugees roasting some free-roaming chickens they had caught, and once some men were trying to catch a cow that had been left behind. I still remember her, bellowing in pain. Mother said she had an impacted udder because she had not been milked too long.

A big, abandoned German shepherd dog chose to follow us one day. Milda instantly adopted him and fed him some of her bread. That night he slept on the briefcase with our vital documents, which we always took in with us to keep safe during the night. However, in the morning, he bit Mother when she tried to get into it. "The poor animal was completely confused about his loyalties," said Father. "Milda was heartbroken, but we could not keep him: a big dog like that needed a lot of food. Fortunately, the next night, we met a prosperous family of refugees traveling with many horses and carts, who gladly took him in as a guard dog. I offered the dog for free, of course, but they gave me a good-sized dried sausage in return: an amazing gift in those days!"

Of all my memories from this period, the one that still makes my heart quake was the need to go begging. Now that I was back to my usual health, if it was not pouring, I had to take my turn to go with Mother from farmstead to farmstead, hoping to supplement our dwindling reserves. Father was too big and looked too imposing to go with us, and besides, we needed him to stand guard over our cart and horse.

A few people, even if they were in need themselves, shared a little with us, but all I remember are vicious dogs chasing us, and doors slamming in our faces, sometimes with swearwords for emphasis. "*Verflüchte Ausländer*—damned foreigners!" still echoes in my ears.

I did not understand that the slammed doors and the curses were not directed at me personally. Each rejection hit me like a poisoned arrow, making me shrivel inside. All too vividly, I saw again the little Jewish girl standing forlorn at our door in Vilnius, and I felt an unidentifiable fear grip me to the point that I'd begin to cry whenever we approached yet another door. The irony is that sometimes my tears helped us obtain a handout.

CHAPTER 10:

A Lucky Meeting

Lina, my companion, was a very quiet little girl, and I felt protective of her. She was a pretty girl with dark curly hair and golden brown eyes, the color of dark amber. She looked small to me, but said she was five. When we stopped to rest, my parents, especially Father, often held and cuddled me and Milda, if only to keep us warm, but I never saw either of the Pranskases show Lina any physical affection. However, they did hold her hand when they asked people to put them up for the night or do them some favor. They were not unkind to her, but I could see Lina craved affection. When her parents were not looking, she would try to snuggle up to my parents or even to Milda. My curiosity was aroused, but days went by and I had no opportunity to question her. Some adult was always hovering over us, and I knew adults would not condone my prying.

We were approaching Königsberg. It was mid-afternoon, and uncharacteristically, the Pranskases stayed with us as we sheltered in a barn with several other fugitive families, a couple of miles away from the center of town, unwilling to risk another bombardment in the city itself.

Father and Mr. Pranskas walked off to find out how to reach the station, and to check the schedule of trains to Berlin. Mother and Mrs. Pranskas went their separate ways to see about food, leaving Milda to keep an eye on Lina and me. But Milda met a Lithuanian teenager her own age, and soon was lost in girlish confidences. It was the perfect moment for me to satisfy my curiosity.

"Lina," I asked bluntly, "does your mother hug and kiss you when you are alone? Because I've never seen her do it."

"No," she whispered. Her eyes filled with tears. "But I must never tell that she's not my real mama and he's not my daddy."

"So where are your real parents? Why are you with the Pranskases?" I asked.

"They found me and took me home," she said.

"They found you? Where?" I said, astonished.

"I was hiding where my *mamusia* told me to, in a railroad station," said Lina, using the Polish word for "mommy."

None of this was making sense to me. I thought about it, then asked, "Your mother told you to hide? How did you get to the railroad station?"

Lina whispered, "Promise you will never tell? Because I'll die if anyone knows, this mama said so."

"I swear I'll never, ever tell," I promised.

Lina leaned over and whispered, "My mamusia was holding me tight when soldiers made us get into a train. It was crowded and people were crying. I was scared. Mamusia kissed me so hard it hurt. Then she told me that a new mama would find me by and by, and I was to go hide in the railroad station. Then she squeezed me out a tiny window. I had to hold on tight to a scarf and then let go. I fell and skinned my knees. It was raining hard. I didn't want to go, and cried and cried—but not aloud, because my mamusia had said to be very quiet. The train left.

"I don't remember much after that. I was very sad. Why did my mamusia make me leave? People came and went at the station, and I cried and I was hungry. And then this mama came and talked to me and said to come with her. I don't think she loves me like my real mamusia did. I'm afraid of going on the train with her. Do you think she'll throw me out of the train too?"

I was speechless. I had no idea what to think. So I held Lina tight and said what I thought she'd want to hear: "No, the Pranskases mean to keep you." I desperately wanted to ask my parents about Lina's tale, but Father had taught me that a promise made must be kept. I regretted having questioned Lina, because now my head was gripped by a distressing story that I did not understand, yet could not forget. Why would a mother throw her child out of a train? The story haunted me for years.

Long after the war was over, when I was eleven, I finally told my father that I kept recalling this strange and painful story. He was not surprised. He reminded me about the Holocaust. He guessed that a year or two before we met the Pranskases, when the Nazis were deporting Jews to concentration camps, Lina's mother had seen an opening in a boxcar and grabbed a chance to save her. A tiny sliver of a chance, but better than the certain death that awaited them. He had heard of many cases where desperate parents had tried to save their children that way. We could not like the Pranskases, but our opinion of them soared once we understood what a risk they had assumed in order to save this child.

Finally the day arrived when we said goodbye to the Pranskases. They had promised to reward us with a piece of good jewelry when we got them to a train running to Berlin. At the Königsberg station, Mrs. Pranskas took out a ring and gave it to Mother, saying, "This ruby is very valuable. It's worth all the trouble you have taken for us." We were grateful, thinking of the help it would be to us in an emergency. Later we found out that the stone was a cheap garnet. Had the Pranskases known and lied on purpose, or had they genuinely believed it was a fine ruby?

With the Pranskases gone, Father and Mother resumed their old disagreement. He wanted to barter the horse and cart, get on the train, and go as far west into Germany as possible. Far from the battle lines, he thought, there would be fewer refugees, the countryside not as denuded and chaotic as in East Prussia, and the conditions of life not as harsh. Mother, however, persuaded him to stay as close to Lithuania as we could, still hoping that when the war ended, we could return to the life we had known before.

In Mother's eyes, compared to our state in July when we had nothing at all, now we were rich. Mother felt comforted by our possessions: we had the cart, which could now hold all four of us inside, and the mare, who continued to look swollen at the buttocks and thighs, but did not seem to be in any discomfort. If worse came to worst, all four of us could sleep in the cart. We still had some food reserves. We had brought a pot and a fry pan and some bowls, we had bedding, we even had a small washboard. True, we were no better off than nomad gypsies, but how could we give it all up? Much to Milda's dismay, Father gave in.

As soon as the Pranskases and their goods were in the station, we hurried away from Königsberg, fearful of another bombing raid. But where to go? Which way to turn? The decision was quickly taken from us. We were on an unfamiliar street, passing mounds of bricks and rubble, the ruins of bombed-out buildings on both sides. The street ended at a wide road that was in total confusion. Men in military uniforms were stopping all civilians and ordering horses and carts that had been heading south to turn around and go north.

Father learned that the German Wehrmacht was engaged in a battle to push the Soviets out of the territory they had claimed in southeast Prussia. An endless military convoy snaked toward the south,
and civilians had to get out of the way. The military guards examined
our documents. Father's wonderful certificate caused a lot of interest.
"You speak German? Then you can act as interpreter to these masses of
Lithuanians and Poles," said an officer, arranging a space for us in the
noisy stream of horses and carts crawling northward.

For a few days, the Germans kept us slowly moving north, whether
we wanted to or not. At least we no longer had to search for overnight
shelter or worry about thieves: the military assigned spaces, and kept
strict order among the refugees.

One bright memory stands out from the damp and gloomy hours
of that period. At a prosperous manor, our military escorts had requisitioned a large hay-barn to shelter several refugee families. It was
already dark, although still early in the evening. Father went to rub
down the horse while Mother, Milda, and I, shivering from the cold
and the damp, had wrapped ourselves in blankets and were cuddling
for warmth. Suddenly Father strode in, a happy smile lighting up his
face. "Come," he said, "we're invited to the manor." Mother became
flustered. How could we go when we looked so shabby?

The prospect of being warm in a proper house overcame her pride.
We were the only ones invited. The landowner, Frau Hofmann, had
noticed Father, who stood out, as he always did, from the other men
near the stables. She asked where he was from, they chatted, and apparently she liked his old-world manners. She was young, perhaps still
in her twenties, left alone to manage the large holdings that belonged
to her husband, now serving with the Wehrmacht and last known
to be somewhere in Romania. She was desperate to talk about anything other than the war. Her cook made us *"Königsberger Klopse,"* a
Prussian specialty of large-sized meatballs covered in white gravy, flavored with capers and served with boiled potatoes. Milda and I could
not remember ever eating anything as delicious. Meat, like joy, was a
rare commodity, and we savored it.

Frau Hofmann and Father discovered a mutual love for poetry and
music. I think they could have talked all night, but I could see Mother
getting uneasy and fidgety. She could not follow the conversation, because her knowledge of German was very limited. She tended to flame

with jealousy when attractive women had Father's attention. It was time to leave the beautiful warm house and its generous owner, and go back to the crowded barn and our spot in the straw.

But first our hostess gave us a parting gift—music. Mrs. Hofmann sat at her grand piano and played for us, a private performance. Milda, whose fingers longed for the piano keys, watched her entranced. There was one piece that imprinted itself on my brain. Father told me it was "Sadness," by a composer named Chopin. I hummed the beginning part for weeks. That one October evening of unexpected kindness we spoke of time and again. A golden spark in a world of grey.

One afternoon, as the convoy was nearing its night-time assignments, word came down from the military that the Germans had pushed the Red Army out of Prussia, and that we could go south toward Germany if we wanted to. Milda was so excited! Mother said dismissively, "We'll see."

That night we were assigned a space in a classroom of an abandoned schoolhouse. Father was called out to translate for the Germans, plus he had to take care of the mare. Mother, as usual, went off to see if there was any bread available to buy. She told Milda to take the pail and find us some water for washing. There were people milling around nearby, many speaking Lithuanian, so my parents felt it safe to leave me alone. Curious as always, I decided to explore what was behind a door next to the corner where we had placed our belongings.

At first, I was disappointed: just a small supply closet with broken shelves, a pile of books and papers on the floor. None of the books had pretty pictures.

Still, during the past months of observing how adults acted, I knew that paper was valuable not only for personal wiping (toilet paper was an unknown luxury) and for starting fires, but also, if it was thin, for rolling cigarettes. It was useful for barter. I was about to haul as much as I could to our corner when a man saw me poking about and strode up. "What have you found there? Show it to me!" he said severely, in Lithuanian. I held out to him a handful of loose papers and a book. "What else?" he growled. I did not know whether to just run away or scream for help.

As I crouched, staring up at him like a bird hypnotized by a snake, a woman called out, "Petras, come here, I need you!"

Saved! As quickly as I could, I grabbed an armful of books and papers and slid them under our bedding, then went back for more. Imagine my surprise: under the remaining pile of loose papers my hands felt—shoes! Two pairs of shoes. What a treasure! *St. Theresa, help me hide them safely until Daddy returns!* I prayed fervently.

If there was one thing everyone living through a war had learned, it was the value of shoes. Even if they did not fit any of us, they were worth gold as barter. These shoes felt like leather, though I barely glanced at them. It did not much matter what condition they were in—any shoemaker would pay well for leather that could be used for patches.

The threatening man was bringing in his family's possessions and admonishing his two young sons, who looked close to Milda's age, while his wife was busy setting up their sleeping arrangements in the corner across the room from us. It was safe for me to act. I hid the shoes and more paper under our bedding, then sat on top as demure as a sleeping cat, my feelings see-sawing between joy that I had found something useful and fear that the man would search our corner and take it all away before the grown-ups came back. I did not trust him.

At long last, there was Milda, staggering in with the pail of water, trying her best not to slosh on the floor. Suddenly the wife of the mean man called out, "Milda Prekeris, is that you?"

It turned out that these people, the Jonynas family, were old acquaintances of my parents. Our two families had not seen each other for a long time; I had changed too much for them to recognize me, but Milda remained unmistakable. When Father and Mother returned, they were delighted to meet them again. They had so much to talk about, to share stories of the flight from our homes. I was trembling with impatience to boast of my find, but nobody was paying me the least attention.

The Jonynases had left their home fully prepared. Two strong draft horses pulled a big cart, protected from rain by a rounded covering of strong tarpaulin. They had brought along an abundance of clothing, many household goods, and a stock of practical items such as camp-stoves, tools for fixing the cart, remedies for people and their animals. They had brought along a cow and an ample supply of food.

Unlike my father, Mr. Jonynas was *apsukrus*—resourceful, quick to assess a situation and shrewd enough to find an advantage. What he lacked—what the entire Jonynas household lacked—was the ability to communicate in German. Unable to understand what was ordered or required, they were at a serious disadvantage.

The Jonynases invited us to travel along with them. Mr. Jonynas proposed to Father: "*Mano galva, tavo liežuvis*—My brain, your tongue—we'll do fine." Mrs. Jonynas added that they had supplies such as dried bread and flour that they could share with us if we ran low.

Mother accepted! In fact, our parents were so pleased to be with friends that they probably needed no extra inducements, just their company. Milda's face shone with relief. We would finally be moving again.

As Mother and Father were arranging our bedding to sleep, they discovered the books and papers and shoes, worn but in good condition. We had so little that anything useful, no matter how insignificant, was a reason to celebrate. One pair had belonged to a child, because it was too small even for me. But when we realized that the other pair fit Milda perfectly, we rejoiced like little children after a visit from Santa Claus. My patient sister had walked all those miles in shoes made of ragged canvas nailed to wooden soles. She almost cried with joy.

Together with the Jonynas family, we turned southward again. When the weather cleared, the Soviets resumed bombing Königsberg, so the adults decided to give it a wide berth. We were a few miles south of the city when military officers blocked our way, once again ordering everyone into organized columns because the road was heavily travelled by military transport. As usual, Father was ordered to interpret for those who did not speak German.

Mr. Jonynas did not like dawdling at tortoise speed in a never-ending caravan of horse-drawn wagons whose pace of progress was limited by those moving the slowest. An ever-present danger was strafing and bombing by Soviet fighter planes. In addition, it was nerve-racking to be constantly under the vigilant eye of German officials who held total power over us.

Although listening to news other than from the official Nazi broadcasts was a capital offense, somehow word got around. Romania and Bulgaria were in Soviet hands, Hungary was under heavy siege and likely to fall to the communists. The Allies were in Belgium. The Nazis had suffered serious losses of life. Their military machine was running out of manpower. Mr. Jonynas and Father were able-bodied men: Father was only thirty-six years old. Why tempt the military to conscript them to labor for Nazi victory? What would become of the women and children? Staying in the convoy, reasoned Mr. Jonynas, may well be orderly and provide secure night shelter, but it also held serious risks.

Our chance to leave the caravan of carts came on a Sunday toward the end of October. We had spent the night in a village some miles north of Elbing (now called Elblag), which lay near the border of East and West Prussia. The refugees were allowed a later start, supposedly because the Nazis respected the people's desire to attend church. The Jonynases and my parents took the opportunity to leave early.

Mr. Jonynas invented a plausible tale to tell if an official stopped us. We would claim that we were related and traveling together, that our mare was ill (she still looked swollen), and that one of the wheels on the Jonynases' cart had a crack that needed fixing. As a result, we were looking for a farmer who would let us stay for a while in return for work. A brown-shirted Nazi did stop to question us, but our story satisfied him. He did not want the headache of a broken-down cart bottling up the road, and waved us along.

The adults spotted a rutted dirt track leading up a slope across the fields, winding in and out of trees, and roughly paralleling the main road on which the regimented column of refugees would be traveling later. We had left before breakfast, so after a while we stopped by a coppice of evergreens to let the horses and the cow graze, and to light the kerosene stove on which to heat water for the ersatz coffee, a fake version made of roasted grains that tasted awful to me, though the adults seemed to like it. It would warm us. The Jonynases had some honey and their cow still gave a little milk, though she was too exhausted from walking day after day, with little rest, to be a good producer. It was a clear morning, and the warm brew and a piece of bread with a whiff of honey made everyone cheerful and unwilling to rush.

As we were enjoying our tranquil Sunday respite, we heard the deep rumbling of noisy trucks on the main road about a third of a mile down-slope from where we sat. Nothing unusual about that, but then we noticed that the trucks were pulling off the roadway and stopping, disgorging dozens of uniformed men. They quickly erected a barrier across the road and posted armed guards. "Look!" said Mr. Jonynas, "I bet they're waiting for the refugee caravan. I bet they intend to collect the men."

We dared not move. A little later, the orderly line of the wagons came into view, accompanied by military guards, as always. At the barrier, the soldiers, or the Brownshirts of the "SA" (*Sturmabteilung*— Assault Division)—it was hard to see details—stopped every cart. From our screened vantage point under the firs we could see that each driver was interrogated and each cart thoroughly searched.

We held our breath for the women and children and old people staggering on the road, trying to hold on to their husbands, sons, and fathers, gesticulating and keening in grief as most of the men were loaded into the waiting military trucks. All was in turmoil and confusion: the most frightening prediction of Mr. Jonynas had come true, but once again, luck—and his astute brain—had saved us. I could see that everyone around me was infected with anxiety: what if someone noticed us? We remained under the trees until the road was empty, the barrier removed, and all the trucks had driven away.

CHAPTER 11

Healed in Time for Christmas

It was not only the adults who were thoroughly shaken after seeing the heartless seizure of the men. So were we—the two Jonynas boys, and Milda and I. We clung to our fathers as if our puny arms could ward off all threats. All of us depended on Father's ability to communicate with and charm the Germans, and on Mr. Jonynas' inborn gift of foreseeing and avoiding trouble. Without them, we would be as helpless as leaves in an autumn gale.

Pulling ourselves together, we continued on our way cautiously, making a wide detour around the busy town of Elbing. Wherever possible, the men chose to drive narrow, rutted country roads that would not attract military convoys. Worry was our constant companion.

We crossed into a contentious territory: "West Prussia" to the Germans, the "Polish Corridor" to the Allies. Prussia had controlled this area from 1772 until German Unification and the formation of the Kaiser's German Empire in the nineteenth century. At the end of World War I, the Treaty of Versailles had returned the area to Poland. In 1939, one of Hitler's first acts was to annex it back to Germany as part of the Third Reich. The population was split between ethnic Germans and native Poles, the German minority dominating the Polish majority.

For our family, the days merged into one another: cold, damp, and hungry. October ended; November was wet with occasional snow flurries. I had a permanent cold; Milda began to complain of sore, weepy eyes. On the road with the Jonynases, when our two families sheltered in the same barn, Milda had tried to teach the two sons how to do the polka and the waltz. One of the boys played the accordion quite well, and it lifted everyone's spirits to watch the three of them having fun. But now Milda had no more energy.

Mrs. Jonynas would often invite Mother to ride along in their cart. She was very happy to have Mother's company, to reminisce about common friends and acquaintances. And she was unfailingly generous, offering us flour and dried bread and occasionally even a few potatoes—though the Jonynases did not carry a big supply of them, because potatoes are heavy. Mother and Father were grateful for their help, but usually declined it. My parents could not bring themselves to live off the generosity of friends. Father said, "We had a horror of being viewed as freeloaders."

With the Jonynas family watching us, Mother felt ashamed to go begging. I was always hungry, but the truth is that our parents were much hungrier. They denied themselves food so that Milda and I could have more. We had flour, but no fat on which to fry anything, and homeless refugees do not carry ovens for baking. Thanks to Mrs. Jonynas, we had the use of a portable Primus camp stove and enough kerosene to fuel it. Sometimes Mother made a sort of soup of barley boiled in water, thickened with flour, and lightly flavored with mashed potato. It was a rare treat. Mother was still saving one pillowcase of dried rye bread from Lithuania for "a real emergency," as she termed it.

While Father led the mare, or rode in the cart when she was calm, usually we three women lay huddled together, trying to keep warm. Mother, Milda, and I sang to keep up our spirits and to distract Father. He would sometimes join in with a sonorous baritone while Milda and I, our voices blending as one, carried the melody in soprano and Mother harmonized in alto. I came to know every song and hymn in my parents' repertoire. We learned to avoid patriotic songs because they made Mother cry, and soon we all would be teary from homesickness and anxiety about our inscrutable future.

Although we travelled with the Jonynas family by day, at night we often had to seek shelter separately. Father always helped the Jonynases get settled first, feeling that we owed them more than we could repay. Mr. Jonynas had a knack for picking out places where the owners would be likely to accept "guests." He had no facility for learning German, but the two boys were interested and were trying to learn from Father how to make requests to stay the night.

Begging for shelter, we experienced many rude refusals, but sometimes we were blessed by extraordinary instances of selfless generosity. All of us long remembered the time we stopped for the night at the home of an elderly Polish couple. Mother and Father spoke good Polish, and Milda and I had learned a little from neighboring Polish children in the streets of Vilnius. Perhaps because of that, the couple treated us like long-lost relatives. They insisted we sleep in the house, in proper beds, and because our clothes were dirty and we were desperate for a bath, they filled pail after pail with water to heat on the wood-burning stove so we could bathe and feel clean again. They filled an old-fashioned tin tub: to be able to actually sit in warm water was an incredible treat.

The woman hung our wash to dry in the warm kitchen, and in the morning produced an antique black iron, which she filled with hot coals so Mother could get the last bit of dampness out of our freshly laundered clothes and bedding. The frequent rejections we ran into when asking for shelter hurt less when we remembered their kindness. They gave us reason to hope.

We kept away from the main roads as much as possible. However, that part of the Polish Corridor is crisscrossed by brooks, streams, and rivers, and in 1944, bridges were few and far between. Often we had to go back to the main roads, to risk the possibility that prowling Nazi officials would conscript Father and Mr. Jonynas into forced labor camps. Approaching Graudenz (Grudziadz in Polish) and its sturdy bridge over the mighty Vistula River, the men chose a stormy night to attempt the crossing, counting on the sleeting rain to keep us out of sight of the military patrols, who would be sheltering in the guard huts. Luck was with us.

Berlin lay about 300 miles west of Graudenz. A considerable number of Lithuanian refugees had reached and settled in or near Berlin, and Mr. Jonynas knew a few who would, he was sure, assist both our families. Father thought that once we were near the big city, we could sell or barter our horse and cart for food and shelter. We needed to hurry because winter weather was upon us, and the sheet tenting over our cart, though strong against the wind, was often soaked through and offered no protection from the rain and snow.

We had traveled about twenty-five miles southwest from Graudenz when luck turned its face away from us. Our journey thus far had been through a relatively flat landscape, but now we reached an area of low hills, the road gently rising, dipping, and rising again. We knew that our little Russian cart had no drag or brake to slow it, and we also knew that the shafts were too short for our big mare's comfort. We had noticed that when the low-hanging singletree (a part of the harness, the crossbar to which the traces are attached) would touch the mare on the hocks, she would almost jump in the air. But there was nothing we could do about it.

The dips in the road on which we were now travelling irritated the mare, because her rear legs were constantly battered by the singletree. Father had been leading her, but could not calm her. He thought he could control her better if he sat in the cart and held the reins tight. He wrapped them around his wrists.

There was barely anyone else on the road that morning, though the Jonynases were right behind us. We came to the top of a rise. This time, the road descended in a steep incline. To minimize the grade, the roadway had been built upon a tall embankment with abrupt ravines on both sides.

As we started the descent, Father had no means to slow the cart, the singletree was drumming on the mare's back legs, and she panicked. She took off down the hill, racing at the speed of a cavalry charge. Her wild dash created a wind that filled the tent sheets like a sail and tore the upper boxy part of the cart from the chassis. Mother, Milda, and I went flying through the air, our possessions spilling all over the road. The body of the cart landed on its side partway over the ravine.

Everything happened at the speed of a film set on fast-forward. Hitting the ground knocked the wind out of me; I revived to a cacophony of incomprehensible shrieking. Next to me, I made out Milda's voice screaming, "Daddy! Daddy!" I jumped up and saw Mother running clumsily down the hill, howling wordlessly, and then my eyes caught the sight of the mare, dragging a body between the bouncing wheels of the topless cart. Father was dead, I was sure of it. I could not find my voice; I started to run to him, but Mrs. Jonynas had rushed over to us and now held me tight, pressing my face against her stomach.

When the top part of the cart had lifted up, the sudden movement pitched Father forward and down to the ground. He was in a helpless situation, the reins cinched tight around his wrists. The frantic mare was dragging him with his hands above his head, upper body suspended, but scraping the road on his knees and toes between the wheels of the cart, inches from her deadly hooves. She ran until the road rose again and she no longer felt the blows to her legs, then finally slowed and stopped.

"They say that before you die, your entire life flashes before your mind's eye," said Father. "In the first few seconds after I hit the ground,

I was terrified; I felt my knees tear into the dirt, and I tried to figure out how to release the reins, but saw at once that it was hopeless. The hooves of the mare thundered and the wheels bounced so close to my head, I knew it was the end for me. But it was not my life that flashed before me, but the peaceful image of the four of us together in the little cart, my three 'girls' and I, harmonizing to the hymn 'Jėzau, pas mane ateiki—Come to me, Jesus'—and I no longer felt terror or pain. And suddenly—all went quiet. The mare had stopped, and I realized that I had survived."

"I rushed up to Father," said Mother, "and fell on my knees, imploring God's mercy. He did not move, but then I heard a groan. He was alive! Mr. Jonynas had driven his cart down the hill and stopped next to the remains of ours, and now he soothed the mare while I crawled between the wheels and unwound the reins from Father's cut and bleeding wrists. Then Jonynas drew the mare forward, tethered her to his own cart, and helped Father turn over on his back. When I saw his torn and mangled knees, I almost fainted. But then, slowly, he sat up and gave me a little smile, whispering, 'Dar gyvas—I'm still alive.' That's when I started to cry uncontrollably: the shock of what might have been finally hit me."

Much later, Mother wrote about the events:

> Your father's knees were scraped to the bone, his only pair of trousers in tatters. The three of us, hurled out of the cart, landed as if on the wings of an angel, without so much as a scratch, though the Jonynases, witnessing us flying out as if carried on a whirlwind, were certain we would be killed—or at least suffer many broken bones. Your father and I recall this experience with deep emotion. We want to believe that God gave us a miracle, or if not a miracle, that He helped ease our plight that day.

Thank God for the Jonynases! All of them flew to our aid. Mr. Jonynas helped Father stand up and take a few steps to make sure no bones were broken. Mrs. Jonynas helped Mother and Milda gather together our scattered belongings. The boys and their father wrestled the boxy body of the cart back onto the chassis. They brought out a hammer and nails and made sure the structure held together securely.

Mr. Jonynas harnessed our mare, who seemed docile in his hands, to his much bigger cart, and substituted one of his smaller horses to pull ours. He also jury-rigged a brake from a piece of wood, to slow our cart down the inclines.

I stayed out of this flurry of activity and just clung to Father's hand, repeating to him Mother's orders that he sit still where he was, on the verge of the road, and not move. But when everything was reassembled, Father had to get up into the cart and drive.

We had to stop at the nearest shelter we could find to take care of Father's knees and the cuts the reins had made on his wrists. It was also essential to repair his only trousers. We were extremely fortunate because the owners of a nearby farmhouse, on seeing Father's injuries and hearing his summary of the accident, took pity on us, and accommodated all of us in their hay barn. They told us we could stay two or three days, if necessary.

Mother could not bear to look at Father's wounds. Mrs. Jonynas told Mother to close her eyes—she was used to handling her sons' scrapes. She had brought with her from Lithuania not only some strong alcohol and a big bottle of iodine, but also a pair of tweezers for plucking eyebrows, which, properly sterilized, could be used to clean foreign matter out of the deep and messy abrasions on Father's knees.

Before the wounds could be cleaned, Father had to take off his trousers. The women gently soaked them off where they had begun crusting into scabs. Left in his underwear and wrapped in a blanket, Father sat by the barn door where the afternoon light was strongest and let Mrs. Jonynas do her best.

It took her a long time to pick the ground-in threads and grit and dirt out of his wounds. Then Mrs. Jonynas washed them with water, and dribbled on the iodine. Mother found a clean cotton pillowcase, washed and ironed days previously at the home of the thoughtful Polish couple. She tore it into strips, and Mrs. Jonynas used them to bandage Father's knees. I had been tempted by curiosity to look at the operation, but the sight of my daddy's face, twisted in agony while Mrs. Jonynas poked about, made me run up to the hayloft and snuggle up to my sleeping sister for comfort.

After eating some rusks of bread, Father stretched out to rest. Mother did her best to clean the blood out of his wrecked trousers. Fortunately, they were dark brown in color: stains would not show.

Mrs. Jonynas rummaged through their possessions and came up with a pair of tweed wool pants that the younger son had outgrown and torn, but which she had kept because they were made of good material and would be good for making repairs to other clothes. Mother and Mrs. Jonynas worked by candlelight until midnight to finish sewing the patches over the holes in the knees. The colors did not match, but in those war years, patches were common and few people noticed them.

We had one additional crisis on our hands. During the accident, Mother, Milda, and I had landed on our bundles and the hay that we carried in the cart for the mare. Outwardly, our bodies showed no wounds. But Milda had suffered whiplash and was in shock. Her eyes had been bothering her for a week; they were red and painful, and she could not bear bright light. And now, late that evening, while Father was resting and the women were sewing, she woke from her nap into a world of darkness. Panic seized her and she cried to Mother to come quick, that she could not see. My sister had gone blind.

Mother's initial reaction shocked Milda deeply. As she told me years later, "I know that Mother was worried sick about Father, but that night, when I was crying in fear that I could not see, the first thing she said to me was, 'Better dead than blind.' If I could have figured out a way to kill myself, I might have done it, I was in such despair."

My poor sister. I could not truly understand her state of mind: I was only seven. Later I realized that the entire war experience was much easier for me to bear than for her. I was at an age where I still believed that Mother and Father had magic powers; as long as I was with them, they would provide for me no matter what. My biggest terror in those days was losing my daddy to the German military. But Milda was adult enough to know that our parents were simply fumbling in the dark, unsure of their decisions, with no set goal on which they could agree.

If she were separated from them, what would happen to her? Men had already tried to grope and kiss her when our parents were not around—she found it both disgusting and frightening. I knew nothing of rape, but she had heard horrifying personal experiences from the maids in the Varnakases' kitchen, leading her to dread it worse than death. For Milda, every day of the war began and ended in a cold sweat. Outwardly, she had been handling it all like an adult, but inside she was just a scared and vulnerable girl of fifteen.

Early the next morning, the adults discussed what to do next. Clearly, both Father and Milda needed urgent medical care. Doctors for civilians were almost impossible to find; all able-bodied medics were treating soldiers on the front lines. However, if lucky, one could sometimes locate a frail old doctor, or one too disabled for active duty.

The family who sheltered us said there was a working hospital in Bromberg (Bydgoszcz in Polish), which was only about fifteen miles away. The town was on the route we had meant to take to get to Berlin. My parents decided that we would have to find help and stay there for a while. We did not want to hold up the Jonynas family, who were anxious to keep going. After a day of rest in the hay-barn of the friendly farmers, we had to go.

Before we parted, Mr. Jonynas asked Father to help him kill the cow. The poor animal had been growing scrawnier by the day, she had stopped giving milk, and the constant walking with no time to chew cud in peace had just about done her in. At Jonynas' request, Father asked permission of the farmer to slaughter it; the farmer agreed, in exchange for some of its blood to make *blutwurst*—blood sausage.

Father was in a quandary: could he refuse to help out? To begin with, he was not in good shape for a strenuous job, barely able to walk or use his swollen wrists. Plus, to kill the patient, friendly creature was for him the stuff of nightmares. And yet, how could he deny assistance to the man whose family had helped us so much? Mr. Jonynas promised that he would let us have all the suet—a priceless offer. Fat was essential, and we had none.

While Mr. Jonynas held the cow roped tight, Father struck a big blow with the blunt end of an axe on her trusting head. She fell instantly. Alas, when she was opened up, there was not an ounce of suet in her body: she was too thin.

Father and Mother were very disappointed. Mother suspected—and of course I agreed—that Mr. Jonynas had dangled an empty promise just to get Father's help with the slaughter. From the first moment I had met him back in the schoolhouse, I had never trusted him. But who knows what our fate might have been if Mr. Jonynas had not been there with us? And Mrs. Jonynas had been an absolute angel to us every mile of the way.

As we left, Mr. Jonynas continued to lend us his smaller horse, and said he would stay close to us until we found lodging. It did not take long. As we were approaching Bromberg, we came upon an old wooden house surrounded by woods. The door was opened by a small woman who spoke German in a strong dialect. We later learned that she was an ethnic German who had been born in Romania. Because Frau Wald was treated as not-quite-pure-German by her neighbors, she had some sympathy for refugees. The house belonged to the *Forstverwalter*—the Forest Superintendent. Frau Wald's own husband was his assistant, but at that time, in the autumn of 1944, he was fighting somewhere in Hungary.

Before agreeing to admit us, she consulted the Superintendent, an old man with the bluest eyes and deepest wrinkles I had ever seen, who lived in a much more modern and prosperous house on the property, and acted like a guardian to Frau Wald. He looked over Father's documentation, smiled over the fancy sealed and stamped certificate, and chatted for a while. I suppose he was satisfied that Father posed no danger.

Upon receiving his approval, Frau Wald let us have the garret room on the third floor. It must have housed servants in years gone by. It had two small, musty beds and a primitive wood-burning stove for cooking and heating. Frau Wald said we could take as much chopped wood as we needed from the enormous pile in the Superintendent's barn.

As payment for the lodging, we had to give them our cart and the mare. Mr. Jonynas took back his horse, the men shook hands and slapped backs, the women cried and hugged, and the boys tried to say their goodbyes to Milda—though she barely responded. Wishing each other good luck and God's blessings, we parted ways. It would be many long years until we met them again, safe and lively, half a world away.

Typical German order still prevailed in Bromberg. Now that we had a residence, we could apply for food coupons. We all went to register at the Mayor's office. The clerk was duly impressed with Father's magnificent certificate. He questioned Father and Mother about the accident, then wrote a note to the city hospital to admit Milda and clean Father's wounds.

The clerk told Mother and Father to get photographs for the documents required to remain in Blomberg. He wrote a note to the doctor at the *Arbeitsamt*, the local Labor Center, asking him to determine whether Father was able to do some sort of work for the Reich. If the doctor signed an official certificate stating that he was currently disabled, we would be authorized to exchange our old food ration coupons for new ones, register at a store, and finally be allowed to buy some groceries.

November 1944. Father in Bromberg.

In the German occupied territories, there were no antibiotics available in those days for regular civilians, and especially not for the *Ausländer*—the foreigners. During the previous forty-eight hours, Father had had no choice but to keep walking and driving, and his knees had become an ugly, infected, inflamed mess. The doctor at the Labor Center confirmed that Father was temporarily disabled. The city hospital placed Milda in the children's ward and cleaned Father's wounds.

On our way back to the forest warden's house, we registered for new food coupons, and walked out with two loaves of bread. Two loaves, each weighing about two pounds, was the ration for all four of us for a week, but oh how good it tasted! We had to save some for Milda, because care at this hospital did not include food for non-Germans.

Milda had a severe inflammation of the eyes, which the doctor could not diagnose and for which he had no medications. The nurses did their best to wash her eyes with salt water, borax, or whatever home remedy they could find. Within a few days, she could distinguish outlines, but bright light stabbed her like needles.

Milda felt safe on the ward, and the nurses treated her with affection. Sometimes they brought her something to eat. Unfortunately, one of these donations did not agree with her: her skin turned yellow, and she developed a fever and intestinal pain. Perhaps it was the same liver infection from which I had suffered as we entered East Prussia. She needed good food, but there was never enough to buy.

By this time—November 1944—stores were always running short of supplies, and the anticipated delivery of food products would attract long lines of housewives, and old men and women, jostling and grumbling, hoping there would be something left when they arrived at the head of the line. Hitler had used the occupied countries to provision his war effort, and now that the Allies had taken back vast stretches of territory, food produced in Germany itself had to do double duty. It went to the military first, leaving little for civilians who were not used to deprivation.

For us foreigners, the ration of food was severely limited. Usually, we could buy potatoes and a little milk for me. If we managed to get to the store right after a delivery, we could also buy a bit of margarine, a little flour, and half a kilogram (about a pound) of beans. All of us were hungry, but most of all Father and Mother, who ate just enough not to die of starvation. As always, the biggest and the best of what little there was they gave to Milda and me.

Father stayed in bed as much as he could. The infection in both knees had turned ugly. A worrisome red stain spread down his legs, discoloring the skin. His immune system was as undernourished and as weak as he was, and Mother was afraid that gangrene would set in. She reminisced, "There were no bathroom facilities in the house, only an outhouse by the barn. We had to walk up and down two flights of stairs and cross the yard, rain or snow. Each trip would open Father's wounds anew. It took a month before he could limp stiffly to town."

In the meantime, I was living a divided life: I was both a carefree child and a child with worries too big for my years. Frau Wald had two little girls, one about eleven, the other five. The older one was a real little Nazi, insisting I greet her with an outstretched arm and a loud "Heil Hitler."

While her big sister was in school, the younger girl, Ilke, asked her mother to let me play with her. Frau Wald first made sure I was a model child. The first week, she would let me come only if she was in the room. I must have passed her test, however, because she soon gave up supervising and left us alone. I knew better than to upset Ilke for even a moment! I had picked up a little German, but I did not know enough to say anything that could rile her.

The girls had a roomful of toys, more than I had ever seen. It was glorious to play with the dolls, push them around in their wicker carriages, and listen to Ilke chatter non-stop, inventing stories about their menagerie of teddy bears and stuffed animals of every kind. And the pile of colorful children's books! As long as I was downstairs with little Ilke, I was just a happy-go-lucky child. The moment I left to go back to our little garret, my anxieties rejoined me at the bottom of the stairs. What if Daddy lost his legs? What if Milda remained blind? What, in heaven's name, could I do about any of it?

By the second week of December, Father's wounds had begun to heal, and he was impatient to explore the town. He hoped to find someone who knew the real news, rather than the Nazi propaganda parroted to us by Frau Wald. She loyally listened to her *Volksempfänger*, the People's Receiver radio, which broadcast only the state-controlled version of events and which she believed with unshakable faith.

Under the Nazis, it was a crime to listen to foreign broadcasts, so nobody would admit to having news from a source such as the BBC. Father and Mother had no idea where the Russian forces were encamped. Desperate to feel safe, my parents decided that we already were, as if wishing could make it so.

Mother was always busy. For one, our garret had no running water. Mother had to bring up buckets for drinking or cooking or laundry or bathing, then she had to take the dirty water outside and throw it out in a designated area. She was our shopper for food and our supplier of clothing. Frau Wald had given her a bag of used clothing she had discarded, and Mother was busy with a needle all day, creating a blouse for Milda from two of Frau Wald's, or—her masterpiece—piecing together a pair of trousers for Father from an old suit worn out by Mr. Wald, whose last news had come from the front lines in Hungary weeks before.

When Father could finally go into town, Mother encouraged him to take me along, ostensibly to make him look harmless despite his height. But I think she hoped my presence would ensure that he would not be tempted to "flirt." She had a jealous streak. I was supposed to report to her if he spent any time talking to other women. From my curious and attentive observation, I saw that the only women he addressed were shopkeepers or officials that he needed to question, but I also noted that many women waiting with us in stores or offices or at the hospital would start talking to him. He was too much of a gentleman not to respond.

Besides, the only way to survive was to learn what was going on. From these casual, friendly chats, he learned important information—such as on which days stores would receive deliveries of margarine or cheese or beans, or where he could find a used bookstore, or which Catholic Church still had a priest.

After our first outing, I reported some details of Father's encounters to Mother, but after experiencing the interrogation which followed, I learned to keep my mouth shut. How could I answer such questions as, "Did she look prettier than me?" For me, Mother had no looks—she was just Mother and therefore incomparable.

Christmas was coming, and my thoughts kept turning with nostalgia to the box of shiny ornaments and tinsel that we had saved over the years, now just part of the debris of our bombed-out home in Vilnius. Ornamental balls were available in Bromberg, but only for barter. By tradition, the first time that German families showed off the decorated and candle-lit tree to their children was in the evening on Christmas Eve.

There was no tree when Frau Wald invited me to watch a small gathering of children and friends on December 6, when St. Nicholas came in his red and white robes, accompanied by a mean, devilish-looking man holding birch twigs to punish children who had been naughty. All the children, except for me, had to sing or recite a poem, then St. Nicholas rewarded them with sweets and little presents—except for me. The black-dressed man swished about and roared, but the only one he scared was me. However, to make me feel better, little Ilke gave me a few of her hard candies, some of which I saved for my sister.

A week before Christmas, the nurses at the hospital said that Milda, though not yet well, had improved enough to be released in a few days. The whites of her eyes were still discolored by the liver infection that had plagued her. The doctor at the hospital joked with her, "See how well I doctored you? You came in with red eyes, you'll leave with yellow." But she could see again, and we felt like celebrating.

Father was like a child when it came to Christmas. He could not bear to go through another cheerless Christmas Eve like the one we had missed under the communists in 1940, when we had sat with no tree, huddled in fear, wondering what had become of him. Now when he and I walked into town, we had a clear focus: to find any object that could be turned into a tree ornament.

Getting the tree itself was not a challenge. Dozens of small firs sprouted at the edge of the Superintendent's property, free for the taking. Father and I decided to make holiday decorations our secret project. We had help: candy wrappers. Whoever had the Reichsmarks could still buy little hard candies wrapped in shiny colored paper, which children typically discarded once the sweet was in the mouth.

The wrappers were perfect for making chains. Father and I had a contest to see who could find more. Father cut the shiny paper into narrow strips, then we glued them into interlocking rings, resulting in long, colorful ropes. During his trips downtown, Father had made friends with a Polish man whose business was thriving: he made coffins. From him, Father got some glue, and also a small bottle each of gold and silver paint. We gathered small fir cones from the forest that Father highlighted in silver. He made a gold star for the top.

From her visits to the vegetable seller, the baker, the grocer, and the dairy store, Mother had squirreled away a beet here, a few carrots there, some salted herring—enough to make some of the dishes for a traditional *Kūčios*, the Christmas Eve gathering that is at the heart of Lithuanian and Polish celebration. The big challenge was to find a *plotkelė*—an unleavened bread wafer which the head of the home shares with the rest of the family. Each family member breaks off and eats a little piece, both in remembrance of Christ breaking bread with his disciples at the Last Supper, and as a symbol of peace and harmony among all those present.

Father approached the priest in the only Catholic Church left open in Bromberg. There were no traditional rectangular wafers to be had, but the priest gave Father two large unsanctified hosts to use as substitutes. Back in our garret, Father placed them in a brown envelope which he put on a small wooden crate that we used for storage.

Around mid-December, our Christmas prospects and our mood had improved, thanks to the friendly and generous heart of a Lithuanian man, Mr. Kamaitis. He and Father met by chance in downtown Bromberg. He came to visit us often in our garret, and took a great liking to me, perhaps because he had no children himself. His job as deliveryman required him to come to town every two or three days, and he had to drive right by us.

Like our friends the Jonynases, he and his wife had left Lithuania unrushed, and had brought with them a horse and a cart full of food and household goods. Now, expecting the war to end any minute, he and Mrs. Kamaitis were working for the owner of a silver-fox breeding ranch, a very prosperous German, who paid and fed and housed them. Plus, as an employed man, Mr. Kamaitis had ration coupons as well. When it came to food, he was the wealthiest man we knew.

At every visit, Mr. Kamaitis brought us some supplies: an extra loaf of bread, a sausage, some ersatz coffee. And he never forgot a treat for me—a sweet roll, a jar of jam, a handful of dried apple slices, some candies. I tried, not always successfully, to save a little for my sister, and was proud of the small pile of treats awaiting her as a Christmas gift.

Milda came home two days before Christmas Eve, looking gaunt, the whites of her eyes still slightly yellow. Bright lights still hurt, but she could see again well enough to read, and was overjoyed to be reunited with us. Father and I brought out our hand-made ornaments, and she helped us decorate a small fir tree. We also hung fir branches from the low ceiling, both to give our garret a festive touch, and especially for the lovely smell.

On the 24th, Mother scrubbed every inch of our space. As the first star appeared in the sky, we put on clean clothes and gathered for our modest celebration, which looked as opulent to me as a feast for princes. Father went to the crate to pick up the hosts to start the ceremony with the traditional breaking of the bread. They were gone!

We searched every corner. Finally, something pricked my memory. "Mama," I said, "wasn't there a brown paper in the trash bucket which you took out this afternoon?" Oh, the consternation! Mother had an aversion to any kind of useless clutter. She had not bothered to check if there was anything inside the ugly brown envelope. She ran outside to the spot where she had dumped the trash, but the hosts had melted in the dirty scrubbing water.

For a while, our festive mood was ruined. Mother was superstitious: she was sure that throwing away "*Dievo duoną*—God's bread" would bring disaster on us. Father was distressed, but for Milda's sake and mine he put on a cheerful face. We managed to have a festive Christmas.

In fact, for the next few weeks, we felt peaceful and hopeful that the worst was over. We had a warm room, everyone's health was improving, we were eating better thanks to Mr. Kamaitis, and we had no news of any Soviet advances.

We were living in fool's paradise.

CHAPTER 12:

The Last Train from Stettin

Winter arrived with a vengeance in January 1945. We were unaware of the true developments in the war, but the Red Dragon was not asleep, and we were in its path. This is what Mother wrote down for me, describing the next few weeks:

One day, in the middle of January, it occurred to us to have our shoes repaired, because they were coming apart and the soles were worn out. Father had met a Polish shoemaker who, in greatest secrecy, repaired shoes for civilians. The government forbade it: he was under orders to work exclusively for the military. He liked Father because he spoke good Polish. The shoemaker told Father to bring our old shoes to him. We would pay him with the extra pair of child shoes Dalia had found in the school closet in Prussia.

But how could Father bring him the shoes? He had just the one pair. He could not drop them off and then return barefoot: it was a terribly cold winter. Father asked Mr. Kamaitis, who agreed to deliver the shoes. And thus Father and Milda and you, Dalia, were left with no footwear. My own shoes did not need fixing, because somewhere on the road I had bought a pair of men's high-top shoes with canvas uppers (which Father contemptuously called "*kiaulviedriai*—pig-slop pails").

The battlefront had been quiet in the east, and we were waiting for spring before continuing further westward. Suddenly, on the evening of January 20, our landlady climbed up to our garret to report she had just heard on the radio that the Red Army had taken Warsaw some days before, and its troops were now approaching Bromberg. She had heard that the Soviets were setting up encampments around the city, but that escape was still possible going west.

At 11 p.m., the Forest Superintendent came to the house, driving the cart and mare that they had taken from us in payment. He set Frau Wald, her daughters, and their belongings on the cart and was about to drive away, leaving us to stay or walk out, barefoot, in freezing temperatures.

Before they left, Milda and I begged Frau Wald to allow us to take some old shoes that she was leaving behind. She gave us permission, but the discards were pretty wretched. Milda took a pair of Frau Wald's that were too big, but could be laced up. She could walk in them. For you, Dalia, we found a worn pair of her older daughter's. Father had the greatest problem, because Frau's husband's shoes were much too small. He managed to squeeze his feet into them, but only if he kept his toes curled. They pinched terribly.

After Frau Wald and her girls left with the Superintendent, we stood as if stunned: what do we do now? Should we remain in the house and wait for the Red Terror to annihilate us, or should we try to get away somehow, hoping for a miracle to save us? We decided to go.

Father lit a candle-lantern and opened the Superintendent's barn, where all the wood was stored. He found some boards and nailed together something resembling a sled, but sleds must have smooth metal runners, and ours had to slide on the rough edges of the wood. On it, we placed the essential things we owned: the bedding, the clothes, the dried bread I had been saving since Jurbarkas, a bag of flour, and on top, we placed you, Dalia. To Milda I gave one cooking pot and our few dishes to carry, wrapped in towels and put in a pillowcase.

By the time we left, it was the middle of the night. The outside thermometer showed minus twenty-six Celsius (about fifteen below zero Fahrenheit). There was no snow on the ground, but it was so cold that the bare wooden runners froze to the road if we stopped even for a moment. And to make matters worse, we had to go uphill. Father and I kept on pulling, but the sled felt so heavy that we needed to stop often to rest, and then it froze solidly to the ground and we could not budge it. It was desperately hard going, but we were desperate to live. You, Dalia, got off to walk, because sitting still you were turning to ice; it helped us a little, but we still needed to stop and catch our breath.

We managed to pull and drag our way for about three or four miles when trouble came. After one brief stop, as Father and I gave the sled a strong tug, the boards separated, and everything we owned scattered all over the road. We were immobilized in the grip of a dark, icy night.

I remember the moment well. My sister was beside herself, but neither of us said anything to our parents, seeing the panic in their faces. For a minute or two, Mother lost all self-control, cursing Hitler and the frozen black night that seemed poised to kill us. Milda and I stood, hopping up and down and swinging our arms to keep warm, our breath sending out little clouds of steam, which then froze on our cheeks. Milda drew me aside, took my hands in hers and said, "We'd better pray, sis, because only God can get us out of this." I concentrated upon our favorite saint, Theresa of the Child Jesus, feeling that I needed her help to persuade the Almighty to get us out of this nightmare. There was nothing Milda and I could do but pray.

Mother's account continues:

Father and I stared into the darkness around us, and saw in the distance a flickering light. Our hearts lifted with hope. He went to investigate while we three gathered everything to the side of the road and waited, stamping our feet and flailing our arms. Our clothes were inadequate to keep us warm in such freezing temperatures. I cannot remember how much time passed before Father reappeared with another Lithuanian, this time pulling a sled with proper metal runners. For that night, at least, we were saved!

The light we had seen came from a substantial farmhouse. The owners had left the day before, and now two Lithuanian families and a group of Poles, all former forced laborers on the farm, were having a party. One of the Lithuanians, an agronomist named Vaškelis, was a dedicated communist who was notorious in Lithuania from the first Soviet occupation. Now he was urging everyone to celebrate the imminent arrival of the Red Army. A bit drunk, he promised that he would put in a good word for us: he would tell the Soviets that the Nazis had forcibly evacuated us from home. It would not do to admit the truth, which was that we had fled in fear of certain deportation to Siberia, perhaps even death. What could we do? Dear God, there was nothing to do but await our fate.

The next afternoon, not long before the early winter sunset, a man drove into the yard, his cart full of hay. Milda yelled, "It's Mr. Kamaitis!" All four of us ran out and threw ourselves at him, ready to beg for help.

It turned out that he was searching for us! When he could not find us at the house in Bromberg, on his way home he questioned everyone he met, asking whether they had seen four people of our description. Finally, one man said that such a family had arrived in the depth of night at this farmhouse.

Mr. Kamaitis settled our belongings and us on his cart and described what had been going on. His boss, the rich German owner of the silver-fox ranch, was in a terrible hurry to leave with everything he possessed, especially his best breeding stock. He could not find enough teamsters to drive the heavy four-in-hand wagons, and to feed, water, and curry the horses.

Mr. Kamaitis described us to the German, saying we were two adults, a teenager, and a child, with almost no possessions. The man, meaning Father, spoke excellent German, could handle horses, and would certainly agree to be one of the drivers, as long as his wife and daughters were taken along. The German owner told Kamaitis to immediately harness a cart and bring us to him, but first to fill it with hay and pretend a delivery in case any military official on the road questioned what he was doing.

Everything was quickly arranged. The German owner loaned one of his horses to the Kamaitises, so they could take our belongings and Dalia on their cart without fatiguing their own horse, which could amble along at ease behind it. Father drove a wagon pulled by four horses and I was allowed to sit next to him, but Milda had to walk. She and I changed places from time to time, because sitting without moving quickly made our teeth chatter, it was so cold. Father had to sit and bear it, because I could not relieve him. I could not learn to control four horses, and even Father had a rough time of it.

The worst part was that his feet turned to ice in shoes that held his feet gripped in a vise, cutting off circulation, with no room to wiggle his toes. When we stopped for the night, his feet were too numb to walk. We tried wrapping cloths around them with little success. If only we had owned a warm wool blanket! It was a hard freeze that January.

After a day of icy rain, Father got very sick, at one point becoming almost incoherent with fever. Because the Russians were so close behind us, we could not stop to let him get well. In fact, the first few days, we didn't stop for more than five or six hours a night.

How well I remember that journey. All day long, I lay on my right side in the Kamaitises' cart, curled up in a fetal position, the tarpaulin just inches above me. Mother covered me with everything she could find, leaving a small opening between the slats of the cart so I could look at the scenery passing by. I see again the dull winter brown of the fields, the black skeletons of trees, and the low grey clouds.

Some days it snowed. I loved the way snow transformed everything we passed into something mysterious: was that soft pile a bush? A wheelbarrow? A kneeling knight cursed to remain frozen until a princess kissed him to life again? But if it snowed hard, the weight of the snow pressed the tarp down right on top of me, a blanket of cold. Then I would slap at it, hoping that Mother or Milda would notice and come to sweep it off me.

I turned eight on the road from Bromberg. Under ordinary circumstances, I might have gone out of my mind or taken to screaming out of boredom, forced to lie in the same position, unmoving, for twelve to fourteen hours a day. But I understood the danger of our situation. Besides, I was used to lying still, having spent much time sick in bed during the previous four years. Time had no meaning for me. And then, somewhere along the way, in an abandoned farmhouse that had been pretty much destroyed by vandals, under a child's bed, I found my own small miracle: a little girl doll, rumpled but unbroken, wearing some sort of regional costume with a black apron. My Laimutė's face had been prettier and more appealing, but this doll had real hair and glass eyes, and her slightly open mouth showed two white teeth. She became by turns my alter ego and my best friend. I named her Ilke, after my recent playmate.

I had a vivid imagination, and would create in my mind long and involved stories in which we played the main roles. Most of them involved enchanted sources of delicious food, which we could enjoy in safe and warm houses, in sunny fields and woods. I visualized in my mind how I would illustrate them if only I had paper and colored pencils.

For a change of theme, I would hum for Ilke my repertoire of songs. At times, homesickness enveloped me in its coils until it was hard to breathe. I still missed my beloved Laimutė, imagining her unbroken and waiting for me in the ruins of our bomb-shattered home. But most of all, I yearned for Šeduva, its soft green fields, bountiful cherry trees, and the taste of the first green peas of spring. I learned not to cry. The tears froze on my face, and besides, I had no handkerchief.

The German owner of the foxes made everyone stop occasionally to feed the horses, which gave the four of us a chance to suck on some of our old dried bread, and to find a bush or ravine to relieve the bladder. Mother and Milda would try to warm up Father's feet, rubbing them in their hands before he painfully imprisoned them again.

It was slow going. Our German master's five or six wagons were just a drop in the stream of humanity on the road. When anyone drew to the side of the road for a rest stop, the column had to slow up and adjust, and even more time was needed to get back into the column when starting on again. Interruptions and slowdowns were constant.

If it was not snowing, I watched the adults scan the skies, worried looks on their faces. Milda explained to me that everyone was on the lookout for Soviet planes. The Russians seemed to enjoy strafing civilian refugees as much as they did military convoys. We prayed for bad weather so the fighter planes would be grounded.

One day, we came to a section of road that had suffered such an attack a day or two before. I saw overturned carts and dead horses, their frozen legs stiff in the air, before Mother rushed up and wrapped her scarf around my eyes, walking next to where I lay in the cart to make sure I did not remove my blindfold and see the bloody carnage.

Mother continues:

> The first week of February ended. Suffering from the bitter cold and the lack of sleep, but happy to be drawing daily farther away from the Russians, we passed a town called Belgard

(Bialogard in Polish) and stopped about ten miles north of it. Our German master needed to procure food for his foxes and horses, and said we would remain there for a couple of days. Father had a vacation!

We looked for a place to stay, and discovered a group of refugee Lithuanians lodged in a small, privately owned dance hall. The floor was covered with long rows of straw for sleeping. A narrow walkway was left open between the rows. On the stage, the landlords had installed a small cooking range. In front of the stage stood an iron wood-burning stove, meant to heat the entire hall. The fire was never allowed to go out: in the dark, the metal glowed red.

Unfortunately, as the latest arrivals, the only place left for us was farthest away from its warmth, and closest to the entryway. People needing to use the outhouse at night, opening and closing the door, constantly let in the freezing cold, and we shivered in our sleep.

Most of the residents were Lithuanian bachelors whom the Germans had released from forced-labor camps abandoned to the advancing Soviets. They were, to a man, thin and worn out, but willingly took care of cutting and supplying wood for the stove and the cooking range.

There were only two other families: an older Lithuanian woman who was an American citizen, trying to escape to the west with her daughter and little granddaughter, and Mrs. Kreivėnas, a teacher, and her four children. Her husband had been deported to Siberia in the terror of June 1941, but she and the children had managed to hide from the communists until the Germans invaded. She was a very dear person and became a good friend.

When we told Mrs. Kreivėnas the conditions under which we were traveling, she recommended that we remain for a while to regain our strength. She said the mayor of the village was a good man who allowed refugees to register for food coupons, and the landlords were remarkably helpful. They sold milk to the refugees for Reichsmarks, plus they had owned a laundry, and there remained a big water heater and tubs and washboards that all of us could use. Heating water was not a problem—the village was surrounded by woods. She also said that trains were still running, so we could leave when we felt ready. Father certainly needed to rest, so we said goodbye to the German fox-breeder and to the Kamaitises, and registered with the Mayor to stay.

The battlefront and the Red Army seemed far away, perhaps still around Bromberg, more than a hundred miles to the southeast. But who really knew? Truthful news reports were hard to get, only Nazi propaganda. We thought we would stay a few weeks, and then, if the war had not ended, take a train west. We had access to food, were warm during the day, and were finally clean again. Our fellow Lithuanians treated us with affection, because when it got dark and the electricity was turned off at the hour of curfew, Father told stories loudly enough for everyone to hear. There were no chairs, so people lay down on the hay on the floor, and listened to him recount fairy tales and myths—Lithuanian, Russian, German, and Polish—he knew hundreds. The bachelors, many of whom had missed out on their education, were fascinated.

Father also gave a moving speech on February 16, the day we commemorated Lithuania's short-lived independence. Dalia recited a couple of patriotic poems, and then we all sang Lithuanian songs until we cried.

Days passed in peace. The Allied government chiefs, Roosevelt, Churchill, and Stalin, met at Yalta and decided the fate of nations, including our homeland, without a word trickling down to us. Ignorant of the facts, once again we stayed put too long. As February was ending, as if from thin air, there came the news that the Red Army was on the move once more, and closing in from the east and south. All of us Lithuanians were in a panic: would we be able to get away in time?

Germany had an impressive network of rail lines, short branches and spurs running everywhere. Mrs. Kreivėnas and I walked the few kilometers to the nearest railroad station at Korlin (now Polish Karlino) to ask about trains that ran to Stettin (now Szeczin). Going west to Stettin was the only way out. The ticket seller was a very helpful young German woman. She said that a few trains were still stopping at Korlin, but because the Russians were drawing near, soon only the German military would be allowed to board them.

Then she gave us a piece of advice that saved us. She said to get tickets for the next morning's train going in the opposite direction from Stettin, back to Belgard, which was the end of that railroad line. She explained that the train running toward Belgard would stop in Korlin almost empty, and we would be able to get on. The same train would then return from Belgard to go to Stettin, but when it stopped at Korlin—if it did—most likely it would be too crowded to find room in it. She had received a message from the stationmaster in Belgard that there were masses of people waiting to board there, everyone hoping to go west to Stettin.

We took her advice, bought the tickets to Belgard and from Belgard to Stettin, went back and repeated to everyone what she had explained. The next morning, our wonderful landlords hitched horses to a large cart and brought Father, all the women and children, and the weaker of the bachelors to the Korlin station; the others walked. All of us found a place on the train. When the train stopped in Belgard, we were amazed at the size of the crowd waiting to get on. People pushed and squeezed until we were literally like packed sardines.

There was a long wait in Belgard, and when the train finally rolled out, it was overloaded. When it reached Korlin it did not even slow down. Had we waited there, we would have been left behind to await our fate in the hands of the Soviets. The thoughtful advice of that good German woman saved us, and I often think of her with loving gratitude, wondering what fate might have been hers if she fell into the clutches of the Red Army.

Father and Milda stood, and I held you, Dalia, on my knees during the eighty-mile journey that dragged on interminably. Around 4 p.m., it turned dark. The train had no lights, hoping to make its way unobserved by the Russian air force. They were bombing Stettin again, and all trains were fair game. Ours crawled in the dark, sometimes stopping for long minutes, making the passengers wonder if the tracks had been bombed. Rumors circulated that the next day would be the last day for civilian train travel in this northern area of the former West Prussia. The air reeked of desperation.

Our train reached Stettin around 3 a.m. Everyone had to get off, as it had to return again to Belgard for military transport. The bombing raid in Stettin was over; we could see parts of the city in flames, the red glare providing the only light as we tried to make our way over to the platform on which the last train from Stettin to admit civilians was expected.

It was deep night when Mother hauled me, dull with sleep, out of the train from Belgard. The need to keep up with my parents and Milda, and also the cold, jolted me awake. I looked around me. The immense central station had escaped that night's bombs, but not previous assaults. Father said it had been a showplace, with high arched glass roofs over the train platforms. These were now shattered, and half of the main building destroyed.

A cold rain was drizzling down, but where some shelter remained, old wind-driven snow covered the ground and the stacks of shapeless refugee baggage piled on the platform. My parents commented that the crowds we had seen in Belgard were insignificant compared to the horde of desperate humanity gathered here, shivering in the cold, each one focused on a single goal: to get onto the last train from Stettin. Our Lithuanian companions formed little groups to help each other, and we said goodbyes with prayers for a happier future.

The situation was dire, and yet, everywhere one looked, the customary German love of order was evident. The glass shards from the ruined ceilings had been swept away. There was a small field kitchen just outside the station run by women from the German Red Cross offering weak ersatz coffee—nothing much, but it was hot and doled out with a smile and good wishes. People waited patiently for their turn, "As much for the touch of a kind word as for the hot drink," said Father. There was a temporary latrine nearby, as the bathroom indoors had been bombed.

Some older men, wearing the armband insignia of the *Volkssturm*—a national militia organized to supplement the military—pushed their way into the crowd, ordering that each person take on the train only one item. All other possessions, they said, were to be left on the platform and would be forwarded to a town called Waren in a few days, when a cargo train could be assembled.

Father and Mother quickly sorted through our bundles, rearranging them into smaller loads, leaving our oldest clothes, the last bag of dried bread, and the flour, to follow us on the cargo train. I clutched my doll fiercely, determined to keep her even if I had to fight Mother.

As we approached the area designated for our train, I recall facing a wall of backs. A multitude of thousands cut us off from the rails. Faced with a choice between survival for his family or old-world courtesy, and urged on by Mother, Father chose survival. At six feet four inches and recovered from his illness, he was a bulldozer on a mission: to get the four of us to the front of the platform. Soon we were standing close to the edge, buffeted by the wind, soaked by the icy drizzle, and our eyes, like those of the thousands around us, looking down along the track on which the promise of escape would come. Everyone worried: when would the train come? Would it come at all?

Hours passed. Rumors flew that the German military had diverted the train to Neustettin (now Szczecinek), which was under attack by the Red Army, to pick up the wounded. The dread that no train would come chilled us more sharply than did the wind and rain. Milda was praying continuously, stiff with anxiety.

At last, as the sky was turning to lighter grey, we heard the screech of wheels. The engine, spewing a cloud of steam, advanced slowly, like a tired animal. The multitude came to life, surging like a wave, straining to get as close to the front of the platform as possible. I was almost swept off my feet onto the tracks. Father and Mother had to use all their strength to push back so we would not fall under the wheels. Everyone was screaming, yelling for family members to stand close, little children shrieking as they were shoved away from their parents or fell under pressing feet. It was sheer pandemonium.

The thrust of the panicked crowd made it clear to my parents that our chances of getting on the train were infinitesimal at best. In 1945, in Germany, two configurations of passenger carriages were in use. The newer ones had two access doors, one at each end of the carriage. If we were not right next to one of the two doors when the train stopped, the desperate crush of the crowd would sweep us away, our hope of escape utterly lost.

The other, older type of carriage had four or five completely separate compartments, each of which had its own door to the outside. We stood a better chance of getting inside, but again, only if we were close enough to a door. The odds were against us. I could see my father's jaws grind in anguish as the deafening roar and the steam from the passing engine enveloped us. Milda was white as a sheet. Mother, in tears, clutched my hand and shouted in my ear, "This is our last chance. Pray to God, ask Him that when the train stops, the handle of the door falls at your father's hand."

I prayed. I, normally shy among strangers, did not care who heard me: I shouted as loud as I could, "God, put the handle in my father's hand! Put the handle in my father's hand!"

The train stopped. The door handle was in Father's hand, but the throng had pushed Mother, Milda, and me far away from him, out of reach.

Mother wrote down her memory of this moment:

> However you look at it, whatever your beliefs, I know God gave us a miracle. He heard the voice of a small, hungry child, and when the train stopped, the door was waiting for your father's hand. He threw it open and stood like a giant, barring entrance, screaming wildly that he would not let anybody in until his family got inside. The crowd, which had pushed us far back, squeezed apart to let us through, and then Father reached out to help others. I cannot find words to express my relief at getting on that train.

Fate, luck, or God's will, we were in. With Father's help, our small compartment managed to fit in about twenty people. The older women and mothers sat with children on their laps, their own or not, and everyone else stood. The shelves above the seating area were sagging, crammed to the ceiling with suitcases and bundles. Those standing became responsible for keeping the pile from falling on everyone's heads.

When the train finally started to move, over the noise of the wheels, all you could hear was a reverent outpouring of "*Gott sei Dank*—Thank God."

CHAPTER 13:

Conscripted by the Nazis

The train from Stettin moved slowly, the engineer and crew scanning the skies for attack planes, unsure if the tracks ahead had been damaged. Not only was every last inch of space inside occupied, but also the outside of the train was encrusted with brave and desperate people, clinging to any handhold and foothold. With every mile away from Stettin, Mother and Father—and especially Milda—looked less fearful.

The entire trip, I sat perched on Mother's knees. Her thighs were numb from my weight. Still, she hugged me tight every few minutes and, smiling, whispered in my ear, "Thank God, once again we've escaped the Red Terror." I pictured the huge Red Dragon, fading away from hunger.

I was fading too, as were we all. I could stand the hunger, but it was becoming pressing for me to find a toilet. Obviously, nothing of the kind was available in the compartment. Mother said, "hold it in"—I would have to wait. The first stop was a slow, slow ninety miles away in Waren, the station to which the extra baggage left in Stettin would be delivered. By the time we got there, all four of us were in misery. Oh, those bodily needs! Mother and Father decided we would get off, wait for our luggage, and then continue on.

Near the Waren station, a school had been converted into a shelter for refugees. We were assigned a small space and given straw for bedding. Hordes of bloodthirsty bedbugs left welts on us each night.

Other than the pests, Waren, located in the lake district of Germany, was a pleasant interlude. Former teachers assisted in organizing and advising the German and Prussian refugees, as well as the Poles, Lithuanians and Latvians, all the throngs of people streaming in from the east, fleeing the Soviets. The administration of the town allowed food coupons to be used in the local stores without proof of residence or incapacity to work, and arranged for soup to be served to the refugees once a day.

When the teachers learned that Father had been a school inspector, they sometimes served us bigger portions, and they also directed Father to a bartering center, where he exchanged his ill-fitting shoes for a bigger pair. Finally, he could walk with his toes straight.

Each day my parents asked about the promised cargo train that was to bring the bundles left in Stettin. We hoped and waited, but in vain. Mother hated to give up on our possessions, especially the dried bread, but for once, she was not refusing to go farther west. She could see that the Soviet threat had not disappeared. After about ten days, we dared not remain any longer.

Trains going west were incredibly crowded, but we managed to board one. It would take us to the Elbe River at *Festung Dömitz*—the fortified city of Dömitz. From there, Father meant to catch another train deeper into the heart of Germany. However, he met an old acquaintance on the train, who recommended that we get off and remain in Dömitz. This man said that the mayor was a known humanitarian, and treated refugees with kindness.

Mother wrote:

> Father told the man that we wanted to cross the Elbe to the west side, where we would be farther from the Soviets. The friend said not to worry, there was a railroad-pedestrian bridge spanning the river nearby, and in case of need, we could simply walk across. So we got off and went to see the mayor of Dömitz.
>
> Farms needed workers. The mayor directed us to stay in a nearby hamlet with the Kochs, who owned a sizeable farm and raised livestock close to the Elbe River, a mile or two outside of Dömitz.

The Koch farmstead was extensive, with many buildings. Frau Koch, a sturdy, graying woman in her sixties, let us use a cozy attic room above the empty dormitories of the farm's hired hands who had been taken away by the military for other service. It had a small window facing south, bright and warm on sunny days. Again, as in Bromberg, we had access to wood for heating: the farm was close to a forest, and the mayor allowed us to cut a generous amount for our needs. We had food ration coupons again, and were pleasantly surprised that the stores in Dömitz still had a reasonable variety of supplies.

The Kochs were hard working, salt-of-the-earth people, and treated us fairly. They assigned Father and Mother to look after the cows and sheep. They took a great liking to Milda, who seemed to have sprung back to life, always smiling and singing, her hair in short braids swinging jauntily at her back. Milda helped out with cleaning and cooking, and ate with the Kochs. She did not need her ration from the store, which meant there was a little more for us—Father, Mother, and me.

It was March 1945. Spring was pushing green blades of grass through the brown thatch of winter and snowdrops shook their little white bells in the cool breeze. Our parents felt they could relax a little, and once again fell into complacency. They persuaded themselves that at war's end, this area would surely be occupied by the Americans or the British, and that it was therefore safe for us to remain with the kindly Kochs until the Western Allies came.

We settled in. Mother and Milda went into the shops in town and bought a replacement washboard, rope and clothes pegs, and a big basin for washing our clothes. Mother was beaming. We would be clean again.

March 24, the Saturday before Palm Sunday, was a lovely spring day. Mother and Father had gone into the forest to cut wood for heating and cooking. They came back to our room in great spirits. That evening, as usual, we lay in the dark listening to Father's bedtime stories. Suddenly, we heard heavy steps thumping up the stairs to our attic.

What could Herr Koch need from us at this late hour? He knocked and came in, holding a lantern (electricity was not available at night) and a paper in his hand, which he handed over to Father. He held the lantern so Father could read it. From the look on Father's face, we immediately knew it meant trouble. Herr Koch expressed his sympathy, and left.

We lit a candle, and Father read the Order from the local SS Unit: no later than midnight on that very day, March 24, Father was to present himself at the market square in Dömitz, bringing with him a blanket, spoon, knife and fork, and a spade. Failure to appear as ordered was punishable by death.

The requirement to bring a spade made everything clear: Father knew at once that he had been conscripted to dig anti-tank trenches. The paper did not say where.

There were only two hours left to midnight. Mother gave Father one of our two thin blankets, and in it placed his clothes and whatever food there was on hand. He had no spade. And so he left us, Milda and I crying our eyes out, Mother screaming curses at the entire mad world loud enough to wake everyone in the hamlet.

The unthinkable had finally happened, and just when we thought we had come to a safe haven. I could not deal with it. My daddy—gone! Taken away who knew where? I tried denial, I tried hope, but only prayer helped to quiet my heart. Evenings were especially bitter. In place of the stories that Father used to tell, Mother, Milda, and I substituted the rosary.

I kept thinking of our recent miraculous escapes: the soft landing when thrown from the cart; Mr. Kamaitis finding us on our flight from Bromberg; the door handle of the train in my father's hand. That there was a God who helped was clear, but why didn't He just prevent all this misery? Everywhere I went I sent silent thoughts to St. Theresa asking her to persuade the Almighty to please return Father to us.

Easter that year fell on April 1. We had not heard from Father. The Kochs gave us half a dozen eggs, but our mood was too bleak to bother coloring them. They brought us some *brötchen*—white rolls, but they simply stuck in our throats. How could we feast, when Father was probably starving? Everyone knew that the rations for trench-diggers were minimal; it was a death-sentence assignment. Where had they sent him? Mother and Milda made inquiries in town, but nobody would or could tell them where he had gone. He had simply disappeared.

Eventually, there arrived a crumpled post card with a short message from Father. It said that his group was at Ueckermünde, north of Stettin. They were being forced to dig anti-tank trenches, and they were weak with hunger. And he loved us for all eternity.

We were stricken with despair for him. What could we do? We could not send food, because it would not reach him. Mother was sure we would never see him again. She spent her days crying, her evenings sitting on the bed and rocking as if her insides were on fire. Why had God not killed us all together, instead of separating us? When black thoughts overcame her and she could not imagine how we three would cope without Father, she threatened to hang herself.

I was too young to know that she did not mean it, that "*pasikarsiu*," meaning "I'm going to hang myself," was just something Lithuanians said when they were at their wits' end. To me her threat was real. What if she carried it out? Milda was safe here with the Kochs, but would they keep me? Where would I go if they chased me away? I would have to go begging to survive. I watched Mother's outbursts helplessly, frozen with fear.

When everything looked as bleak as it could get, there came a distraction. The German Army units deployed along the Elbe River had been ordered by Hitler and his generals to fight off the approaching Allies to the last man. The British and Americans were advancing from the west, and the Soviets from the east. A Wehrmacht infantry company installed its field kitchen by the Kochs' barn, and ordered Mother and Milda, who was almost sixteen, to help with the cooking and cleaning.

Mother had to dry her tears and learn to keep quiet if she wanted to remain where we were, in hopes that, if he survived, some day Father would find us. The Kochs advised the three of us to say that Milda was only thirteen. "You never know with soldiers," they said. I had no idea what they were talking about but, of course, I did as told.

At first, I spent my days alone. When it rained, I would sit in the sheep pen, watching lambs play, holding my doll tightly to me, and pleading with heaven to keep my daddy safe and bring him back to us. When the weather was clear, I took her along to keep me company as I searched the fields for new sorrel and dandelion leaves. When Mother sent me to find dry bark and small twigs for kindling, Ilke and I found solace in the woods full of birds and their carefree music. But then the military hid its artillery among the trees, so the woods became off-limits.

When I felt especially despondent, I would lean against the wall of the barn. From there I could watch Mother and Milda working in the field kitchen area, and feel calmer knowing they were near. One day, a young captain (*Hauptmann*) noticed me hanging around. I reminded him, he said, of his youngest sister. He took me under his wing, and soon the men treated me like their unit's mascot. Whenever the soldiers had time, they would ask me to sing for them, even though the words were in Lithuanian. Our sad melodies suited their mood. Often Milda would join me in a duet. In return, they would give us a taste of their small ration of chocolate.

The men liked to sit me on their knees and tell me about their sisters or daughters, though sometimes their dialects were so thick I could not understand a word. I did not feel shy with them. I could feel that they were worried and lonely for their families, just as I was for Father.

Toward the end of April, we heard the rumble of plane engines descending toward Dömitz, and then the muffled thunder of bombs exploding. A large section of the bridge over the Elbe was completely destroyed. When Mother learned of it, she was dismayed. Another option taken away: if we needed to get to the other side, we would have to swim—and the three of us did not know how.

The battle lines were getting closer. German tanks and military vehicles of every description choked the roads and byways and farm tracks. An American bomber crashed and burned in a nearby field, shot down by the anti-aircraft guns at the edge of the woods. At night, distant fires lit up the undersides of clouds, and during the rare moments of relative quiet, we could hear a constant barrage of explosions somewhere far to the southeast. There were ever-increasing numbers of American, British and Russian aircraft roaring overhead. Mother kept repeating that, living in the midst of a German battalion, we three would certainly die when the battle lines reached us.

It was a warm April in 1945. One day, when there were ominous clouds of smoke rising to the east, I saw barn swallows looping in the air above the farm, their elegant V-shaped tails spread out behind them. Many returned to nests left over from the previous year under the eaves of the barn, and busied themselves repairing the old or constructing new ones.

I remembered Father's regret that we could not fly like the swallows, that there was nowhere for us to build a home. "God, give us wings," I begged, "We have to get away from here. I'm really, really scared! But we can't leave without Daddy. God, hurry, bring him back, please?"

I imagined the boundless freedom of flight, picturing Father flying back to us on large white wings. I knew my prayer was impossible—only an empty wish, but repeating it over and over comforted me. I clung to the hope that Father would return. "Fly to him," I urged the swallows, "show him the way back here."

But what of Father's experiences during those five weeks of our separation? This is his written account, starting with the night of March 24, when the Nazis took him away from us.

From the farm to Dömitz is not far, about two miles. Gathered in the *Marktplatz*—market square, I see more fellow foreigners, also Nazi storm trooper guards in their brown shirts. Everyone is quiet, morose. A couple of hours later, trucks pull up, and our guards order us to mount. We move away from the river and reach the town of Ludwigslust. Here, the Brownshirts make us get off in a garden area next to the train station, and we join a crowd of other trench diggers: men and women, French and Polish prisoners-of-war, laborers from many countries, farmers and refugees. Some have brought a spade or an axe, but most have only a small bundle on their back or held in their hands.

After a long wait, the officials herd us from the garden onto a freight train. We get into boxcars or open-topped carriages. Accompanied by Brownshirt guards, we move east. It's a long trip; we are crammed together and hungry. It's a sunny day, but cold.

In the evening, the train maneuvers onto a siding next to a huge brick factory. Everyone gets off and guards direct us into the empty buildings. There are many more people already inside. The guards line us up, and count over 2,000. Somehow, I quickly find a considerable group of Lithuanians, numbering about 120–150 people. Other nationalities soon separate into their own groups. French, Russians, Poles, and Ukrainians make up the biggest numbers. We stay in the factory for several days.

In the morning, a field kitchen serves us a piece of military bread and ersatz coffee. Then local Brownshirts and old men assigned to the Volkssturm, the national guard, hand us shovels, and "Raus!"—we get out into the fields and dig. Our work is supervised by men in military uniforms who show us where to start the trenches.

All around us stand old men of the Volkssturm, armed with old-fashioned hunting rifles, making sure that nobody escapes and nobody gets tempted by the potato silos on nearby farms. A few brave souls try to sneak away to grab some potatoes, but are beaten with sticks to get back in line and dig. Along the roads, farms, and villages, the Nazis have posted warnings that those who walk away from their assignment will be executed on the spot.

From the guards we learn that we are digging near the mouth of the Oder River, an area known as Stettiner Haff—Stettin lagoon. The nearest village is Ueckermünde. With some difficulty, I obtain a post card to tell my dear ones where I am. Soon they transfer our Lithuanian group to a nearby hamlet and lodge us in a small church with straw on the floor for sleeping.

Early in the morning, we leave to dig; in the evening, on our return, we receive some bread with jam, and hot soup made from old, moldy sauerkraut or pickled turnips, flavored with salted horsemeat. My digestion cannot handle it. After a few days we all start to itch from fleas, because we sleep in our clothes. After work, we rush to wash up in a nearby stream or by the well, but there are no facilities for bathing, and it is still cold. Constant hunger tortures us. Each day, I feel weaker.

One day, I ask our group supervisor, a kind fellow, for leave to go to the village of Ueckermünde. It is beautiful and clean. The German love of order is apparent: all offices and agencies are working, despite the sound of heavy artillery in the distance and the scream of sirens announcing a bombing raid. First, I go to the Arbeitsamt—Labor Center. I hope to get permission to leave this war zone.

On entering, I approach the woman sitting on the other side of the counter. When she stands up, I unthinkingly put my hands on the counter. She starts to scream like a madwoman, "*Hände ab!*—Hands off!" I lower my hands and start to explain my mission, but she rudely retorts, "*Raus!*" and that's that. I go.

On a house in the street I see a doctor's signboard. I think to myself, *I'll go ask for a certificate that I am no longer able to work; perhaps they'll let me go.* I do look like Lazarus in the grave, or one of those old emaciated saints you see on icons. I enter, explain. He looks me over, feels my arms, and gives me his diagnosis: I need a beating. Once again, "Raus!"

On the way back, I stop to look in the window of a bookstore. Two books catch my eye: a history of German music and an old 1928 calendar, opened to a beautiful etching by Dürer. I go in. The owner sells them to me cheap, so I put them under my arm and make my way back, pleased to have obtained at least some food for the soul.

Soon, we finish the trenches in this area, and they move us farther out. We are lodged in a straw-filled loft under the roof of a stable, part of a large manor house. The house itself and the surrounding area are lovely, there's a stream close by for washing, and several dammed ponds. After work, some of the more energetic go fishing.

One day, a man succeeded in catching a river otter. He was fishing near a dam when he spotted the otter, grabbed a big stick, and his throw caught the otter on the head, stunning it. The man threw himself into the water and hauled out his prize. Dealing with the otter made entertainment for everyone. The lucky man carefully removed its skin and prepared the meat for cooking.

A delegation took the pelt to the owner of the manor house, hoping they could exchange it for potatoes. The landowner accepted the pelt, thanked the men, and led them to an immense potato silo, showed them the best place to access, and told them to take as many as they want, and tell others they can take them too.

The flesh of the otter had a disgusting, fishy taste, but the potatoes became our salvation. We boiled them, sprinkled them with salt and wild onions from the fields, and felt less hungry. Some of the group owned a tin or two of margarine, and shared a little of the fat with me.

Most of the Lithuanians, especially the unmarried young men and women, had brought with them all their belongings, which they had to leave in the loft when going to dig. When the group left for the trenches, the guards went with them. The group decided that one of us should remain behind to watch over everyone's possessions, and since I looked so frail, they kindly chose me to be the watchdog.

In the morning, everyone goes down the ladder to the stables, in the farmyard the supervisor counts heads, everyone leaves for the fields and the trenches. I remain on guard, reading. At times I descend to the yard to stretch my joints.

One day, I meet the landowner. He says hello, we chat, soon we are deep in conversation. I thank him for the potatoes; he waves the thanks away, as if it does not matter any more, as if he has lost all hope. He asks me to come inside the house. His wife comes in, we talk. They are anxious, apprehensive: what awaits them? Not a word about the Führer or the invincible Wehrmacht.

Our goodbye is warm and polite, and I leave these two worried people, carrying their dread with me. It is as if they were seeking my help to alleviate their fear and disappointment. But I too am losing all hope.

One morning, I am sitting on the straw near the small opening that provides the only entry into the loft, reading the thick volume on the history of German music. I hear steps on the ladder. I raise my head—there in front of me, outlined in the opening, I see the upper portion of the *Feldwebel*, the sergeant of the Volkssturm in charge of monitoring us. His eyes pierce into me as he growls, furious, "*Was machst du hier?*— What are you doing here?"

"The group asked me to stay to look after their belongings," I reply.

"What? The world is turning upside down and you just sit there? Heraus!"

"If you wish it, Herr Feldwebel, then I'll go." I start to rise, place my book on the straw.

"*Was lesen sie hier?*—What are you reading there?"

"The Cultural History of German Music," I answer, showing him the book. I see he is startled.

"*Wer sind sie?*—Who are you?" he asks.

"*Schulrat*—school inspector," I reply.

"*Bleiben sie hier!*—you stay here!" And he slowly goes down the ladder and leaves for the fields.

Each morning we notice that our numbers are dwindling. And nobody seems to be getting upset about it. But the thunder of artillery gets louder each day, and there are more and more warplanes in the sky.

One evening, Butkus, a younger man, approaches me. He murmurs that he has two loaves of bread, but he does not know any German. Could we make a break together? He offers, "*Mano duona, tavo galva*—My bread, your brain, perhaps we will get through." I have nothing to lose: if I stay, I die. We decide that the following day, we will leave the group as if going for a bathroom break. I warn our Lithuanian group leader that I'm going to vanish.

So we leave. It's a beautiful, sunny day. We walk through field paths and along byways. We see many groups in the fields digging trenches. Every path, track, and road displays warnings that those fleeing their assigned work duties will be shot on sight. Butkus and I get our story ready: if asked, we will say that we are refugees from Stettin, which, at that time, the German residents were evacuating in droves.

Luck is with us: we get beyond the trench construction zone with no problems, and in the afternoon we reach a small village from which a narrow-gauge train is available within the hour to go further west. We stay on the train a couple of hours, but then it starts to get dark. The train stops in the village of Rathebur for the night, and will continue only in the morning. The stationmaster does not allow us to sleep in the station.

I propose to my companion Butkus to go directly to the police: they will tell us where we can find a place for the night. He does not believe me; he is frightened of the police, but he agrees to go with me. At the police station I show them my documents, my impressive certificate, and ask for their help. An elderly veteran immediately leads us to a restaurant-pub, presents us to the owner, and orders him to give us something to eat, and after the clients leave at curfew (10 p.m.), to let us sleep on his benches.

We do not have long to wait until the tranquil burghers of the village finish their beet-based beer, extinguish their cigarettes and go out into the dark. The owner gives us each a bowl of *Schtammgericht*, a mixture of vegetables that can be bought without food coupons. We eat, and then we are left alone in a big room. I immediately stretch out to sleep, but my companion cannot rest for happiness. The ashtrays have not been emptied! From the stubby butts, he carefully loosens the remaining herbs that pass for tobacco, composes something resembling a cigarette, and smokes it down to his fingers, sighing contentedly at each puff.

In the morning, the little train takes us a few more miles west. From there, when we can, we take trains, when we can't, we walk. We finish the two loaves of bread, but always find some potatoes along the way. At last, we reach Ludwigslust. Trains are no longer available. Here we part: my companion goes on his way, and I turn my feet toward Dömitz.

On the roads, nothing but military vehicles and trucks, coming and going. A couple of times, soldiers give me a ride, a couple of times I have to throw myself into a ditch to escape from fighter planes strafing the military convoys on the road.

I reach the hamlet where I had left my dear ones early, before dawn. Everywhere I look, signs of Wehrmacht soldiers. In the yard by the barn, a military field kitchen. I dare not enter the dormitory building; it may not be safe. I pick up a pebble and throw it at the window of the attic, once, twice. Suddenly, there is my Stasė at the window. "Is it safe to come in?" I ask. She flies down the stairs—as do my beloved girls.

I sit wrapped in a blanket in the little room, all my clothes left on the stairs because they are full of fleas. I sit, I recount my experiences. I listen to how you three spent your days. Morning is bright. The western powers are at the Elbe. I listen to my dear ones, interrupted by the thumps of cannons, by the roar of airplanes overhead. Stasė had given me a small loaf of bread; I realize I have eaten all of it.

We hear thunder and the explosions of artillery all around us. In the yard and the nearby field, a commotion of soldiers, each man nursing one solitary wish: to fall into the hands of the Western Allies. But in our room, there is peace. We four, for this hour, for this day, are simply content to be together again.

CHAPTER 14:

The War Is Over—but not for Us

There are joys so intense they hurt like pain. I sat on the floor, leaning against my daddy's thin legs, staring without thinking at his big, bony, blistered feet, almost every toe deformed by angry-looking corns. How far had he had to walk to find us? I was wrapped in the sound of his voice but not really listening. I absorbed his presence like a sponge does water. I was so happy my chest felt tight, I could hardly breathe.

How many minutes or hours did it take for me to accept that Father was really real, that he was actually sitting here with us, slowly eating a loaf of bread, his dear familiar voice telling us an amazing story of ill-treatment and kindness and escape? Finally he fell silent and the spell was broken. We could see that he was exhausted.

Mother and Milda had to report to work. I promised everyone that I would sit quietly and let him sleep. After they left, Father reached out and squeezed my hand, murmured my favorite endearment, "*Saulute Mylimiausia*—Dearest Sunshine," and was asleep before I could say a word.

We could not let anybody know that Father had returned. Although the vast majority of Germans, military and civilians, knew that the war was lost, there were still fanatical Nazis around who would shoot Father as a deserter from his "service" to the military. He stayed hidden in our little room, slowly regaining strength, our own secret joy.

It was the very end of April 1945. All around us, military preparations for battle were in full swing. My special friend and protector, the captain, in the face of certain German defeat, broke all rules and told Mother that the war was almost over, that there were rumors that Hitler was dead, and that Berlin had fallen to the Red Army. Nonetheless, the remaining Nazi generals demanded that German soldiers fight to the last man, and anyone caught deserting was to be shot on sight. He said a final battle would be fought any day.

He spoke again and again of the fervent prayers of his men to surrender to the Western Allies, to escape the Soviets. In the beginning of May, anticipating the approach of the final battle, and knowing that if he survived he would be a prisoner-of-war, the captain gave me his well-used, silver-plated spoon to remember him by. I treasure it to this day.

The captain took two of his men and dug a trench away from any structures, because buildings were the primary bombing targets. He helped place sturdy logs over the excavation, covered them with leafy branches, and then poured a small mound of dirt over everything. He and his helpers made a steep sloping entryway so that Mother, Milda, and I could slide into this makeshift bunker. He told us to rush out and hide there when the fighting erupted. We would be protected as long as our shelter escaped a direct hit. He shook Mother's hand and held me close, repeating softly, "*Ich hoffe du vergesst mich nicht*—I hope you do not forget me." "*Nimmer*," I replied, "never," and I kept that promise. It was the last time I saw him.

On the evening of May 3, if my parents remembered the date correctly, a deafening roar announced the approach of a squadron of Allied warplanes. From the verge of the forest, the hidden German artillery made frantic attempts to shoot them down. It was useless to worry about Father's status as a deserter: all four of us ran for our lives to hide in the trench.

It was a tight fit with Father there, but we squeezed in, one partly on top of the other, and prayed for another miracle to be spared once again. We begged that at last the final bomb would fall, so the world could resume living in peace.

At first, the bombing and the anti-aircraft artillery raged all around us. Every explosion shook dirt on us, both from the "roof" and from the sides of the trench. I lay rolled up into a ball, clutching my doll, trying to convince her—and myself—that we would be safe. Father and Milda started to feel claustrophobic. They stuck their heads as far out into the open as they dared. After a while, battle noises in our area diminished, with lengthening silences in between.

Toward dawn, all noise ceased. At sunrise, Father crawled out to look around. The farmstead buildings had sustained some damage, but only the barn was gone, nothing now but a ruin. The dormitory structure with our attic room was untouched. Then he exclaimed, "Come, look!" From every window in every house, white sheets fluttered in sign of surrender.

"Is the war over? Is it over? It's over, isn't it?" exulted Mother. "We made it! We survived!" We stood there hugging and laughing and crying. I can only imagine the relief felt by my parents and Milda. I felt their joy. But then I noticed the swallows flying around aimlessly, chirping in confusion, searching in vain for their nests, which had fallen down with the barn. When I pointed them out to Father, he told me not to worry, that within a day or two they would find another structure on which to rebuild. I smiled to myself, taking this as an omen that we, too, could now go home again; we too could rebuild our nest.

We strolled back to our residence, arm in arm, feeling euphoric. We could not see any of our soldier friends. The Kochs said that their commander had taken the entire contingent over to the Elbe, to surrender to the Western Allies. I imagined my friend, the captain, offering a prayer of thanks that they had escaped the Soviets.

As for us, we did not know what to do next. People came out from the scattered farmhouses to the main road leading to Dömitz and clustered together, discussing the night's events, the numbers of wounded, the damage to their farms, and wondering what would happen now. Everyone was relieved that there would be no more bombing and burning, but who would be in charge? With Hitler gone, what changes were in store for them?

Around 10 a.m., we saw a long line of soldiers approaching from the direction of Dömitz. Unlike the German military, they did not march in step in neat columns. They slouched along, some swaying a little bit, their baggy pants and rounded helmets a stark contrast to those worn by the Wehrmacht. Word spread among the people lining the road: Americans. Almost all of them had jaws constantly working. They did not appear to be actually eating, so what were they chewing?

And—oh my goodness, I saw the first chocolate brown faces I had ever seen! I thought that only in Africa did people tan so deeply. I had a lot to ask Father, but he was calling out to the passing soldiers asking for news. For many minutes, nobody responded—nobody spoke German. He was ready to give up when he caught the sound of familiar swearwords. Polish! He rushed up to the men and greeted them enthusiastically. The men, somewhat drunk, stopped and answered back in heavily accented Polish.

"We're from Chicago," said one.

"What are you doing out of Poland, were you prisoners of the Germans?" asked the other.

"No, we are Lithuanians, Poland's neighbors," replied Father. "Has the war really ended? Have the Germans capitulated?"

"No, it hasn't quite ended everywhere, but here in northern Germany, the fighting is now over. We are on our way to meet up with the Russkies."

"The Russians?" asked Father. "Are they close? Are you Americans going to be in charge here?"

"Only till the Ivans get here, which should be in three–four hours. Everything this side of the Elbe will go to them. That's what we've been told. You'll be able to go home now, you know. *Pożegnanie*—goodbye!"

We four stood there, looking at each other in disbelief, turned to stone. We had come so far, gone through so much, only to lose it all at the finish line. The bridge over the Elbe was gone. How could we get to the other side? Father started hurrying down the road, shouting "Where is the nearest bridge?" to the onlookers and to the passing soldiers.

"These men just crossed over in Dömitz; there's a pontoon bridge!" someone shouted back.

A bridge in Dömitz! There was a temporary bridge! Hope flared again. Father appealed to the Kochs for a handcart or a wheelbarrow, but most of their smaller farm equipment had been lost in the bombed-out barn. They let us look through their dump of discarded parts and spares. Father found a wooden axle with two wheels still attached, full of wood rot, but at least they turned. The Kochs willingly let us have the lot. From loose boards, father hammered together a narrow box and nailed it to the axle, on each side of which he cut a groove to hold a rope in place. Mother chose the most essential things: food, clothes, and bedding, which she placed in the box.

We left behind the last of our cooking utensils, the washboard, the basin and the empty jars and bottles Mother had collected dreaming of summer canning. They made me sit on top. Father attached the clothes-line rope on the right and left sides of the axle, then, pulling like two oxen at the plough, Father and Mother hurried as fast as they could down the road toward the pontoon bridge, Milda helping to steady the thing from behind.

As we approached Dömitz, traffic on the road increased. It was the same old story: a stream of bewildered refugees, those who had reason to fear the Soviets, making one last effort to escape their clutches. Access to the narrow bridge was severely limited. It was mid-afternoon by the time we set foot on it. The bridge was very long and narrow: wide enough only for pedestrians and one line of trucks. Our clumsy wheels had to be pushed close to the edge and turned sideways to let military vehicles go past. The rope was wearing blisters on my parents' hands, even though they had wrapped them in rags to protect against the rough chafing.

The pontoon bridge we struggled to cross, May 1945.

The American infantry unit in charge of the bridge that day was not in a kind mood. To begin with, the American soldiers had no idea why so many civilians were trying to get to the other side of the river. *What did these people want? Where the heck were they going?*

In addition, signs of celebration were obvious: many soldiers staggered about drunk, and many stopped the fleeing civilians and by hand gestures demanded rings and watches. We were in trouble. The ruby ring that the Pranskases had given us was hidden in a corner of a suitcase at the bottom of the pile, and Father had no watch.

One drunken soldier became very angry at our lack of booty. When his yelling did not produce results, he pulled out a deadly looking pistol and, weaving unsteadily on his feet, aimed it at Father's head. In unison, Mother, Milda, and I started screaming for help: "*Hilfe! Hilfe!*"

An officer in a jeep, a chauffeur driving, heard the commotion and zoomed up to investigate. In one fluid motion he jumped out of the vehicle, snatched the pistol out of the soldier's hand, grabbed him by the arm, and pulled him into the jeep, all the while motioning for us to get moving—traffic was backing up behind us.

Time played tricks: it seemed to take hours to cross the bridge. As we were approaching the western bank of the river, traffic stopped again. The Americans had erected a barrier across the exit from the bridge and were checking everyone's documents.

They seemed to be in a foul temper. They motioned for us to take out our belongings and leave our wheeled contraption in a ravine. They then pushed all of us confused civilian strays into trucks, and when one was filled to capacity, so crowded it could not hold any more, drove us a couple of miles to a staging area between two sizeable farms. They motioned for Mother, Milda, and me to walk to one of the barns, and separated the men to walk to the other one, farther away.

We had absolutely no idea of what was going on. All four of us were carrying suitcases or bundles taken out of the cart, but the little bit of food we had hurriedly grabbed on leaving was with us women, so what would Father eat? There was no sign of anyone preparing a meal for the gathering crowd at the barn. And what a crowd! By the time it was dark, there were nearly two hundred women and children trying to find a bit of straw and a few feet of space for the night.

In addition to those of us whom the Americans had coerced into the barn, there was a large group of French women whom they had liberated from a work camp nearby. Apparently, the American soldiers had a different opinion of their value. The French women were enjoying a large supply of donated C-rations and bottles of liquor, chocolate, and cigarettes. And they intended to celebrate their freedom in their own Gallic way—singing and talking at the top of their voices all night long. When some of the refugees tried to hush them, their answers, given in the universal language of hand gestures and rude noises, let all of us know we could shut the %#&* up.

Perhaps we would not have slept even if we had been fed and had a quiet corner. We were in a tizzy of anxiety. Would Father be allowed to rejoin us? When? How could we get food to him? How could we find out what the Americans meant to do with us? We did not speak English, and they did not answer to German.

I remember feeling completely befuddled. First, my daddy had miraculously reappeared; now, the American soldiers had whisked him away again. Everyone was saying the war was over, but clearly not for us: the Red Dragon was still clawing at our backs.

I remembered a two-person swing I had seen at a park once. The occupants had pushed it to a dangerous height, and I thought: surely they'll fall out? But no, the swing dropped down in a whoosh, only to go up again on the other side, and drop again and up again. This was the image of our lives since Daddy had come to the Varnakas farm, many months ago in July, to tell us that the Red Army was back in Vilnius and our home destroyed. Thinking back over our ups and downs, our narrow escapes during the past ten months made my brain hurt.

Sometime in mid-morning, a number of trucks pulled up to the barn. With sinking hopes, we saw that they were decorated with the banners and flags of the Soviet Union—the hammer and sickle on a red background. Leaving the French women to stay, the American army soldiers unceremoniously herded the rest of us back on. The women in the trucks raised an unholy uproar, demanding news about their men. Somebody in the group grasped enough English to pass along the information that the men had already left, and we would be taken to the same place.

Imagine our despair when the trucks trundled back over the bridge to the east side of the river, which we now knew had been given to the Soviets.

In about an hour, we arrived at the former Luftwaffe flight training school in Ludwigslust. The parade ground was crowded with milling humanity, searching for their separated family members. Thanks to Father's height, it did not take us long to find him.

Rumors were flying that the Red Army would immediately take all those gathered here back to whichever country they had come from. In the meantime, we were kept on the field, the sun beating down on us, with no water or food, and closely watched by armed military guards. After a few hours, a translator for the administration shouted through a loudspeaker to separate by nationalities, indicating who was to gather where. There were thousands of Poles and hundreds of Ukrainians who had been brought by the Nazis to Germany for forced labor. There were also over a hundred from the Baltic countries: Lithuanians, Latvians, and Estonians.

We joined a group of about forty Lithuanians. It was a quiet group, standing together disconsolate and forlorn, expecting the Soviets to come for us any minute. Our situation seemed hopeless. An hour or two later, American soldiers marched us to a military barracks that had housed the Luftwaffe's students and officers. Had we not been so downcast, we might have appreciated the quarters assigned to us: a cheerful, sunny room with four bunk beds, shaded lightly by a big birch tree.

Toward evening, a loudspeaker announced, in German, that everyone was to go to the school's large dining room. We did not know what to expect, but word sped down the waiting line that the Americans were giving out food! Milda quickly ran back to grab our silverware and our all-purpose bowls.

When it was our turn to be served, we were amazed: each of us received a quarter-loaf of bread, our bowls were filled to capacity with a stew of chicken, potatoes, and peas, and we were told to help ourselves to thin, sweet cookies, as many as we liked. We noticed that in another section of the kitchen, the Americans were pouring out as much milk as anyone wanted. We sat at a long table and appreciated every bite, although Mother kept muttering, "*Pirma pašers, paskui paskers*"—First they'll fatten us up, then they'll slaughter us."

An American soldier took up a loudspeaker and, with someone translating, asked if there were any volunteers to help with food preparation and distribution. Mother jabbed Father: "Do it! Food!" Father's hand shot up at once. Later, at the organizing meeting, he was made the assistant director of the kitchen, primarily because he could communicate in the three languages that most refugees understood: Russian, Polish, and German. We need not have worried about food. The kitchen prepared such quantities that much was wasted every day.

Shortly before midnight on the eighth of May, everyone in camp was jarred awake by the noise of rifle and pistol shots. Magnesium flares, emergency and signaling flares lit up the sky. What on earth? When the shouting, hooting and hollering became intelligible, we learned that the American and Russian soldiers were celebrating the official end of the war in Europe.

The Russians brought a huge supply of vodka from their camp, and proceeded to get falling-down drunk. Our American guards were drunk as well, not only with alcohol but with joy, and could not understand why the mood of the refugees, especially of the Estonians, Latvians, and Lithuanians, was so gloomy. Were we not pleased that we would be going home soon?

Our entire stay at the Ludwigslust assembly center lasted less than ten days. There was plenty of food, but little cheer. The Camp Commander, an American, made it clear that we were in a transit situation, and that everyone would be moved out before the end of May. At first, the Commander and his assistant administrators repeated the propaganda that the Russians fed them: "Stalin forgives you for running away; you'll be welcomed at home."

The Balts sent delegation after delegation to speak to the Americans, to make them understand why we did not want to go home while our countries were occupied by the Soviets. We would rush home the minute the Western Allies guaranteed our independence, but the Soviets were not our friends. The translators described the destruction and terror that the Soviets had unleashed on the three little nations in 1940–1941. They petitioned to be allowed to go to the British or the American Zone—anywhere but back to the Soviets.

The Commander was not a bad man, but he had his orders. He said he knew nothing about any plans to restore self-determination to the countries now occupied by the Allied victors. The Soviets were valued allies, they had helped win the war, and the US was not going to upset them. This was his final word.

On May 10, the management posted a notice that camp would be closing on May 13. Most of the Poles and Ukrainians had been sent away, though a hundred or so remained, as did all the Balts. We were to be packed and ready to go early that morning. The finality of this news hit my parents like a tocsin of doom. The hardships of our flight had been for nothing: the minute the Soviets had us in their grasp, we would be on our way to Siberia. Mother and Father encouraged each other to prepare for whatever suffering came, hoping they could help Milda and me survive.

They looked through all of our documents, and tore to pieces anything that could be construed as "working for the Germans." Father incinerated in the kitchen his imposing certificate from the Gebietskommissar in Lithuania: no longer an asset, it was now a dangerous liability.

I saw the despair on my parents' faces, but could not accept that now, after so many miracles, God would simply let us perish. Were we to be handed over to the Red Dragon like so many meat dumplings? Milda had simply given up at this final outrage: she would not eat, and hour after hour she lay on her bed prostrate with misery.

The next morning, at breakfast, the dining room rumbled with lowered voices spreading the news that a dozen or more Balts had committed suicide, preferring a quick death by hanging to the hell the Soviets had in store for them.

We children were not supposed to listen, but nothing can be hidden from sharp little ears for long. Soon, an older boy who seemed to have insider information led a group of us to a coppice of thick chestnut trees, and pointed out the branches from which two bodies had been cut down. His brother was one of those who had found them. He described what the corpses had looked like, the protruding tongues, the twisted faces. It made my stomach heave. He asked if we wanted see where other suicides had hung, but I rushed off to hide in Father's arms.

The number of suicides shocked the Camp Commander. He had heard the petitioners explain what the Soviets had done, but it had not really persuaded him. Policy was policy. Then suddenly, on May 12, he had a change of heart. He announced that the next day there would be both Soviet trucks and American trucks, and we could choose which ones to take. But first, he said, we had to gather in the parade ground and listen to the Soviets assure us what a glorious future awaited us in "liberated" Soviet Lithuania, Latvia, and Estonia. Everyone went, as ordered—but nobody listened.

The morning of May 13 dawned brilliantly warm and sunny. The mood of the refugees was dark. Rumors flew that the Camp Commander had lied, that he only wanted to avoid more suicides.

There was no choice, however, but to stand and wait for whatever fate would bring. American soldiers lined us up by the side of the road leading out of the compound. People sought to stay together with their own countrymen. "Pray, girls," said Mother. Milda and I did not need urging.

At 9 a.m., a convoy of open-bed trucks sped by, turned around in the parade ground, and screeched to a halt alongside the joyless crowd. Not one of the trucks carried any signs: no Soviet red flags with hammer-and-sickle, no British Union Jacks, not one American Old Glory. What did it mean? How could we choose which truck to climb into if there was no identification? More rumors, more fear.

Given no choice, and urged on by guards, everyone climbed into the nearest truck. Word travelled from one truck to another: if, after we pass the town of Ludwigslust, the trucks turn right, we are heading deeper into Soviet territory; if they turn left and cross back over the Elbe River, we will be with the British.

A few minutes more, and the trucks roared to life. Everyone, every single person I could see, was praying with desperate concentration. There's the town—now which direction? Every truck turned left! An explosion of clapping, shouts of "Alleluia," people hugging and kissing, families, friends, and strangers. Another chance at life! Still, a little anxiety remained: would we really be taken across the river to the free side of the Elbe?

A couple of wind-blown hours later, the convoy reached the pontoon bridge near Bleckede. Slowly, noisily, the trucks swayed over the bridge. At a checkpoint just beyond the bridge, British soldiers walked up to each truck, greeted everyone with a smile, asked if anyone needed to use the "WC," and if anyone needed water to drink. They handed out chocolate to the children. After the disastrous impression made on us by the Americans at the Dömitz bridge, in comparison, the British were true "gentlemen."

Secure on the western side of the Elbe River, once the trucks were moving again, we Lithuanians, who celebrate everything in our lives with song, wanted to give voice to our gratitude. By tradition, everyone called on Mary the Mother of Jesus first: "*Marija, Marija, Skaisčiausia Lelija*—Mary, Mary, lily most pure," a heartfelt appeal to the Mother of God to intercede for us before the Almighty. And then, realizing that it might be long years before we saw our homes again, all of us on our truck began: "*Lietuva brangi, mano tėvyne*—My fatherland, beloved Lithuania," a melancholy song of nostalgia for the cherished homeland to which we could not return.

The distance driven that day was modest, but the heavy vehicles could not go fast because the roads were in shambles. Sitting in the open trucks, we were sunburned and wind-whipped, and covered with dust. Toward evening, we grew miserably chilled. At last, the trucks came to an endless collection of military buildings at Wolterdingen, just north of Soltau.

Wolterdingen had been a very large German military installation, but now its wooden barracks were crammed with humanity to the point of explosion. There was not an inch of space inside. We were the last arrivals, and had to sleep in the open, under the pines. There was just the tiniest sliver of moon, but the stars in the Milky Way shone all the more brightly, and despite the lack of warmth, we were blissfully happy. We were with the British and felt that surely, finally, at last for us the war had ended.

CHAPTER 15:

Life in Displaced Person Camps

Sleeping under the stars may have been fine on a clear night, but the very next day it began to rain. It is hard to appreciate the bliss of freedom when one is wet, cold, hungry, and completely dependent on strangers whose language one cannot understand. What would be our fate under the British military administration? Those of us who had been brought to Wolterdingen the evening before, now wet and bedraggled, picked up all our bundles and baggage and gathered in front of the administration building with an interpreter to find out what plans, if any, they had for us.

It was clear even to me, an eight-year-old, that something was not right. British military personnel kept coming in and out and slamming the office doors, zooming off and hurrying back in jeeps, while inside, telephones rang constantly, and loud, impatient voices ranted in a language almost none of us listeners, dripping outside, understood. Some countrymen did grasp a word here and there, and explained to the rest of us that the Commander was trying to get a grip on a situation that was out of control.

Mother and Father worried that there was not enough space or food to provide for those of us already there, and viewed with alarm the influx of refugees who were still arriving, brought in by various military units, or appearing in droves on their own. The barracks buildings had been filled already by two thousand or more liberated forced laborers and prisoners of war, most of them from Poland.

Father later explained, "The British in charge gave preference to the laborers and the prisoners of war, because it was clear that they had suffered at the hands of the Nazis. It was not clear to them why so many Lithuanians, Latvians, Estonians, and Ukrainians had left their countries voluntarily and now refused to go home. For all the British knew, we were secret Nazi sympathizers.

"They had no idea what life was like under Soviet rule. Their Soviet allies continued to demand that we be turned over to them at once. The British had an additional headache: the hordes of German nationals arriving destitute from Prussia and Poland—former German territories now gripped by the communists. Truly, it was chaos."

The British sent translators to tell us, in German, that in a day or so conditions would improve. They explained that the British military had designated Wolterdingen as a collection center for persons displaced by the war, but that a tidal wave of refugees was surging in when only a stream had been expected. They assured us that the British were requisitioning food from the German farmers in the area, and had ordered tents, which should arrive soon, for temporary housing. In the meantime, they said, the administration had designated some makeshift shelters for those who had children under twelve. I was eight and felt very important. My family qualified because of me.

The only "shelters" available, however, were damp, smelly, cement artillery bunkers or wooden ammunition storage crates, which looked like overgrown doghouses. These large, rectangular boxes were lined up in neat rows among the pines. They stood raised on stilts about two feet off the ground. They were open in front, and their roofs sloped slightly toward the back. They must have measured less than six feet across because Father's long frame did not allow him to stretch out. I do not know how wide they were or how tall, but I remember that Father could not sit up straight inside.

One of these crates was to be our shelter until the British came up with a better solution. In daytime, when it rained, we had to squeeze in, all four of us, with Father half reclining, the rest of us sitting cross-legged, barely able to move. At night, Father lay on his side with his knees bent: he took the position closest to the opening. I occupied the space above his knees, and Mother and Milda squeezed in, head to foot, at the back. We had to remain lying like spoons on our sides, and if one of us wanted to change position, everyone else had to do the same. It was torture for Milda, who complained she was suffocating, and it was cold and miserable for Father whose back got wet sticking out of the opening. Our possessions stayed under the crate, lifted off the wet ground on bricks we scavenged from a nearby pile.

The next day, there was some sort of hot porridge for breakfast, and bread and ersatz coffee. The kitchen facilities could not cope with the demand. The British organized a distribution of potatoes and eggs, urging the refugees to cook for themselves in the open, and demonstrated how to make cooking pits using bricks.

Since we no longer had any cooking utensils, Mother arranged to borrow from those who did, but we had to wait until they had prepared their own food first. Milda and I went looking for dry branches and twigs. There was no lack of wood, but it was all soaked through from the rain. I remember the adults grumbling bitterly that the Polish men assigned to hand out the supplies took much more than their share, and favored their friends and countrymen. But I was used to life not being "fair," and as long as I had something in my stomach, and no longer needed to fear bombs or separation from Father, I was content.

Children need so little for happiness, but life in a crowded and chaotic setting presented a hard challenge for our parents. An immediate danger threatening the camp was the lack of sanitation. The toilets in the barracks were overflowing, so everyone did their business in the woods, creating a health hazard for everyone else. Mother grumbled about the lack of bathing facilities. Within two or three days, German prisoners-of-war were brought in to dig and prepare proper latrine trenches. I recall that women and children were assigned to one area and men to a distant other.

It didn't take long for the women to discover a stream not far from camp, which became the bathing and laundry area. I remember an incident when several young girls, apparently determined to wash everything they owned, were working away in the nude, out of sight of the rest of us women and children who had modestly kept some clothes on. Suddenly, we heard the young ones screaming and the sounds of a struggle. Many women in our group ran to see what was happening, and found three young men wrestling some of the girls to the ground. The women grabbed whatever came to hand and attacked the men with sticks, stones, teeth, and nails until they begged for mercy. One was almost drowned.

Our British administrators were appalled. They threatened harsh military discipline to anyone who failed to obey the camp rules. Father's opinion was that after years of forced labor and slavish obedience, these men wanted nothing to do with authority, and considered the women their rightful reward for years of deprivation. However, their resistance to following rules put the rest of the camp in danger.

Everyone was required to undergo a thorough spraying, body and clothing, with DDT powder, but many men avoided it. As a result, fleas proliferated, and typhus, typhoid, and dysentery menaced us.

When the weather turned sunny again, Father slept outside. Within the week we had a large tent to share with another Lithuanian family of four. It was crowded, but at least we could stretch out.

Father spent his days meeting with other Lithuanians to discuss how best to organize ourselves as a separate voice among the refugees. Everything depended on the plans the authorities at SHAEF (Supreme Headquarters Allied Expeditionary Force) were making to deal with the hordes of homeless scattered all over demolished, gutted Germany. Everyone rejoiced when it was announced that the British and the Americans had decided to separate the refugee groups by nationalities, to make communication and administration more efficient. So the next question became: into what conditions and in what location would they place us Lithuanians?

Mother was, as always, the one to provide us with food and to enforce cleanliness. Milda disappeared all day with newfound friends, and I soon ran free in the woods with dozens of other children of every nationality. My only experience of children my age had been my miserable year in first grade, but here, we were all in the same boat: all homeless, ragged, ill-shod, speaking broken German as our *lingua franca*—common language.

Our only goal was to amuse ourselves. The areas surrounding the camp provided playthings galore, though bristling with sharp metal edges and broken glass. We had a choice of burned-out tanks, broken down military vehicles, abandoned artillery pieces of every size, and our favorite—anti-aircraft searchlights. Although the lights were broken, and glass shards posed constant risks, we favored them because we could make them swivel from side to side.

We children vented our feelings of frustration and revenge on these war machines, which had brought us such fear during the war. They were now under our command, and we tore them apart with gusto, using whatever weapons of destruction came to hand. Of course, many of the wilder boys suffered cuts and lacerations, but nothing stopped our persistent demolition.

We stayed in Wolterdingen less than three weeks. Then the administration moved us Lithuanians thirty miles eastward, to Hassendorf.

We were to occupy an installation composed primarily of wooden barracks, but no abandoned military machinery was in evidence. Perhaps this small *Lager*, or camp, had once been a hospital, or a rest and recuperation facility. It was located in a clearing surrounded by a forest of young trees.

There were many young Lithuanian men, mostly former forced laborers, already in the barracks and in the few smaller buildings, but there was enough room inside for us, and the additional truckloads of our countrymen that soon arrived. Among them were an opera singer and a choir director that my parents knew from Vilnius, and their spirits rose at once.

The British commander gave the day-to-day operation of the camp into the hands of a committee elected by the residents, but under close military supervision. The best news in Mother's estimation came when Father, who was a member of the Executive Committee, was put in charge of food services.

It was June, warm and beautiful even when it rained. But after a couple of days sharing quarters with over seventy other people, sleeping in bunk beds stacked three-high, it became clear that something had to be done to protect the girls and women from the young male workers, who had reverted to a really low level of uncivilized behavior.

The Committee asked the British supervisors for permission to move families into the smaller buildings, and segregate the young single men to lead their wilder and noisier lives in separate barracks. This was readily approved. There was also a barracks building designated for the single women, monitored by several older former teachers.

I remember my parents arguing about the conduct of the younger men. Most of them had been forced by the Nazis to work in factories, in appalling conditions. A few had spent the last months of the war in prisons not much different from concentration camps. Mother, and most other adults in the camp, found them disgusting: unwashed, untidy, uncouth, wanting nothing but liquor and cigarettes, noisy, foul-mouthed, and immoral, playing cards all day and night. A litany of sins. She was ashamed to belong to the same nationality as these hoodlums.

Father made excuses for some of their bad behavior, though he condemned those who stole from other Lithuanians or from the local German inhabitants. He tried to make everyone understand that the

Nazis and the war had destroyed the best years of their youth, deprived them of an education, wrenched them away from their families, housed them in degrading conditions, and now had left them, like so much flotsam, without training or jobs, with no real hope for a normal life. No wonder they were wild, living only for the pleasure of the moment.

The Executive Committee foresaw that trouble would result if these young adults were left to their own devices. Children and teens also needed guidance and direction. Immediately, volunteers came forward, willing to organize whatever activities were possible considering our total lack of money or equipment.

Overnight, it seems, soccer teams formed thanks to a few balls donated by the British. A Catholic priest among the refugees asked for a chapel. Someone dashed off a primitive design, and the young folk scrounged whatever boards and nails could be found and constructed it forthwith. Within weeks, the Lithuanians could celebrate Mass in a stark but clean chapel, decorated with wildflowers.

The makeshift chapel at Hassendorf.

Other adults took charge of organizing work brigades to improve camp sanitation and beautification, and proposed such activities as folk dancing, accordion lessons, an a cappella choir, theater and scouting for every age group. Volunteers supervised younger children as they practiced folk dancing and singing, created skits, and learned the rudiments of scouting. In the evenings, the dining room, rearranged as a performance hall, welcomed musical presentations and educational lectures.

By June 24, everyone in camp, it seemed, was ready for an extravaganza of singing, dancing and skits in honor of "St. John's Night," the traditional summer solstice celebration. Younger women, Milda among them, wove wreaths of wild flowers to crown every man named Jonas and every woman named Jonė or Janina. Many brought fronds of fern from the forest, to decorate the periphery of the performance area, and elaborated for us children the old legend of the fern blossom. It is well known in Lithuania that at midnight on the 24th, a magic fern produces a blossom lasting just the blink of an eye, but that whoever succeeds in plucking it can see gold, money hoards, and treasure troves buried underground.

We, the younger children, all dressed up in improvised costumes as bats, evil spirits, and little *"velniukai"*—trickster imps, were told to accompany the witch of the night. She went around foretelling romances for the girls and dramatic fortunes for the adults, and scaring the more rambunctious youth with dire predictions, while we, her entourage, swept through the crowd of onlookers, hissing and moaning and poking and pulling hair ("but not hard, mind!").

Dressed in white sheets, an ancient druid and several vestal virgins—keepers of the sacred flame—impressed on everyone that the fire of love for our fatherland would never die, and that wherever we ended up, we should do our best to work for Lithuania's liberation.

The skit I remember best, however, taught me something new about adults. One of the mature women, whom everyone considered a very plain "old maid," tricked herself out as a white-faced, wild-haired ghost. She stuffed her clothing with pillows to look as fat as possible, then staggered around the bonfire, moaning and letting out little shrieks as she grabbed at the younger men.

When she had everyone's attention, she brandished a huge kitchen knife, and started caterwauling melodramatically about the fickleness of her young lover who had abandoned her for a sweet young thing. She wailed that her only recourse had been to take a sharp knife and stab herself in the heart (appropriate gestures) so that the world would know how scorching was her love for him (*"Pasiėmus aštrų peilį širdį sau pervėriau,/ Kad žinotu visas svietas kaip karštai mylėjau"*). I had never heard a mature audience laugh so hard, and was amazed. It was practically unheard-of among Lithuanians for a woman to make herself look ridiculous, and the entire camp gave her a standing ovation for being such a good sport.

The celebration lasted until sunrise, and included many rounds of jumping over burning logs by the younger folk. Milda enjoyed every last minute, but I fell asleep long before dawn. The evening's activities had impressed me unforgettably—it was the first time in my memory that I had seen adults act silly and laugh uproariously without being drunk. It was a liberating revelation. Apparently, it was finally safe for the adults to let go their worries, their gravity, self-control, even their dignity, and act as merry as kids. *If they can have fun, I can too*, I thought. I felt a huge relief thinking that I could finally give up trying for adult wisdom.

Excitement gripped the camp on July 9. News had reached us that a solar eclipse was coming that afternoon. The wiser and better informed tried to explain the science behind an eclipse, to minimize the superstitious fears that troubled many of the less educated. The morning was spent in searching out pieces of glass and darkening them with smoke so that we could look at the sun without blinding ourselves. Wiser folk insisted that glass smudged with smoke did not provide enough protection from eye damage, but who listens to the wise? Smarter heads followed instructions to make a tiny pinhole in one piece of paper and then place another piece some distance behind it. The advancing shadow the moon spread over the sun became visible, projected through the opening onto the second piece of paper.

The eclipse was deep, though not total. It was an eerie feeling to see the early afternoon turn to twilight. I noticed that the birds became confused. As darkness increased, they stopped twittering and settled down on their nests to roost. Crickets, who hide during the day, started to chirp as though night had come. The normal order of things was going haywire! I saw many older people glancing at the disappearing sun in consternation and crossing themselves fearfully. The eclipse became the chief subject of conversation—and instruction—for days.

The weeks in Hassendorf were a restful period. Everyone in camp needed to recover from the years of war and the flight from Lithuania to escape the terror of the returning communist regime. All conversations eventually returned to those two themes: fear and flight.

Many families had been torn apart by the recent events. Administrators of the camps in the British and American Zones set up a postal delivery system so people could search for friends and relatives. Almost daily, there were cries of joy as news arrived from other camps that a son or a daughter, parents or siblings, had survived.

We began to put on weight. There was enough food for everyone, although Father, as head of food services, had a constant challenge due to the hit-or-miss British delivery of supplies. One week, only potatoes would arrive; another, a truck full of cherries. Refrigeration was unavailable. When meat was delivered, the kitchen staff had to cook it at once. Nonetheless, there was always bread, we often had eggs, and summertime produce made good soups. I had barely grown since I was six: now, at eight-and-a half, I started stretching upward.

As August arrived, the camp organizers realized that they could no longer put off dealing with a problem that had been staring them in the face from day one: there was no building available in camp Hassendorf to use for a school. Every child and teen of school age had lost a year of instruction in 1944–1945, during the final struggles of the war. The Germans made it very clear that they would not accept foreign children into their school system: they had their own surplus of refugees to absorb. Of course, most of us younger children didn't care, but wiser, older teens were beginning to worry about their future.

The Executive Committee appealed to the Commander in charge to do something about a school, but the British military was not interested in constructing a building for what had been designated as just a temporary assembly center. Toward the end of August, the Commander offered a choice to families of school-aged children. He would transfer us to whichever bigger camp we selected where schools were planned. He mentioned that authorities were in the process of organizing a large camp for Lithuanians, Latvians, and Estonians at Dörverden, located about twenty-two miles south of Hassendorf. The camp was to be named "Camp Montgomery" for the hero of the British troops, Field Marshal Bernard Montgomery.

From the Commander, we learned two new acronyms that thenceforth ruled our lives: "UNRRA" and "DP." He said that starting in September, 1945, the United Nations Relief and Rehabilitation Administration, always referred to as UNRRA, would take over the running of all the Displaced Person, or "DP," camps in the American, British, and French zones of occupied Germany. The occupying military forces would remain responsible for maintaining order and dealing with crime.

Finally we refugees had a special designation: we were "DPs." Lithuanians soon invented a nickname based on the acronym DP. We called ourselves *Dievo Paukšteliai*—God's Little Birds.

After the meeting with the Commander, families gathered to confer. Everyone who had school-age children insisted on relocating to a camp with facilities for their education. The majority chose the camp still under construction, hoping to have some influence on its character. I remember Mother and Father inviting friends, old and new, to join them in the move. Many residents who did not have school-age children, but who had an interest in teaching or providing cultural activities for the younger generation, wanted to come as well, especially those who enjoyed working together in Hassendorf. As August ended, the British provided a fleet of trucks and moved us to our new home, Camp Montgomery in Dörverden.

I remember the disappointment we all felt when we saw our new quarters. The location of this camp had been an enormous gunpowder factory. The sight of black, soot-covered concrete blocks caused instant depression. The buildings assigned to the refugees were the barracks, kitchen, offices, and administration buildings formerly occupied by slave laborers and their supervisors.

Once again we were assigned to a barracks of triple-tier bunks, indiscriminately housing a mix of freed men and women laborers, family units, priests, single people, and couples—if you were a DP, in you went, first come, first served. Once again we faced a dangerous lack of sanitation. It was the most uncivilized, bug-infested, frightening place imaginable. There was no privacy at all. The constant din of overcrowded humanity arguing, babies crying, men drinking and yelling—Mother said it felt like a madhouse.

For the first time, I experienced a new kind of unidentifiable fear whenever I went to bed, though I should have felt safe in the middle bunk, my mother below me and Milda above. There was one man in the bunk across the aisle who gave me the shivers. Every time I had to take off my clothes to get ready for bed, I saw him staring at me in a way that I could not identify but did not like. He never touched me, but there was something about him I instinctively knew was not right.

It was worse for Milda. Many men considered my sister, a real beauty at sixteen, fair game—whether she was willing or not. Because of misplaced shame, it took her a few days to confide to Mother that in the wee hours of the morning, presumably when everyone was asleep and snores shook the air, she would feel searching hands trying to get under the covers of her top bunk. She did not know whether to scream or pretend to be asleep in hope that whoever it was would go away. She was embarrassed to raise a fuss and wake everyone, but finally she complained to Mother and Mother went berserk.

Mother told me, years later, that she called together an urgent meeting of women who, in a vocal crowd, marched to the UNRRA administrator's office and declared that enough was enough; that they had not escaped from the Soviet rapists just to be molested by their own twisted countrymen.

Husbands and fathers were equally appalled. However, the UNRRA personnel, composed predominantly of U.S. civilians who had just arrived in Germany, seemed completely incapable of dealing with the situation. They were just beginning to learn what chaos they had been given to organize. The angry delegation of parents asked the camp's administration to grant to the Executive Committees of each nation the right to make rules for their fellow nationals, and to police and expel troublemakers, with military police escort, if needed. Such committees had worked well in the other camps under British military supervision, so why not under UNRRA? The proposal was accepted with relief.

Job one was to put some order into the way space had been assigned to the residents. As in Hassendorf, unmarried men and women were segregated into separate, supervised buildings. To give a little privacy to families, men removed half of the bunk beds in the barracks. They then erected wood partitions or hung old surplus tent material donated by the military to create tiny cubicles. Living conditions were still noisy and demeaning, but Milda and I no longer had to endure leers and groping hands.

Soon after our arrival in Camp Montgomery, Father discovered that his brother Karolis, his wife and son, had arrived at a DP camp not far from ours. As soon as could be arranged, they came to visit us, and to check out if our living conditions were any better than in their camp. Father was excited: what a treat it would be to have at least one sibling for company.

As they were approaching to greet each other, the first words out of Uncle Karolis' mouth were, "Felicius! You're completely gray!" It was true, but I had not noticed because it had happened imperceptibly over the past year. Even though he was eight years older, Uncle's hair was still dark and curly. He wanted to move to Camp Montgomery to be near us, but his wife objected. She could not stand how ugly it was, or how primitive the living arrangements.

Father was elected by all three Baltic nations to be the leader uniting their separate Executive Committees. Everyone called him the camp's "Commandant," but his powers were extremely limited. Above him was the UNRRA Director and his staff, and above them the British Military Commander of the region. However, Father accomplished a significant turnaround from chaos to order because of his diplomacy, understanding, reasonableness, and sheer charisma.

The first order of business at Dörverden was sanitation and health. I remember undergoing another thorough dusting with DDT. Children were repeatedly vaccinated against who knows what, because the interpreter did not know how to translate the medical words.

Every day, before the midday meal, we children lined up to swallow a spoonful of cod liver oil. The first few times the slimy taste made me gag, but then I got used to it. Most of my little friends raised a huge fuss, and tried every trick to avoid getting the stuff in their mouths. The grownups said it would keep us from getting sick. It must have worked because, despite the autumn weather, the rains, and the unremitting closeness of people around me, I stayed healthy.

Second on the list was the establishment of elementary and high school classes. Among the Lithuanian DPs there were many who had been teachers; they were not only willing, but eager to educate the young, who had forgotten so much during the past year of war and destruction. Really, what else was there for them to do with their time? However, they faced a serious problem: no books, no notepaper, no pens or pencils.

At first, all we had was a cracked blackboard and some chalk provided by one of the UNRRA staff. There were no desks, only old dining-room tables, wobbly chairs, and rickety benches. Available space was scarce: grades had to be combined, and double sessions were held in the same room. Milda's classes started in the morning, mine in the afternoon.

Two weeks or so after our arrival at Camp Montgomery, a Red Cross truck delivered a pile of packages from the US, resulting in much excited speculation about the contents. The majority of the boxes contained second-hand clothing and shoes donated to the refugees by kind Americans, but some intelligent person had thought to send along a supply of used pencils and erasers and notebooks. Many of the notebook pages were already covered with writing, but nonetheless—what a lifesaver for the school. At last we young ones could copy notes and sums from the board. We were told to write as small as possible, to make the paper last.

Milda was in her element among her peers in high school, but I languished in my grade. This time the problem was the teacher, not teasing by other children. In fact, there was one little girl in particular, Neria, who was only six, and attached herself to me like a loveable puppy. She was in my class because first and second grades had been lumped together. There were more than thirty of us, our ages ranging from beginner six-year-olds who had never been to school, to older children like me, and some already nine.

The teacher failed utterly to gain our interest. She was so intent on maintaining perfect discipline that she neglected to actually teach. I complained to Father that she was mean, smacked the unruly, and called us names. As a former school inspector, he knew she should be reassigned, but nobody else would agree to teach this chaotic class.

Camp life had its brighter side: scouting and folk dancing groups, theatricals and choirs. And it so happened that Dörverden had many artists among the 700 Lithuanians gathered there. Their eyes could not bear the ugliness of our surroundings. From day one, they formed a group to do something about it.

In front of each barracks, there was a narrow strip of ground covered with weeds or gravel. They persuaded the Executive Committee to sponsor a contest to see which barracks could turn this neglected area into the most attractive ornamental display. Soon the strips blazed with autumn chrysanthemums, or were turned into pretty patterns or slogans using different colored pebbles and stones. A couple of artists carved a tall traditional Lithuanian cross and erected it outside, in a square between the barracks. It became the focus of Lithuanian gatherings and especially of scout meetings.

One artist appropriated a pile of dirt: he wanted to mark the Lithuanian area with a *Vytis,* a representation of a knight, sword raised, galloping on a white horse—the emblem of Lithuania. Fortunately, September had many days of decent weather, which meant that young folk could go into the fields in search of flowers to transplant, and we elementary school children go on a quest to find white pebbles and stones for the Vytis. The artist used pieces of broken brick to make the red background. It turned out very well. It was the first time I had worked physically on a communal project, and I loved it. I was definitely growing more social.

The Vytis in Camp Montgomery. Mother stands above me; little Neria next to me.

My companion, Neria, was an only child, much cherished by her parents, so it is still a mystery to me how she had learned to wheedle and cajole so successfully when she had no need to do it at home. Whatever she wanted, in the end she got. True, she was a gorgeous child. Every boy and girl wanted to do whatever Neria wanted—and she wanted my doll. "You are so much bigger than me, you are too old to play with dolls any more; I'm still a little girl and have no toys at all," she persisted over and over, until she wore me down, and in a moment of blind generosity I gave my Ilke to her. I instantly regretted it, but it was too late.

"You silly girl," scolded Mother, "why did you do that, knowing there are no other dolls to be found? Now don't ever bother me again about wanting a doll, understood?" Oh, I was so sorry I had given my doll away, and Neria did not even play with it once she had it. I learned the hard lesson that sometimes the pleasure of giving costs too much to the giver.

With October came the winds, the rains and the cold. I had outgrown all my clothes. Just as my mother was about to pull her hair out with worry, the Red Cross delivered more trucks with used clothing and shoes donated in the U.S. Of course, wars erupted among the DPs over the distribution: who would be in charge, and would the degree of need be considered?

Poor Father had his hands full trying to ensure fairness. He persuaded others to agree that the neediest would choose first. I thought, with good reason, that our family was among the most destitute in the camp, but Father's ethics decreed that, as the family of the "Commandant", we would be last. He could not bear to be accused of taking advantage. Nonetheless, even scraping the bottom of the barrels, with Mother's clever sewing and knitting skills we finally had something to wear for the winter.

In the autumn of 1945, a young Lithuanian journalist, Algirdas Gustaitis, wanted to see how his fellow countrymen were coping five months after the war had ended. He got permission from the authorities to leave his own DP camp to gather material for a report. He came to visit Camp Montgomery in October. A few months later, UNRRA printed his observations in a slim book titled "Between Switzerland and Denmark."

In the book, the author heaped praise on our camp, describing its beautification, admiring the activities for the young and the mature, commending the leaders for their outreach to well-known Lithuanian musicians, artists, and intellectuals. Concerning Father, he wrote: "The leader of the Dörverden camp, Felicius Prekeris, was elected by all three nations. A great optimist and public servant. Commandant of the Balts, scout leader, high school teacher, member of the literary association, active chorister."

I know that Mother was proud to be the wife of the Commandant: we were poor, but we had status. Unfortunately, Father's health, severely impaired by the yearlong flight to escape the Soviets, was not up to all the tasks which he had undertaken and which seemed to increase daily. As the weather worsened, people became more demanding about every defect and shortage.

Father was not in control of the housing situation, the heating, or the food supply, but he was the one the residents came to with all their complaints, demands and opinions. Mother, Milda, and I saw how exhausted he was. He confessed that all he wanted to do was teach and keep on with scout leadership, but he didn't know how to resign without appearing to be a quitter.

Fortunately, in mid-autumn, there was a Lithuanian refugee leadership conference held in the DP Assembly Center ("DPAC") in Detmold, during which Father was elected school inspector for all the Lithuanian DP camp elementary schools in the British Zone of Germany. Now he had an excuse to resign from his post as camp "Commandant." Moreover, the Lithuanians in Detmold were organizing their camp as the headquarters for scouting in the British Zone. They invited Father to move to their camp. It offered better accommodations: a room in a private house instead of in a barracks.

Father applied at once, but sadly, Detmold had just reached its quota and was no longer a possibility. It was considered a prestigious location, and available space had quickly been filled. UNRRA administrators told Father they still had room for a family of four in the nearby town of Blomberg, thirteen miles to the east of Detmold. Father went to check it out and was charmed by the attractive old architecture of the town's center, the many gardens, and the surrounding fields and forests.

As in Camp Montgomery, the assembly of refugees in Blomberg encompassed all three Baltic nations. Each had appointed its own Executive Committee and set up its own schools. Members of the Lithuanian Committee told Father they would welcome him as teacher and scout-master, and suggested he apply for the transfer immediately: the camp was small and in high demand, and there remained almost no openings. Father did so.

When the date of our move came, Milda was ill with bronchitis. Our parents worried that we would have to delay our move and perhaps lose our reservation in Blomberg. But sociable Milda had made friends even in the administration. Thus, mid-November 1945 saw us on our way to a new home. Father, Mother, and I huddled in a bone-chilling truck, but Milda made the trip in a comfortable, enclosed military ambulance.

CHAPTER 16:

Will We Never Escape
the Soviet Menace?

lomberg's DPAC (Displaced Person Assembly Center) administration assigned our little family to a private house full of other
Lithuanian refugees at #1 Jahnstrasse. We had a room to ourselves on the second floor. It was barely big enough to contain three
small beds hugging the walls, and one small table with just two chairs
in the middle. Mother and I shared one bed—Milda claimed I was too
restless in my sleep to share hers.

There was also a small wardrobe for clothes, quite sufficient for our
meager supply. This small, crowded space was to be our study room,
living room, dining room, and sleeping space. In bad weather, Mother
strung a spider web of cords on which to hang our drying laundry. But
what joy! At last, when we closed the door, we were alone, just the four
of us. And after a few months, when the family in the room next door
moved to another camp, we were allotted their bigger, brighter room,
and considered ourselves to be living in luxury.

The house had not been constructed to accommodate the number
of residents now assigned to live in it. With so many people, from babies to elders, crowded together, there was the constant noise of neighbors talking or singing or arguing or dealing with their children. Walls
muffled the worst of it. Having experienced life in the barracks, where
there was no escaping anyone else's eyes or voices, the neighbors' vo-
calizations beyond our walls became like the background buzzing of
bees, a white noise that we could ignore.

Crammed into this modest-size house were seven families on the
first two floors, and two bachelors in tiny loft rooms beneath the roof.
Imagine one single toilet and one small bathtub for about twenty-five
people. The residents had to agree on a schedule for bathing. Heaven
help you if you needed to use the toilet while someone else was taking

a bath! Necessity obliged all residents to acquire some sort of bucket to use in their rooms for emergencies.

Had there been a regular kitchen in the house? Had it been gutted to accommodate a couple of refugees? For us residents of #1 Jahnstrasse, the combination kitchen/laundry was located in the basement. I remember it as perpetually sunk in obscurity—the low-watt bulb in the ceiling only accentuated the dark, rather than providing illumination. Father considered it a punishment to go down there, so he jokingly named it the "Purgatory." There was an old-fashioned wood stove and a large laundry sink, plus a scarred, stained table for the preparation of food.

Actually, craving privacy, most residents preferred to cook in their own rooms. Wherever I went visiting, I saw a pot or a pan on a small electric ring or on a wobbly-looking Primus stove. Amazingly, nobody started a fire.

A radiator provided heat when it got really cold, but because the men who lived in the house had to take turns chopping wood into pieces small enough to fit into the furnace—a hard chore with blunt axes—there was seldom enough fuel to heat around the clock. In winter, at daybreak, our breath came out in clouds of condensation. I admired the intricate ferns and feathers of frost that formed during the night, ornamenting the glass in the windows.

The number of refugees in Blomberg was small compared to the big "barracks" camps such as Camp Montgomery. But housing the DPs in private homes upset the German residents of the town, with good reason. The occupying British military had requisitioned a number of houses from their owners, like it or not, assuming they would go live with their relatives or friends—though families with children were not touched.

Right after the war ended, the Allied military that occupied Germany were not feeling well-disposed toward the natives and could not have cared less about their wishes. This was especially true of the British, who had suffered so much from Hitler's bombs and rockets during the infamous bombing campaigns over England. Those targeting London alone had killed over fifty thousand civilians, and wounded hundreds of thousands more. Every British soldier in occupied Germany had a score to settle.

On the other hand, the German civilians, trained since the early 1930s under the Nazis to view themselves as superior to the rest of the world, were outraged at the assistance bestowed upon us Ausländer, the foreign invaders. They were sure that we primitive, uncultured Balts would ruin their well-kept homes. As a result, throughout most of our stay in Blomberg, the Baltic refugees rarely interacted with the German citizens, except when bartering: money had become worthless, but clothing, valuables, and cigarettes were always in demand.

As for us children, we knew never to go out alone. If a group of us refugees met a group of Germans, and if either side felt stronger or was more numerous, a battle would ensue. When evenly matched, we taunted the German children with the ditty: "*Deutschland, Deutschland über alles, /Zwei Kartoffel, das is alles!* (Germany, Germany rules over all, /Two potatoes, that's their all!)"—an insulting version of the Nazi's patriotic anthem. In return, we were called many choice epithets, in which the word *Schwein* (pig), and every possible variation on the word *Scheiss* (shit), got top billing.

This was our fourth camp in the seven months since the end of the war, and we found that some arrangements were already familiar, even "traditional." Each nation had its own Executive Committee to issue and enforce rules for its compatriots, and act as liaison with UNRRA and the British Commander. By 1946, the Lithuanian contingent in Blomberg numbered 377 adults and about 150 minors. A certain number of activities—schools, scouting, sports, music, ballet and folk dance groups, adult choir, theater, and literary associations—had by then become not only expected, but taken for granted. The greatest worry of all the DPs was to keep their young ones from getting into mischief. If someone was caught committing a crime, the punishment could go as far as expulsion from the camp.

Later, when emigration became possible, everyone knew that a criminal record would disqualify you from entering any other country. Activities helped keep youths engaged, and serious crime among the refugees in Blomberg was rare.

Father's duties as the alleged elementary school inspector for Lithuanian schools in the British Zone took little time, as they were more honorary than factual. He was delighted to throw himself into teaching and scouting, his two favorite activities, and Mother found a group of women with whom she liked to sew and knit and brainstorm creative ways to make the food doled out at the DP pantry last longer.

Like many other women, Mother was totally smitten by the strikingly handsome choir director, Mr. Vaičiulėnas, whose thick, black eyebrows both frightened and attracted the women he directed. She never missed a rehearsal. Father did not like him. "He's only good at showing himself off; he knows nothing about getting the best out of the singers," he said. I wondered if it was his turn to be jealous.

In the beginning of our stay in Blomberg, for all four of us, but especially for Milda and me, life seemed wonderful. I was born an introvert, self-aware, and still somewhat shy, but Milda was the exact opposite. She was completely natural, and not self-conscious in the least. She did not grow tall: her final height barely reached five feet two inches.

Older boys and young men appreciated my sister's charm, easy laugh, and ability to put them at ease. They circled around her, swooning over her blue eyes and honey-blond hair like lovesick adolescents. Her inborn sociability, repressed during our flight, and threatened by life in the barracks, effervesced and sparkled now that she felt safe. At long last, she could be carefree.

Milda took full advantage of the activities available at camp, such as scouting. She especially loved dancing. Fortunately for her, there were dances every weekend enjoyed not only by the young but also by the adults. Accordion music was always on offer. Some musicians were true virtuosos. "*Gyvenimas virte virė*—Life was boiling and bubbling," said Father.

My class in 1947.
I was not ready to give up wearing a hair ribbon.
Our teacher, Ms. Domeika, stands third from left.

As for me, I loved my class in school. There were only eight of us, six girls and two cowed boys, seriously outnumbered, whom we kept in their place. We were motivated to get through assignments as quickly as possible so we could go out to play or attend various activities. Our teacher, Ms. Zuzana Domeika, was a serious, traditional "old maid schoolmarm," determined to help us make up the year of schooling we had lost in the final upheavals of the war. We learned to appreciate her dedication and fairness. In those few months of schooling during the winter and spring of 1946, she gave us so much attention that, despite the lack of textbooks and scarcity of paper, my classmates and I completed both the second and third grades. We glowed in the praise lavished upon us by our parents and the entire community.

The other girls in my class were better off than I was. They had dolls. I still longed for a little girl doll to be my confidante and my companion in the stories I invented. Mother had not forgotten that I had recently given away my doll, and I knew better than to trouble her for one. I berated myself every day for having given in to that sweet-tongued Neria in Camp Montgomery. It was hopeless: we had nothing we could barter for a doll, anyway.

Sometimes my classmates would invite me to play with their dolls, but not often. Their parents did not welcome other children as frequent guests. By Lithuanian custom, it is rude to give food to your own child without offering something to a visitor, but nobody had food to spare—so visitors were discouraged.

My father had more tolerance for childish desires. He must have written to my cousin to see if he could find me a doll. Vytas Vaikutis, the son of Mother's brother Jurgis, was registered in a DP camp somewhere, but had received permission to continue working for the German railroads, a job he had held back in Lithuania. Travel had its advantages: it allowed him to pursue a sideline selling saccharin on the black market, a forbidden, though lucrative, activity. He had a network of contacts.

One day Vytas showed up in Blomberg, glowing with pride, carrying a huge doll that he was sure would send me into transports of joy. He was astonished when I took a long look at it, burst into tears, and handed it back: "*Ji sena boba! Jos nenoriu!*—She's an old granny! I don't want her!" I did not even thank him. In my disappointment, I quite forgot my manners.

How was a young man in his twenties to know that a child like me craved a little girl doll to love as an alter ego or a friend? He brought me what appealed to his taste. This antique doll dated, I later discovered, from the nineteenth century. It had a sawdust-filled body, wooden arms and legs, and a wax head molded to simulate wavy hair. Its faded wax face depicted a mature woman. It wore an ivory colored costume fussily ornamented with fancy lace, ruffles, ribbons, and furbelows like an overdressed opera singer.

How could I play with an old woman? Vytas left the doll with me and forgave me, but he never looked for another one. Mother persuaded Father to trade it in for something practical, like several pounds of buckwheat groats.

Just like Father and Milda, I thrived on scouting. The rules we followed were those written for "Girl Guides" in 1918 by Agnes Baden-Powell, sister of Lord Robert Baden-Powell, the founder of scouting. The adults wanted to instill in us, even under the problematic conditions of DP life, the basic scout principles of character development, respect for religion, good works and generosity, healthy bodies, and love of nature and country.

There were no uniforms or equipment available to buy, but somehow, by scouring the bins of donated clothing or bartering with the Germans, DP mothers soon had enough fabric in the requisite colors to sew into proper scouting blouses and skirts.

We, the younger girls, wore a navy colored skirt and a navy blouse with a red tie. Some DPs protested that we should shun red ties, because red was the color of scarves worn by the Young Pioneers in the Soviet Union. However, tradition won out against political objections.

The Lithuanian name for Girl Scout Brownies is "*Paukštytės*—Little Birds," and our membership pins portrayed a swallow within a ring. I felt a glow in my heart whenever I thought of swallows: their snug little nests, their untrammeled flight. I considered them to be my good-luck charm, and it felt comforting to wear their image on my uniform.

During our meetings, we smaller girls shared ideas about the good deeds we could do for others, even in our limited DP circumstances. We spent happy hours learning songs and thinking of skits to present at the "bonfires" which gathered together the various troops for story-telling, songs, and performances

True to the foundation of scouting, we learned nature lore, tracking, tying knots, and signaling. When the weather permitted, all scouts went on outings. The routine was for a couple of older scouts to go out early in the morning and mark a trail leading to a specific gathering spot. There was good-natured rivalry among the troops to be the first to locate the chosen site. Often, the "clues" were hard to distinguish from twigs that had fallen by chance.

Tracking was my favorite activity, because I could pretend to be an American Indian. I practiced walking soundlessly as described in the stories Father remembered from the "Leatherstocking Tales" of James Fenimore Cooper.

Senior scouts, 1946. Milda stands above and to the left of Father. Directly above her stands Jonas who became her second husband.

I linger on the good days because they did not last long for our family—or for most other DPs, exception made for the shrewd and the cunning, those who did not mind running risks and had little fear of dealing on the black market. Others who had assets to barter with the Germans did well, too, but my parents had no such assets or talents. I remember Mother sighing enviously about one particular group of energetic twenty-somethings. She would point out to Father, as a shining example, that young Mažeika's family never lacked for attractive clothes or fresh meat.

During the first months after the war, while the DP camps were under military rule, the British and American soldiers treated us with as much kindness as they could summon while trying to get a grip on the millions of refugees scrambling to survive in a country that was largely devastated. As Displaced Persons, we received food and rudimentary medical care, and parcels of donated clothes and shoes from the U.S. We were allowed to run our own schools. We were given access to printing equipment to republish textbooks and manuals used "back home" in our own countries.

Under the management of UNRRA, the climate of care cooled. The Allied nations had formed the United Nations Relief and Rehabilitation Administration in November of 1943. Governments foresaw that war-torn Europe would be full of displaced populations, similar to the up-heavals after World War I. UNRRA's immediate task after Germany's capitulation was the support of foreign refugees to prevent epidemics and starvation. However, its primary function was the return of these refugees back to their own countries. We were to feel the unwelcome weight of that policy for years.

With the coming of spring in 1946, conditions in camp began to change. First, food allotments were reduced, then came a campaign to repatriate us. UNRRA employees warned adult refugees to expect a summons to an official interview. Each person would have to prove his or her eligibility to receive services and aid as a DP. Rumors flew that the real reason for the interviews was to strong-arm us to go back to our own countries, Lithuania, Latvia, and Estonia—though our countries were gone, having officially become part of the Soviet Union.

Once the management of DP camps passed completely into the hands of UNRRA, politics took over, and we refugees were caught like flies in a bottle trap. UNRRA employees were not from the military services: few had fought in the war, and the great majority of them were American civilians who had not experienced battles or bombings or destruction at home. They had no empathy for the homeless victims of Nazi invasions and Soviet aggression, no motivation to help them, and no deep feelings of revenge directed against the German citizens. Few cared to learn the real reasons why so many DPs resisted going home to live under communist rule. For them, policy was policy.

The Soviet contingent in UNRRA spread propaganda that only former Nazi collaborators during the war were unwilling to return home—and collaborators were strictly excluded from claiming aid as DPs. Soviet colleagues badgered the American and British UNRRA employees to interrogate DPs at length, to examine their histories and make sure they had not helped the Nazi regime in any way.

Soviets urged the Western Allies to likewise interview as many neighbors and acquaintances as could be found to corroborate the deposition of every DP. Father complained, "It felt like a repetition of life under the Soviets in 1940–41: anyone could accuse you of having aided the Nazis, and how would you prove you had not?"

Giving in to such pressure, on May 13, 1946, the administration of our camp organized a "Poll on Repatriation." The results of the votes cast by Estonians, Latvians, and Lithuanians were tabulated, and on May 18, a report on the poll, approved and signed by the camp Director, H. Thuret, was sent to the regional office of UNRRA. This report was obviously not written by a native English speaker, but I transcribe it here unchanged, leaving in the typing mistakes and the awkward English.

18 May 46

SUBJECT: Poll on repat.
TO   : UNRRA Distr Dir MG 1 Corps Dist

ANALYSIS OF QUESTION 3.

The poll on repat held in Blomberg's AC 33/131 Is very significative.

Of 1237 DPs allowed to vote, only three were not participating, 10 said yes and 99,4% answered in a negative way.

Three nationalities are living in this camp, namely Lithuanians, Esthonians and Latvians. Nevertheless all their replies express the same feeling and the same basic ideas e.g. "We love our native country, we want all to return but never as long as our country is not free and under a foreign dictatorship."

Enclosed please find some copies of several answers taken from the ballots, which could be considered as an average answer.

No political propaganda took place in this camp and an absolute freeness was assured. Questions of economic un- certainty or difficulty of travel conditions were solved at the same time.

All these Baltics are prepared to face life with courage as long as their freeness is guaranteed. All of them have a very steady idea of living free in the democratic way they had organized. They hold their flag and traditions, culture very high.

All the answers explain a real terror of the actual regime carried out in their country at the moment. Most of them having relations there who have told them or have seen it themselves, how life is going on, if they had to return without the protection of the Allies.

Signed: H Thuret
Director
164 UNRRA
Blomberg

Out of 1,237 Baltic nationals, only ten Latvians wanted to return home. It should have been clear to UNRRA officialdom that the Balts wanted to live in a free and democratic environment, and not under Soviet rule. The news of the period showed that Stalin was refusing any limitations on the way he treated the territories under the heel of his armed forces. Although Churchill had warned as early as March 5, 1946, that Stalin had drawn an iron curtain to hide what he was doing in the territories he controlled, officially, the Western Allies still acted as if their Eastern Ally would allow for national self-determination in the lands it had occupied.

Privately, Churchill was strongly advising the Western Allies that they were in danger of an imminent Third World War against Soviet aggression. In that case, they would need Germany's resources and manpower.

In the spring of 1946, the focus of UNRRA veered from supporting foreign refugees, to alleviating hunger among the Germans. The country was devastated, overrun by the homeless, millions of them ethnic Germans—*Volksdeutsch*—from areas now occupied by the Soviets. Rather than continuing to punish Germany, the Western Allies decided it would serve their own interests better to help it reconstruct its industries. German coal and steel were essential to rebuild Europe, and a healthy Europe meant a healthy market for British and American products.

Policy makers, short on facts, decided that if the DPs were given barely enough food to survive, perhaps they would find jobs and become independent, thereby helping to rebuild Germany. But for DPs to find jobs in Germany, the employers would have to be the Americans and the British. With seven million ethnic German refugees clamoring for work, German employers would never hire the despised DPs. Germans deeply resented the foreign refugees in their midst, and especially what they perceived as their pampered lives, receiving largesse from UNRRA.

Let's face it: the presence of the DPs complicated everyone's greater political concerns. Officially, the American and British governments refused to acknowledge the legality of the Soviet occupation of the Baltic nations, and therefore did not agree to use force to return the Lithuanian, Estonian, and Latvian refugees against their will—but at the same time, they did everything they could to make us go home voluntarily.

Mother and Father were well aware of these political undercurrents, because many newssheets circulated in the camps. I remember hearing them discuss, in hushed tones, the terrifying prospect of forced repatriation to Soviet Lithuania. I also remember that the bread handed out to us lost its flavor and became full of bran that tasted like cardboard, that powdered milk (often spoiled by humidity) replaced fresh, that cheese and butter and sugar disappeared, and that our hot school lunch more often than not consisted of a pale green watery soup which was supposedly made of split peas. We blessed the can of corned beef or Spam we got for the four of us each week.

Rumors flew: many thought that the Camp Director was stealing the supplies to sell on the black market. Actually, he was not the guilty party at all. The volume and quality of aid to the DPs had been cut off at the source, and theft by UNRRA employees added its own evils.

Apparently, the drivers of the trucks who brought supplies to Blomberg from the warehouse in Detmold were siphoning off a large portion of the goods, which they later sold on the black market. One day, they stole the contents of an entire truck, which, in addition to food, had carried the monthly cigarette ration for the camp—and cigarettes made you rich. The thieves then set the truck on fire to hide the evidence.

The cunning and unprincipled lived well. For those like Mother and Father, who were unable to cheat others, the question of how to provide enough food for the family was always the first thought in their minds.

I tried to do my part. Whenever we had time and the weather permitted, my two favorite classmates, Siga, Dita and I would play in the meadows near the watermill, where we could pick wild sorrel to take home in our aprons for our mothers to add to soup. On our scouting expeditions we paid special attention to anything we could forage in the woods.

In spring, we looked for the exquisite, wild forest strawberries, though they were few and far between. Later in the summer came the gratifying bounty of wild raspberries. There was a hill not far from town made impenetrable by tangles of raspberry bushes. I recall making several visits with Milda, during each of which we filled a sizeable pail. Mother boiled them up with locally grown sugar beets to make a sort of jam.

In the fall, there was the delight of mushroom picking. The surrounding woods and forests were full of them. Our scout troop leader taught us to distinguish between the poisonous and the edible. Most of them were familiar from my earliest summers with the aunties in Šeduva.

When conditions were just right, the crowning glory of the mushroom world, the *boletus edulis*—bolete or porcini, would emerge, and every Baltic DP man, woman, and child would head for the forest. Everyone had a favorite spot, and people fought, sometimes with fists, to protect their personal patches from intruders.

On one such mushrooming expedition, Mother gave me a lesson in morality I have never forgotten. In the autumn of 1946, I was studying the Catholic catechism to prepare for my First Communion. Aware of all possible big and little sins, and inspired by the ethics I had learned in scouting, I was very sensitive to any wrongdoing.

Mother and I had not been lucky that day, and only a handful of low-quality mushrooms lay at the bottom of Mother's pail. It was drizzling, and to return to our room more quickly, we carefully cut across a farmer's field, thickly covered in rutabagas ready for harvest. Mother stooped down and pulled up four of these turnips and put them in her pail. I was horrified.

"Mama, that's stealing! That's a mortal sin!" I admonished her self-righteously.

"I wish I didn't have to do it," said Mother, "but we have nothing else to eat tonight. Perhaps, if he knew how hungry we are, the farmer would let us take them."

"No, Mama, he would not. You know the Germans hate us," I said.

Mother paused, looked at me, and said, "Do not worry, *mano vargšele*—my poor girl. God understands, and will forgive me. He knows that only desperation forces me to take these few rutabagas, which the farmer will not even miss. I'm sure he's only growing them to feed his pigs. It is not a sin to take something to keep yourself alive." Tears were running down her face as she said this, and I felt so ashamed. Ashamed that my mother had to steal, and ashamed of myself for making her cry. I racked my brain trying to think of ways I could help out.

When the butter ration disappeared, finding a fat substitute became urgent. In late September, my classmates and I went searching for beechnuts, which, when pressed, make a usable cooking oil. Oh, but what a chore to pick enough of them to obtain even a cup of oil! The nuts are tiny, barely larger than half an inch, and finding whole ones is not easy—birds and squirrels find them faster than humans.

It takes at least three pounds to squeeze out eight ounces of low-quality oil, and only if the nuts have been ground up a little to open the shell. But necessity left no other options, and long after my friends had given up and were playing around, I was on my knees, scrabbling among the fallen leaves. Every nut was a gift for Mama.

The lack of proper food was hardest on Father. As always, our parents fed Milda and me first, and—gentleman that he was—Father always took the smallest portion. I remember hearing him lament that his tongue felt swollen, and he suffered constantly from indigestion. "It's this sawdust bread," Father would say. I often saw him rub his hands and massage his feet. "They tingle as if I'd walked through stinging nettles barefoot," he complained. The doctor at the camp clinic could not make heads or tails of the symptoms to reach a diagnosis.

It's ironic that for a while, our survival depended on cigarettes. UNRRA paid Father four or five packs of cigarettes a week for his work as a teacher and school inspector. With the German economy shattered and the Reichsmark almost valueless, *Zigaretten* were the new currency. Early in 1946, a single pack would buy ten pounds of potatoes. But soon, soldiers of the occupation and employees of UNRRA, who had access to many cartons of cigarettes, flooded the black market in expectation of instant riches, and ruined it for everyone. By summer, each pack brought in only two pounds of potatoes.

In other camps, starting in the early summer of 1946, DPs often received Red Cross and CARE packages which contained sugar and coffee and chocolate, products much prized by the Germans and thus invaluable for bartering for meat or shoes. We received very few of these packages in Blomberg—someone was stealing them.

For me, the winter of 1946–47 meant schoolwork, scouting and sledding; for Milda, it was the last year of high school. It seemed to me that there were as many activities and events in camp as ever. I was not aware of many problems other than hunger and the lack of heat (it was hard to write in school when you needed to wear mittens). I saw that my parents were anxious, but I thought it was the usual worry about food. Just approaching age ten, I was too young to understand their concerns about our long-term prospects for the future.

Years later, reminiscing about life in Blomberg, I asked my parents, "What troubled you most during that awful winter? How did you feel?"

"In despair," said Father.

"In a panic, is how I felt," said Mother. "The same thoughts, over and over: what was to become of us? Of you and Milda? We could not survive on the scant rations doled out to us. We had no money or items to barter. There were no jobs. We could not go home. We had no relatives in a more prosperous country who might obtain documents for us to join them."

"I was only thirty-eight," said Father, "but I felt death breathing down my neck. I felt so weak. I could not bend down without going dizzy, I was out of breath, my heart was racing. Who would ever hire me outside the DP camp? The worst part was that we still felt pressured to go 'home.' Our UNRRA administrators continued to remind us that we would get a free train ride and a sixty-days' supply of food per person if we agreed to return to Stalin's Soviet Lithuania."

The issue of repatriation came to a head on October 11, 1946. On that date, our camp administrators welcomed the Soviet envoy, Colonel Kutuzov, and his staff from the UNRRA Repatriation Commission. Their declared purpose was to describe to the DPs from Estonia, Latvia, and Lithuania the renewed prosperity in our countries, which had now been officially integrated into the Soviet Union, and to answer any questions about returning "home."

Colonel Kutuzov's attempts to persuade the Baltic nationals of the good life at home were met with incredulity and jeers. The Latvian contingent, by far the most numerous in Blomberg, was especially vocal. In the subsequent report, one exchange (which I copy verbatim) clearly made the Soviet visitors squirm:

Question: "Had the Government of the Soviet Union given an order to displace (sic: to deport) thousands of Estonians, Latvians and Lithuanians from their homes to Siberia?"
Answer: "Yes, in summer of 1941 our Government gave such an order because the Soviet Union was menaced by the danger of a war with Germany, and for its security it was necessary to send people who were politically untrustable from the Baltic states. But there were made a lot of mistakes and there were many innocent people among those who were sent off."
Question: "What was the crime of these you suppose to be guilty? Why there was no court of justice?"
Answer: " ------- "(The Russians did not give any answer to this question).
(The public asked many questions on the same subject)
Colonel: "I am now for two years hearing always the same questions (about the displacement), and I don't want to discuss this problem any longer."

Concerning the validity of the occupation of the Baltic nations by the Soviets in 1940, one of our fearless young men, Mr. Mažeika, asked whether the takeover had been part of the Molotov–Ribbentrop secret treaty of 1939. Col. Kutuzov answered with this amazing lie: "Such a treaty has never existed at all. Ribbentrop's account of such a treaty in the court of Nurnberg was only an attempt to accuse the Soviet Union and to save himself and his companions."

Apparently Col. Kutuzov was not aware that a copy of the pact had already reached the hands of the British government.

When the meeting ended and the two Soviet vehicles were pulling out of their protected parking spots into the street, someone threw a grenade in their direction. A window nearby shattered, and three bystanders claimed injuries. No Russians were hurt, but they decried the act so loudly, it made headlines everywhere in Europe. They demanded—and were granted—the right to conduct weeks of interrogations. They attempted to implicate every attendee of the meeting as part of a huge conspiracy. However, no guilty party was found.

Mr. Mažeika explained to me, years later, that one of his friends had kept a training grenade as a war souvenir. It made noise but had a minimal charge. Egged on by others, this man threw it under the wheels of the departing delegation, primarily to scare one of the drivers, who was a Lithuanian Communist Party member and therefore considered worse than scum.

Later, when the authorities questioned the men, they laid the blame back on the Soviets. They alleged that they had seen the driver of one of the cars toss something into the street, and then heard the explosion. "Typical commie disinformation tactic!" they said. "Probably just looking for an excuse to torment us poor Balts, who detest all they stand for."

Our new camp Director, Major Defise, was not a friend of the Soviets. To keep the peace politically, he decreed a punishment on the entire camp. He ruled that the DPs in Blomberg must remain confined within the town limits for a month. But nobody in charge ever checked to see if any of us disobeyed.

CHAPTER 17:

Long-Distance Lifesaving

As 1946 came to a close, my parents wondered how much longer we could endure the depressing conditions of existence as unwanted DPs. Returning to Lithuania was out of the question, life as resented interlopers in Germany was robbing us of what little self-respect we had left, and thoughts of the future were bleak. The free countries of the world were exceedingly slow to accept DPs from Eastern Europe. "We're poor *Dievo Paukšteliai*—God's Little Birds," the Lithuanian refugees said. "We're expected to build our own nests, but we're not welcome anywhere."

Existing immigration quotas were totally inadequate, and UNRRA had no authority to promote the resettlement of refugees outside of Germany; such a task was not in its charter. Moreover, its charter was to expire on June 30, 1947, which meant it was in a hurry to end its involvement in refugee affairs.

Before it handed us over to a successor, however, one additional task had to be done. UNNRA's top administrators in Germany felt that there were too many DP camps. They decided that the smaller ones should be disbanded, and the DPs moved into bigger "Assembly Centers" for the sake of efficiency. We read that our small camp in Blomberg was among those to be closed, although no date had been set. Where would they place us now? The thought of returning to a noisy barracks hung over us like a menace.

Finally, early in 1947, there came a spark of hope for my parents and the other DPs frozen in no-man's-land. Father said, "That winter there was talk that Belgium had requested men under forty to work in the coal mines, though their families would have to wait two years to join them. At last, someone wanted us, if only a select few. I was thirty-eight, but too weak to even think about it."

Father was fading, but Mother was still strong. She was forty, but she was sturdy and looked younger. Soon another encouraging rumor swept through the camp. Someone had heard that the Labor government in Britain wanted to recruit two or three thousand Baltic women between the ages of eighteen and forty to work as domestics for affluent Britons, or as cleaning staff in hospitals and care homes. Room and board and a small wage would be provided. However, no husbands or children would be accepted.

Around February 1947, our camp administration confirmed that this was a concrete proposal. The Ministry of Labor in London called it "Operation Baltic Cygnets." The contract was for two years, to be reviewed after one year and extended at the employer's discretion. The employee was forbidden to break the contract without official permission based on good cause, but could be sent back to the DP camp at any time for any reason.

These were effectively conditions of serfdom. However, our family's survival in the DP environment was so precarious that Mother jumped at the chance. Not only that, but she made Milda apply as well, much to my sister's chagrin. "I was not ready for adulthood; I wanted more time to be carefree, and Dad did not want me to go," she confided to me. But Mother thought that the two of them working and saving together could soon send us food and perhaps other items, such as nylon stockings, which Father could use for barter. When it came to decisions regarding Milda, Mother always trumped Father.

Milda was still officially underage, but she would turn eighteen on April 24, 1947. She was readily accepted: in fact, the age limits were quite flexible. Other women flocked to sign up, although no one else with underage children was brave enough to leave them behind.

Before the date of the departure, much had to be done in the Lithuanian community. The traditional Lithuanian ordeal of written and oral examinations, which would allow us fourth graders to enter "junior high school," was advanced to April 14 because our teacher, Ms. Domeika, was going to England. This was Milda's last year of school. Her teachers gave her early exams so she could receive her diploma.

On April 21, a gloomy, overcast morning, a military truck picked up about twenty women from our camp and drove them away, full of dread and hope, to try their luck in England. Mother did not want me present, fearing that she or I would break down in front of everybody and create a scene. Before leaving, Mother reminded me to get my hair cut and to bathe myself as she had taught me. I remember how I hugged her and Milda, and how we made the sign of the cross over each other asking God to bless us all and let us meet again.

As they were leaving, I dared to whisper to Mother, "If you get the chance, please send me a doll." Father went to see them off, but I wrapped myself tight in my blanket and lay in bed until he returned, thinking of everything and anything except that Mother was gone, and what life would be like without her.

With Mother and Milda's departure everything changed, of course. The administration of the camp reminded us that our big, bright room was too spacious for just two people. In the same house, one of the tiny loft rooms under the eaves had become available. This was an L-shaped space with scant room for furniture. There was a little table under a small gable window facing east, and Father nailed together a rickety bookcase that served to hold our folded clothes, as well as books and food supplies. There was a small wood-burning stove that did not draw well, and often flooded our "cell" with smoke.

Mother and Milda leave for England.

We had one single narrow bed that we were obliged to share. We managed to fit in by placing my head at Father's feet. It was very uncomfortable for Father, but I liked having his feet at my back. I felt secure.

Fortunately for us, it was spring. Father did not have to bother lighting and cleaning out the stove unless we had something to cook. But there was no water on this floor, so he had to go all the way to the basement to fill a container. It took him a long time to walk back upstairs. I was still too young to really grasp how weak he was. He was my emotional tower of strength, therefore indestructible and immortal.

In reality, by mid-May of 1947, Father could barely walk, and I noticed without understanding that he had begun to forget appointments, or repeat the same questions. Father joked about being the typical "absent-minded professor," making sure I would suspect nothing. He felt his motherless little girl had enough to worry about.

The camp doctor was seriously concerned, but there was no equipment in the DP clinic for in-depth tests. The UNRRA Director of our camp, Major Defise, was a great supporter of scouting, and had a special liking for Father. He arranged to have him tested at a German hospital. This facility, located about eight miles from Blomberg in a beautiful pine forest, had once been a sanatorium. Father was placed in the main building and endured test after test.

Because there was nobody in Blomberg to look after me, I was sent along as a "patient" to the women's building. My roommates were new mothers. Although, for the sake of officialdom, the nurse took my temperature and checked my pulse every morning, I was free to come and go as I pleased. In those days, many German women brought along their other small children when they came to deliver their babies. I had a lovely time babysitting in the playroom.

Every day, I walked across the spacious grounds to visit Father. Here and there, wild strawberries made a groundcover. It was a warm spring and a few were beginning to ripen. I'd pick as many as I could find for my daddy.

The doctors had discovered that his stomach lacked enough of the hydrochloric acid needed for digestion, but they did not know why. When they brought him his meals, which were of much better quality than those we were allotted back at camp, they also made him drink diluted hydrochloric acid, which burned his esophagus. His health failed to improve at all. After about two weeks of torturing him, the doctors gave up and sent us both back to Blomberg.

Mother, Milda, and most of the other Lithuanian women from Blomberg had been assigned as cleaning maids to a very large facility, Mount Vernon Hospital, located in Northwood, a pleasant suburb north-west of London. The hospital specialized in cancer research and treatment. The women lived in a medium-sized barracks building, their small private areas separated from their neighbors by thin hospital curtains. There were thirty of them, Lithuanians and Irish, all in one long room. In the winter, it was very cold. In one of her letters Mother wrote: "When it's time to leave my warm bed, it's like jumping into ice water."

The maids had to get up at 6 a.m., and were done for the day only after washing up the dishes of the evening meal. In the barracks, there was a big sitting room where they could gather to sew and talk and sing. And write letters. Many of the women had left husbands behind, but only Mother had left a child.

Sometime towards the end of May, Father wrote a letter to Mother explaining how precarious his health had become, and suggesting that perhaps she should prepare for the worst. Mother wrote to us later that she went into hysterics: what would become of me, just ten years old, if Father died? How long would it take the authorities to release her from her contract?

Given the urgency of the situation, Mother had to approach the head of the hospital, a woman known as "The Matron." Everyone was in awe of her; on all matters at Mount Vernon Hospital, she was the Court of Last Resort. Because Mother as yet spoke very little English, she asked a fellow Lithuanian, who was more fluent, to help.

The Matron, Miss Sterlini, was an outstanding administrator who demanded from every employee total dedication to service. She was thin as a stick, a very proper maiden lady who appreciated those who worked hard, such as Mother. Mother's tearful account of her poor child, left behind in the care of a dying husband, touched a soft spot in the Matron's heart. She asked her staff to call to her office the doctors who were doing rounds in the hospital that day, and had Mother repeat Father's symptoms to them. Before she had even finished, one doctor said, "Sounds like pernicious anemia. All he needs is a regimen of liver extract injections and he'll soon be right as rain." He explained that people with pernicious anemia were dangerously low on iron and vitamin B12. Their digestive systems were malfunctioning, and they could not process these essential nutrients from the food they ate.

You can imagine Mother's reaction to this sudden lifeline of hope. The Matron had her staff send a telegram to the Camp Director in Blomberg, asking him to pass along the diagnosis to the doctor for the DPs who should immediately give Father shots of liver extract. A day later, a telegram came back saying there were no supplies of liver extract available anywhere in Germany, let alone in Blomberg.

The Matron helped Mother find a supplier. Mother bought some immediately, but she knew that trying to mail the medication would be futile: it would never reach Father. Postal workers in Germany were notorious thieves, and medication such as this would be worth its weight in gold on the black market. Mother's hopes crumbled. "I could not stop crying," she told me. "In my thoughts, all I saw was Felicius dead, and you an orphan with nobody to take care of you, starving alone in the attic."

Sometimes, when help is most needed, help appears: call it luck or the will of God. Milda and the other younger Lithuanians had quickly picked up sufficient English to leave the protective circle of the hospital. On their days off, they explored London and its attractions. They had located the one Lithuanian Catholic Church in London, St. Casimir's, where fellow countrymen gathered each Sunday to go to confession, receive communion, and celebrate Mass in their own language. It took hours to get there from the hospital by subway trains and busses, but all the women who could manage it got up at 5 a.m. to make the trip.

Sundays at St. Casimir's were a magnet, not just for the religious service, but also for sharing information and advice. Through the parishioners' grapevine, Milda met Mrs. Liudžius, a Lithuanian woman who had resided in London for decades, and whose son was a consular courier between England and the British military officials in Germany. Would he—could he—carry to Germany the medication to save Father's life?

Milda immediately arranged for Mother to meet Mrs. Liudžius and explain her plight. Within the week, Mother received a letter stating that the son had agreed to personally deliver the medication to Detmold, the military administrative center nearest to Blomberg. Everything happened so fast and efficiently that by mid-June, Father was receiving the liver extract injections three times a week. Slowly, he began to recover his health and his will to live. However, he needed good food, and that continued to be a problem.

In a letter dated June 14, 1947, Father wrote to Mother:

> I've so many errands, so many details to take care of. One has to live, to keep moving. There are vegetables, and something with more calories to find and to cook, our little cell to keep clean, clothes to wash, and I have to stand forever in line at the food pantry for a quart of milk and a loaf of bread. Let's face it: other than bread and corn flour, the pantry doles out enough food for only two days, and even then not in full measure. It's up to the DP to find how to provide for the other five days. Even so, it's better now than when you were here, because I receive

some milk also, since I'm still not well…. Dalia is looking sturdy. It's harder for me because I cannot digest many foods—
black bread, especially, gives me problems…. It's black only in
appearance, but who knows what it's made of. According to
the recipe, it's supposedly corn and wheat, but according to my
taste buds, it's sawdust.

"Oh, I remember that bread," said Mr. Mažeika to me, remembering our life in Blomberg. "It disgusted people, but my horses loved it!"

I became re-acquainted with Mr. Mažeika in 2011, sixty-three
years after leaving the DP camp. He was well into his nineties, but
as bright as ever. His memories of those years were the very opposite of ours. He had been one of the few in the camp who found life
there more of a merry challenge than a grim battle for survival. "But
you see, I was lucky," he said. "I had left our farm in Lithuania with
my wife and two toddler boys well ahead of the approaching Soviets.
I had a cart full of supplies, and two fine horses to pull it. I spoke
German, and stopped to work at farms where my horses were in great
demand and where we received free food and lodging. Most farmers
had lost their horses to the military, which had seized them to haul
war materiel."

During the years in Blomberg, Mr. Mažeika rented his horses out to
nearby farmers and, in return, received fresh meat and other supplies.
One payment of a piglet, through a chain of bartering, netted his wife
a manual sewing machine. She and her friends set up a *Nahstube*—a
sewing room, in which the women transformed the worn clothing donated to the DPs into attractive women's and children's apparel. Their
husbands then bartered them with area farmers for food.

"It was forbidden to raise any live animals: the German owners
of the DP houses were rightfully afraid of damage to their property,"
said Mr. Mažeika. "A special inspector was appointed to make unan-
nounced visits. But if everyone in a house agreed to keep quiet, it was
possible to raise chickens, rabbits, and even pigs in the basement, or in
a shed close by. I remember the trouble I had with a pig we slaughtered:
how were we to get rid of the bristles? We had no way to singe them
off. The solution? Every man in the house donated his razor blades,
and two of us spent a tense but hilarious night shaving the porker from
snout to bitty tail!

"And then there's the tale of the unwilling cow. The inhabitants of one house, a bunch of bachelors overseen by the young priest, Father Demeika, were keeping a cow in the back yard. One day, a boy came rushing up to warn them that the inspector was on his way. What to do? Imagine their panic. The guys managed to shove the poor animal up the narrow stairs into the attic and to convince the inspector, with a few glasses of schnapps, to go away without too much snooping around. But you know? A cow will not willingly climb down stairs, and it took all of them some heavy lifting to extricate her back to the yard!" He chuckled at the memory.

"I did get caught once bringing home a pig," he continued, "and Major Defise, our camp Director, asked me if I was not ashamed of my behavior. I got mad. I told him I had two little boys who needed meat to stay healthy. I said I would be ashamed before God if I let them fall sick because the Germans had persuaded UNRRA to pass that idiotic rule against our raising animals. UNRRA did not provide enough food for our needs, and yet forbade us to get it for ourselves. The Director thought about it for a minute, then said, 'You may go.' I never heard any more about it. And while he was in charge, the inspectors somehow never found anyone to punish."

But Father had neither the means nor the cunning to outwit the bureaucratic food restrictions, so for us, hunger was always a threat. The packages Mother sent were often stolen, but the ones that came through were a godsend. They truly saved our lives.

It was summer vacation; it was warm. I continued foraging for sorrel, blueberries, raspberries, and early mushrooms, and going on outings with my scout troop. Father lacked energy, but refused to miss any scout meetings. He even participated in a Baltic Scouts camp in July, primarily because there was better food at camp than the rations given out at the DP pantry. He needed to rest a lot, and he still sometimes stumbled when he walked. Some scouts made him a nice walking stick. I enjoyed camping, despite the rain leaking into our "army surplus" tent.

Mother and Milda continued their best efforts to ensure that Father and I did not go hungry. Everyone smoked in those days, but not Milda, and Mother only rarely—though she loved the occasional indulgence in a Benson & Hedges, a luxury brand of cigarette. She and Milda saved every penny they could spare to send us coffee, sugar, canned lard, and even nylons, which were in short supply in England as well, but invaluable for us because young German women craved them.

It was not easy for Mother to help us. England was still on rationing for clothing and food. Mother and Milda received far fewer ration coupons than the norm—after all, the hospital provided their meals and uniforms, so the Ministry of Food determined they had minimal need to shop for clothing or groceries.

The "cygnets" from Blomberg soon learned, however, that, for a price, they could get extra coupons sold "under the table." Every week, Mother and Milda would send us a package containing items Father could use to barter for meat or eggs, but, until late 1947, almost every package arrived sliced open, some of its contents stolen, sometimes replaced with a rock to make it feel heavier. Mother was beside herself with anxiety and rage: why had she left us, a sick man and a child, if she could not do anything for us?

Mother was born with a gene to worry and foresee troubles at every turn, but Milda was eighteen, hungry to live and laugh. Mother wrote: "She's always happy and never cries. As if made of steel." Well, she was young. On Sundays at the Lithuanian church, everyone stayed after Mass to socialize. Milda met many young men who vied for her company. Her mind was already set on the future; Mother's was still in the past, bound to the needs of her husband and child.

Mother's strength and persistence came from the hope that Father and I would soon be able to join them in England. What an emotional seesaw she endured! The few surviving letters she and Father wrote to each other reveal their constant worries. When would the omnipotent "they" permit him and me to come to England? Where would Father be placed? What kind of work could he do?

The delays were endless, and the threat that the camp in Blomberg would be closed added its own stress. When would the authorities transfer Father and me to another DP camp? Where would it be? They had no solid information, only rumors.

In the letter of June 14, 1947, Father warned:

Don't expect us, Stase, to arrive soon; it does not appear that we'll be on the early list.... In the DP newspaper today there is an announcement that the Ministry of Labor cannot reach a solution on what to do for people with families. Neither can UNRRA decide on the question of transfers to another camp, nor on immigration as laborers to England.

September came and school started again. My curriculum now included a class in "sewing," but with a DP refugee twist. We younger girls were not instructed in how to put together a blouse or a dress. Instead, our teacher, Mrs. Tamulaitis, focused on the skills most essential to the needs of a DP: sewing up hems, fixing unraveling buttonholes, darning socks and gloves, and patching up garments, from tears in our dresses to holes in our fathers' jackets. Some of my more lively classmates hated this class, but I found it restful, and was proud of the professional-quality darning I did on Father's socks. And my buttonholes were in a class apart—works of perfection worthy of a medal, I felt.

Father's liver-extract shots were painful and irritating, resulting in skin rash and swelling, but by degrees, he regained his strength. He enjoyed teaching, mostly Lithuanian language and literature, but also art. He continued as the chief scoutmaster for the Lithuanian camp.

He and I spent happy hours on mushrooming expeditions. We dried the delicious boletes to enjoy over winter. Father loved to cook. He created meals for us by combining whatever unlikely ingredients we happened to have on hand, like canned mackerel and potatoes. He liked to discuss food preparation with the two older ladies who lived in the same house, and carefully wrote out into a notebook the delicious recipes they remembered, even though we never had the ingredients for him to actually use them. Like remembering a piece of music, he could taste them in his mind.

CHAPTER 18:

Father and I Take Wing

I missed Mother, but also did not: life with Father was always calm and interesting, even if our clothes and our room were not as clean as she would have kept them. Without Mother to restrain him, occasionally Father's impractical side came out. He believed that childhood should be a time of lighthearted gladness. It grieved him to see me "living off crumbs," as he put it.

Fall, 1947. Father and I:
ragged, but always hopeful.

Father was always on the lookout for something interesting or playful with which to surprise me. For example, instead of saving cigarettes to barter for food, he spent them to acquire an old, shabby German atlas, which had several pages in color. I would get lost in it for hours, marveling at the world, repeating the names of islands—Barbados, Madagascar, Tasmania—as if they were candy in my mouth.

And that irresistible siren call of "*Terra Incognita*," labeled on portions of South America and Africa. Unknown lands. What amazing discoveries would be made there? Dream worlds! Father acquired a few stamps from all over the world so I could search out in my atlas the countries where they had originated.

Father felt sad and diminished that it was Mother and Milda who were working so we could survive. He felt keenly that it was his job to provide for all of us. He often worried about Milda. He was guilt-ridden that she had to waste her youth scrubbing floors and washing dishes to help us. He missed her sunny disposition, her light-heartedness. "I hope your mother is treating Milda with great kindness," he would sigh. "She deserves our special gratitude."

In the autumn of 1947, the number of Lithuanians in camp decreased significantly as more and more people were transferred out to bigger DP Assembly Centers. We were no longer under the management of the United Nations Relief and Rehabilitation Administration, whose charter had expired in June.

UNRRA's duties had never included finding new homes for the non-German refugees in Europe, but now that changed. The task of our new guardian, the International Refugee Organization (IRO), was not only the maintenance of European refugees, but also their resettlement.

IRO spent its first few months ineffectually fumbling and blundering, trying to understand the magnitude of the work it had to tackle. Nobody seemed to know what specific plans might be in store for us in Blomberg. We lived on rumors and a sorry dose of paranoia.

In December 1947, Mother's fear that I would be left an orphan with nobody to take care of me, "starving alone in the attic" almost came true, if only for a few days.

Early in December, an epidemic of mumps broke out in Blomberg. One morning, I developed a fever and at the same time so did Father. My ears ached and it hurt to open my mouth. Father had a bad headache and a painful, ugly red area on one hip—the site of repeated liver-extract shots.

Because he was still far from recovered from the pernicious anemia, Father knew he had better get checked out at the clinic. He told me to stay in bed until he returned, and not to venture from our room for fear of infecting others.

At the clinic, the Doctor ordered Father's immediate transfer to the hospital unit for observation. Father knew he had no choice but to go, and he asked one of the nursing staff to tell Mrs. Gailiūnas, a kindly older woman who lived in the same house as we did, to look after me.

Father's fever was spiking dangerously. Some kind of blood infection, thought the doctor. Knowing how much the Camp Director—a dedicated scout—liked Father, the doctor alerted him that the prognosis was bad unless some better medication than the usual remedies available for DPs could be found. Major Defise quickly obtained a supply of the marvelous new wonder drug, penicillin. Two or three days later, Father was sufficiently recovered to return to convalesce at home.

The outbreak of mumps in Blomberg spread with the speed of a hurricane. Some children had a terrible time of it, even ending up with meningitis. Apparently, the son of the woman who was to tell Mrs. Gailiūnas to look after me suddenly developed dangerous symptoms, and she completely forgot about the message.

I knew my daddy had gone to the clinic, but I expected him home soon. Night came, but not Father. In my fevered state, I did not have the presence of mind to go down the stairs to the second floor to find help, and I did not like to speak to the man who had the little loft room opposite ours. He was very tall and severe, and he scared me.

I am not sure if anyone realized that I had been left by myself. In those days, the only way to communicate among the DPs was face-to-face, in person. There was no telephone in the building. It is also possible that if the neighbors knew I had mumps, they might have avoided me intentionally, afraid to spread the illness to other children. Whatever the reason, nobody came to check on me.

I remember being very, very cold. I did not dare light a fire in our little stove to heat our winter garret: even Father had difficulties with it. On a shelf in our "cell," there was always a jug of water, usually some bread, a can or two of lunchmeat, and a few of cans of evaporated milk. I must have helped myself to something because I certainly did not starve. However, I was heartsick over Father. *Daddy, where are you?* I worried. What if he did not come back soon? Could he have died? What would I do if he did not return?

I probably slept a lot, but I remember sitting on the bed, wearing as many clothes as I could put on, including Father's suit coat, wrapped up in our two blankets, rocking back and forth for distraction and mentally singing to myself all the songs I knew. My fevered brain was not thinking rationally—I was terrified that I would die there alone, even though I knew every one of the other people who shared the house and were one short staircase away.

When, after three days, Father walked in through the door, I had hysterics from sheer happiness. He could not believe I had been left to cope alone while sick with mumps. He did not write to Mother about this episode, knowing she would never forgive him for failing to make sure, somehow, that I had care. I never told her either.

By Christmas we were both recovered and ready to celebrate. In autumn of 1947, German postal services had instituted "Registered Mail," which ensured that most of Mother's packages now reached us. This time, we had enough food, which Father obtained by bartering with the local Germans for the coffee, soap, and the two thermos flasks Milda and Mother had sent us. We even had a tiny Christmas tree in the back corner of our small table, decorated with angel hair that Milda had thoughtfully included in one of the packages.

1948 arrived. Early in the year, I turned eleven. And Mother sent me a doll! I had not reminded her, but once Father's health had stabilized, she recalled my parting plea. I loved the fact that this was a doll with a little girl's face, blue-eyed and brown-haired, wearing clothes lovingly crocheted by Mother's own hands. Her grey sweater, edged in blue, was a work of art. She was made of some metallic material, which made her unusually heavy. I named her "Lucia" in honor of the little girl in Fatima, Portugal, whose visions of the Blessed Virgin were described in a book I had just received as a gift for my Confirmation in the Catholic faith.

One would have thought that my obsession was finally satisfied and I was content. But when it came to dolls, I was a demanding critic, and this doll had shortcomings. Quality control was sadly lacking in the place of her manufacture, I thought. In a letter to Mother dated March 11, I wrote:

At first, the doll made a bad impression on me, but later, as I kept looking at her, I found her quite pretty. But facts are facts: you can't compare English-made toys with German. The English are not conscientious and don't pay attention to detail. When it was time to paint the doll, paint was slapped on just anyhow. On my doll, the paint for her lips is on her chin, the dots for the nostrils are on the tip of her nose, the eyebrows are high up in the middle of her forehead, and as for her hair—too much glued in one spot and half-bald in another. But the shape of her body is pleasing, and she can sit in a place of honor in a DP girl's home.

Mother and her co-workers found this critique hilarious. When we finally left Blomberg, I gave my Lucia to another doll-deprived little DP. I was a little puzzled at myself for parting with her so easily, but she was a cumbersome and heavy doll and I was hoping to find one more to my taste once we reached England.

As 1948 progressed, more people were transferred out of Blomberg, or departed to work in England or even Australia. Canada was asking for loggers and farm hands. By now, Father was strong enough, he thought, to work on a farm. The main topic of discussion in camp was where people would go and how soon. But talk was all we had: there was nothing on the horizon for families with children.

Our new administration at the International Refugee Organization appeared stumped, unable to find a way to resettle refugees with unproductive minors. In the meantime, at the start of the year, Major Defise, our old camp Director who had been easy-going and enthusiastically supported all our scouting activities, had retired. The new one, a prime example of a micromanaging, bean-counting bureaucrat, aroused immediate and universal dislike. Even from my tolerant and forgiving father.

It was the beginning of March, about three weeks before Easter. "*Po šimts velnių*—by the hundred devils!" exclaimed Father one afternoon, using an old Lithuanian curse. I looked up from my book to see him frowning, scanning one of a fistful of printed forms.

"What's happening?" I asked, alarmed. Father never swore.

"It's the new Director; he's sticking his long nose into everything," said Father, flinging the forms on the table.

"Are we in trouble?" I asked.

"*Tas rupūžėnas*—that toad wants to know if we DPs have any animals, and reminds us that keeping them is strictly forbidden."

"Oh, no," I cried, "will they take away our Whitey?"

A couple of weeks before, Father had exchanged another thermos flask sent by Mother for a young white hen. We called her *Baltukė*—Whitey. She was an excellent layer, giving us four or five eggs a week. She was very tame and undemanding. We kept her in the small, empty attic space next to our garret, where she could strut about freely. We covered the floor with newspapers to allow for easy cleaning. I brought fine gravel for her to scratch about and swallow to help her digestion. From a pile of shredded rags, she had made herself a warm nest into which we placed a chalk egg to encourage her to lay.

Spring was coming, and fresh grass and weeds were poking through the rough winter's thatch, so whenever the weather allowed, we tied Whitey up by her foot in the back yard, where she could peck away at the greens. Father dug up earthworms for her and treated her with great affection. He was not going to give her up.

"I'm not going to tell them a word about her," he declared. "If they find out and confiscate her, well, let them. They should be ashamed! They don't want to waste food on us, but won't let us try to feed ourselves." I had seldom seen him so upset. Fortunately for us, none of our neighbors squawked: Whitey continued to provide us with protein till the day we left Blomberg, when we passed her on to a family that had five children to feed. We knew they would treat her like royalty.

The new administration made Father very angry. In a letter to Mother, dated March 6, 1948, Father wrote:

> We're having a break in correspondence—this is the third week with no news of you. Perhaps it's a repeat of last summer, when the administration changed and everything disappeared into UNRRA's or DPAC's basket. Our new Camp Director is formulating reforms with the goal of avoiding any dealings with DP affairs. One exception: his kitchen. He can't find a permanent cook, because Mrs. Director not only has everything under lock and key, but also thoroughly frisks the poor wretch before she leaves....
>
> An envoy from the Director came to the house to deliver and explain the man's new regulations. First document: we have to show in writing where we obtained the furniture we're using. Did we buy it? From whom? Are we renting it? Second document: explain and sign if you have any domestic animals, and third, state if you have any foreign currency or gold. I did not list our Whitey; let them confiscate her.
>
> The war on our nerves continues, played to a Soviet tune. Our Gentlemen Guardians do not want to resemble the Soviets, but follow their prescription—never let people relax. It all begins again: will they move us—will they not move us— from here to Gostau, four kilometers (two-and-half miles) from the Soviet border? They seem to want all the DP camps

next to the Iron Curtain, to make it easy for the NKVD to abduct us and solve the messy problem of what to do with God's Little Birds. Our Guardians want to keep their hands clean. Their conscience is always clear. Whatever goes wrong, the blame is ours.

Father had his worries, but Mother too had something troubling her that she needed to discuss. It concerned Milda. But this time, the news was good: she had been invited to apply to nursing school!

It happened as follows:

Around Christmas of 1947, Milda, who had finished cleaning up in her own ward, went over to her friend Hilda's so they could walk back to the barracks together. The two of them were inseparable. Everyone confused their names.

Hilda was still mopping the kitchen floor, and Milda took up a broom to help sweep the corridor. But then, Milda spied an upright piano standing by the barrier that separated the two sides of the ward. "Hilda! Look! A piano," she said, all excited.

"Do you know how to play?" asked Hilda.

"Yes, some. I played a lot at home," said Milda.

"Play something," urged her friend.

It had been months since Milda had last played, in Blomberg, but her fingers flew into her favorite Strauss waltz, the Blue Danube. The patients who were strong enough sat up to listen, smiling. The nurses and the Staff Sister (the head nurse of the ward), who were meeting in the staff room, poked their heads out.

Milda noticed the Staff Sister watching and quickly closed the piano, but the patients clamored for her to continue, and the Sister told her to go ahead and play. When Milda finished the piece, the Sister asked where she had learned to play. "At home in Lithuania. We had a piano," said Milda, still anxious that perhaps she had broken a rule. She and Hilda fled back to the women's residence. "You made me do it, and now we'll be in trouble," grumbled Milda.

Sure enough, the next day, the two girls were summoned to Matron Sterlini's office. Milda and Hilda were literally quaking.

"What are your names?" the Matron asked, writing down the answers. "I heard one of you played the piano on the ward last night. Which one of you was it?"

"She did," yelped Hilda, pointing at Milda, who had turned bright pink.

"How is it that you know how to play a Strauss waltz?" asked the Matron, looking more curious than upset.

"I've been playing since I was little. We had a grand piano at home," explained Milda.

"You had a piano at home?" repeated the Matron, a bit astonished. It was most unusual for a maid to play classical music; in class-conscious England, maids did not get piano lessons.

She asked Milda and Hilda to sit down. Then, in a friendly manner, she had them describe their lives in Lithuania. She was clearly intrigued and also surprised, because at that time, Britons considered all "foreigners," but especially the stateless refugee DPs from Eastern Europe, as a bit primitive and lacking in refinement. And here she had two maids, the lowest rung on the employment ladder, who described living cultured lives.

Some of the Lithuanian "Cygnets" in Mount Vernon Hospital. Top row: Milda, 4th from left. Bottom row: Mother, 1st on left, Hilda, 3rd and Ms. Domeika at the end.

At the end of the interview, the Matron asked how they spent their time after work and what their hobbies were. Then she said, "Have you two considered going to nursing school? There is a severe shortage of nurses. Schooling, room, and board are provided free, and you are given a uniform. However, until the second year, your pay is only sixteen shillings a week."

Hilda knew she could not afford to give up her job at the hospital; she needed to help her parents and sisters, who were still in a DP camp in Germany. But my sister found the prospect appealing. The Matron told her to discuss it with the Ministry of Labor at the annual review of her contract.

The day following the conversation with Matron Sterlini, the piano from the ward was delivered to the maids' sitting room in the barracks, and a Ping-Pong table was installed in the storage room. Milda and Hilda had mentioned they used to play the game back in the DP camp. The other maids in the barracks, who had always felt that they were below anyone's notice, were amazed and very pleased.

In March 1948, Milda had a pre-scheduled appearance at the Ministry of Labor. It would decide whether to renew her contract, or cancel it when her year of service ended in April. After the committee had discussed her work record, Milda mentioned Matron's suggestion to attend nursing school. She asked the interviewers if they thought she would qualify as a candidate.

Mother wrote to Father on March 18, 1948:

When Milda asked about it, they answered, "We'll let you know soon by letter." Well, we thought, judging by the typically slow pace of decisions in England, half a year will go by. But only a few days passed and today we received a letter asking her to go to a certain office next Tuesday. Included was a ticket for the trip. Of course, they may reject her because her language may not be good enough…. The whole training takes four years. The pay is minimal. But she would have a profession; she would not need to scrub floors the rest of her life. Let me know at once what you think!

Father urged Mother to let Milda go to school: he believed that women should be able to lead independent lives. Milda did get accepted, and threw herself into her studies at Charing Cross Hospital. She soon had a circle of English friends, and her language skills improved tremendously.

As for Father and me, spring brought us no better prospects. He could get permission to work in England, but children were not included. The letters my parents exchanged show their deepening depression.

One day in early June 1948, Mother was washing the dinner dishes in her ward, crying silently to herself out of frustration about the impasse of our plight.

"What's wrong, Stasė?" came the cheerful voice of Jean Bell, the Staff Sister on the ward whom Mother liked very much.

Mother could speak enough English by then to communicate without a translator. "I will never see my child again!" wailed Mother. "My husband can come, but the Ministry of Labor does not allow children. So they are rotting in the DP camp and I can do nothing!"

"Can't you find her a foster home? That way, the Ministry of Labor would not consider her a problem. They don't have the personnel to deal with childcare."

"I have heard of this," said Mother, "but I don't know anybody with a home in England who could take her."

"Don't give up," said Jean. "I'll talk to my parents."

She was as good as her word. Returning from her next visit home, Jean greeted Mother, smiling broadly. "My parents want to meet you," she announced. "They want to discuss giving a home to your daughter."

Mother, overjoyed, dissolved in tears of gratitude. But when she did meet the Bells, her first reaction was uncertainty. Jean's father, a taciturn man, intimidated her. However, Jean's mother seemed as cheerful and easy-going as Jean herself. Before long, Mother and the Bells agreed on the cost of my support, filled out reams of paperwork, and sent it to the Ministry of Labor. We waited patiently for developments.

By mid-July, "the gates of our prison," as Father said, at long last swung open. The Camp Director sent word that a truck would come for us on July 25 to transport us to a transition camp for final medical reviews. And then a boat would take us to England. We could not believe that the wait was finally over.

Both Father and I found the transition camp thoroughly unsettling. I did not know a soul there, and there was nothing for a child to do but walk around the barracks, go to the communal kitchen for meals, then sit in our hot little room and just wait. We had packed away the few worldly goods Mother had advised us to bring to England. We had kept a change of clothing on hand and little else. There were no books to read.

I spent the time drawing and daydreaming and worrying about my life to come. I knew only a handful of English words from school. How would I communicate with my foster family? How would the students at school treat me? What if they decided to bully me: who would come to my aid when I could not even explain what was going on? I was exercising my inherited version of Mother's worry gene.

Father, in the meantime, was floundering blindly in bureaucratic Limbo. So many forms to fill out all over again. One doctor thought he was not well enough to immigrate as a laborer. Father managed to get an urgent appeal filed. The next doctor thought that he could manage janitorial duties at the hospital, which was the job he had waiting for him. Matron Sterlini had made sure that the Ministry of Labor would assign him to the same hospital as Mother.

The delays caused us to miss the boat we were supposed to take. Mother sent frantic telegrams. Finally, it was done: we had our permits. A military truck conveyed us to the port at Cuxhaven, where we boarded a small ship for the rolling, jarring, seasick crossing to our new home.

We were leaving the Displaced Person life behind us: God's Little Birds had taken wing.

CHAPTER 19:

Our New Home, England

Father and I arrived at the port of Harwich, England, early on Saturday, August 14, 1948. Mother and Milda were waiting impatiently for us to get through the interminable debarkation procedures, but by afternoon, we were together again, laughing and crying and unable to get our fill of one another. Mother kept saying to me, "I had no idea you could grow so fast! You're as tall as Milda!" Yes, I had shot up in height, thanks to her and Milda—thanks to the lifesaving packages they had sent us, every week, at the cost of sacrificing their own desires for our sakes.

Mother had saved all of her vacation days, and the Matron had given her permission to spend two weeks with Father and me. Milda had only the weekend, because she had internship training during the summer for her nursing school. As the ultimate treat, Mother had rented two connected rooms for two nights at a modest hotel. I thought I had fallen into the lap of luxury. I had forgotten, over the years since leaving our home in Vilnius, the simple pleasure of having a bathroom and toilet just for the four of us.

The hotel was within easy reach by Underground (the British subway) of Regent's Park, home of the London zoo. Our little family, united again, spent the entire Sunday meandering in the park, looking at animals I had only dreamed of seeing, and others I had never known existed. And I tasted my first ice cream. It was bliss.

I confided to Mother how worried I was about living with strangers whose language I did not understand. "The Bells are a bit frightening at first," Mother said, "but what generous people! You'll be fine. They arranged for us to stay for the next two weeks at the home of Mrs. Bell's sister, who went to spend August at some seaside resort. It's what the English do in August: they head to the beach."

"Are there more children, or only Jean?" I asked worriedly. I had visions of being pushed around by wicked stepsisters and made, like Cinderella, to work like a slave. "When do I have to go live with them?"

"We'll take you to the Bells on August 29," said Mother. "They have a son, who will be away at his university so you won't even see him, and also a daughter, Brenda. She is sixteen, Jean said, and wild about boys. She won't bother you."

I was not so sure. A little worm of anxiety gnawed away inside, even while the three of us spent happy days getting re-acquainted. Mother soon resumed bossing me around, but Father agreed that I had become sloppy with him as my caretaker. Mother said I needed to be very clean, very polite, and very obedient if I wanted the Bells to like me and keep me. Both Mother and Father stressed that if the Bells rejected me, it was likely the Ministry of Labor would send Father and me back to Germany, to who-knows-what camp.

Blomberg had definitely been scheduled to close by the end of the year. It was up to me now to ensure that we remained in England. The weight of that responsibility felt overwhelming. I distracted myself during the two weeks by learning to ride a bicycle that stood in the garage. And on a shopping outing, in a Woolworth store, I found a six-inch composition doll with moveable arms and real-looking hair that I could actually buy! During the coming lonely months, I sewed for her and knitted little outfits; I almost destroyed her from an excess of love.

And then, all too soon, our time together ended. Sunday, August 29, 1948, walking from the subway station at Hatch End toward my new home at 85 Sylvia Avenue, I tried hard not to cry, to be brave, to act grown-up. I was terrified. Even during the worst of our experiences since we left Lithuania, other than the few days when Father was in the hospital, I had always had at least one parent to cling to. And now that all four of us were in England, I was to live with strangers who had the power to ruin our lives if they did not like me.

Oh, I understood well enough why this had to be. After all, I was eleven-and-a-half, and life had walloped me with many hard lessons. Nonetheless, my heart was breaking from fear and anticipated loneliness. How I wished that my teacher in Blomberg had made me learn more English than to conjugate irregular verbs like "I am, you are, he–she–it is."

I saw by their faces that Mother and Father were worried too. Who knew how these proper Britons would treat me when no one was looking? Mother was very insistent that I behave properly and not "bring shame upon us," as she put it.

The closer we came to parting, the worse it got. Father's face was drawn tight. I realized that he was trying to encourage himself as well as me by repeating how bright I was and how quickly I would pick up English. He reminded me, over and over, that I was allowed to visit them at the hospital every weekend, that the most I had to make it on my own were five days at a time. To me—an eternity.

I was predisposed to fear, and the first view of my foster parents was not encouraging. Doris Bell seemed to tower over her husband, a giant Valkyrie—big bosoms, big around the middle, a cigarette dangling from her mouth, speaking with an accent that was so British even my mother could barely understand her. Fred Bell hardly said a word, but his high forehead, black, slicked-back hair, and nose pointing down to a chin that reached up toward it, showed, I thought, a cruel streak.

However, their gestures seemed kind enough. They escorted my parents and me around the house, indicated where I would sleep and where I could put away my small supply of clothes. I was given to understand that I should call them "Uncle Fred" and "Ahntie Doris." Repeat: Uncle Fred and Auntie Doris. Brenda, a well-developed young woman, looked bored with my arrival and barely said a word to us. And then my parents left. What was I to do next?

Later I wondered what Uncle Fred and Auntie Doris thought of this frightened, mute, gangly adolescent dropped into their safekeeping. Did they have qualms themselves? They had raised three children. Actually, raising me was not the problem—but making sure that this little foreigner learned to conform to British standards, that was the issue. To start with, they would show me the proper way to partake of the meal called "tea," served around 5 p.m.

My first tea, I still remember, had toast with sardines as the main offering, and the inevitable currant cake as dessert. I was used to eating in the European style—fork in left hand, knife in right, held thus throughout the meal. But sandwiches we just picked up in our hands. I reached for the toast. Oh dear, was that a major infraction.

Auntie Doris stood behind me, put the fork, tines facing down, into my left hand, then the knife, cutting side down, into the right, and instructed me to hold it like one holds a pencil. Then she showed me how to start at the corner of the toast and cut off a piece, place the knife down, transfer the fork into my right hand, spear the morsel, place my left hand on my lap, and then finally place the food in my mouth and chew with my teeth clenched tight. Or so it looked to me.

Brenda demonstrated how to hold the teacup just so—watch that little finger!—and how to stir the sugar into it by swishing with the teaspoon back and forth gently because one must not clink against the sides of the cup. She also showed me how to place the knife and fork, tines up, at the top of the plate to indicate I had done eating, and how to wipe my mouth properly with the cloth napkin and then fold it up again. I was scrutinized throughout the meal to make sure I did it right. I was close to tears with mortification.

That first evening, after tea, we took the dishes to the kitchen, I helped dry them, and then we went to the sitting room at the back of the house. It had French doors leading into the garden. The sunset had begun, but it was lingeringly bright. Uncle Fred beckoned me outside. He showed me his pride and joy, the neat rows of strawberries and vegetables and exotic-looking, smelly, large-leafed plants—tobacco. I noticed he always had a plain wood pipe with a gently bent stem clenched between his teeth.

He showed me the fruit trees at the very back of the property. Late-ripening plums still hung on one tree. Uncle Fred picked one for me. It tasted sweet and comforting. He took me to a snug, warm shed to show me his strings of drying tobacco leaves, indicating they were meant for his own pipe.

I had to repeat the names of everything just the way he said them. I noted all the special nooks where I could hide if I had to. I was fascinated by the miniature pond, made from a plugged-up bathtub sunk into the ground and overgrown with waterweeds, around which small newts were catching the last of the day's sun. It reminded me of a toy, a perfect playground for my new little doll, and made me think for the first time that I might like it there.

The Bells spent their evenings in the sitting room, which had a coal fireplace, and in which pride of place went to the imposing console radio around which the family's life revolved. Sport broadcasts were a favorite.

The first night I was there, Brenda demonstrated what was, to me, a new technology: the phonograph. The turntable was inside a lidded cabinet, and on the right, there hung a long side handle that had to be wound up every two minutes or so to maintain turning speed. I giggled as it slowly ground to a halt, the melody descending from high notes to a mumbling bass.

Brenda had only a handful of records that she liked to play. Her favorites, both imports from America, were "Mairzy dohts an dozy dohts" (Mares eat oats and does eat oats) and "East is East, and West is West, and the wrong one I have chose." The first song I never did understand, and from the second I picked up some rather doubtful grammar.

Was it on the first evening or the second that something completely unexpected won for me the Bells' admiration and even affection? Brenda was probably out with friends, because there were just Uncle Fred, smoking his stinking tobacco and reading the newspaper while listening to something on the radio, Auntie Doris looking with disgust at a large basket full of wool thread and socks, and me, observing them and paging uncomprehendingly through a children's book Brenda had loaned me.

Auntie Doris chose one of Uncle Fred's socks and slid it onto a wooden darning egg, revealing a big hole worn in the heel. She threaded a needle, lit a cigarette—which never left the corner of her mouth—and proceeded to torment the sock in a most violent manner. Clearly she detested darning, but clothing was still on rationing in 1948. Undoubtedly, the Bells were short of coupons, and buying new socks was not an option.

"What is she doing?" I asked myself. She was using the wrong color and thickness of thread, and was just pulling the sides of the hole together with no thought for the wear in the underlying material of the sock, and certainly no concern for the beauty of the thing. I debated with myself for a minute, then dared to tap Auntie Doris on the arm and say, "Please, I do"—the extent of my English.

I still recall the look of incredulity on both their faces. However, Auntie Doris handed me the sock and watched with curiosity what I would do. The first thing—I undid her work! Then I picked out a more appropriate thread, settled the sock in the right position on the wooden egg, examined the extent of the hole and the weakness or strength of the surrounding material, and proceeded to rapidly weave a work of art, a miniature tapestry of thread. I noticed, as I was coming toward the end, that my audience was so engrossed in my fingers that they were almost holding their breath.

When I finished, they both applauded. Auntie Doris smothered me in a huge hug, which surprised me no end because I had heard that

Northern Europeans hugged only their children, and the frosty British? Nevah! She then disappeared into the hallway to make an excited telephone call to someone. I heard "Dalia" mentioned. Uncle Fred nodded at me approvingly and said, "Good, very good," then went back to his reading and his radio.

Auntie Doris came back, picked up the basket, and handed it to me almost ceremoniously. "You do!" she said, smiling so wide that the cigarette almost fell out of her mouth. I was thrilled: I had something to do that I knew I excelled in.

Thank God for my DP camp training. I became an asset to the Bells, and it endeared me to them. I enjoyed the evenings when, after finishing my homework, I would darn their socks, repair loose seams, fix hems in fraying sheets, create admirable buttonholes, and sew on snaps and buttons.

One day, I noticed how unhappy Uncle Fred looked. He and Auntie Doris were examining his favorite jacket, which had suffered a highly visible burn right in front, where a cinder from his pipe had landed. I didn't yet understand much of what was said, but I saw that, against his objections, Auntie Doris put the jacket into the ragbag.

The next day, immediately on returning from school, while I had the house to myself, I rescued the jacket and examined the damage. It would be a challenge to fix, but I thought it was worth a try.

Fortunately, the pre-war tweed wool was of prime quality, and I was able to cut a large enough patch out of the inner hem not only to cover the hole, but also to match the pattern. I thought that Mrs. Tamulaitis, my sewing teacher from DP camp, would have given me the topmost grade had she seen the result. The patch was invisible, unless you knew where to look from up close. I hung the jacket on the back of Uncle Fred's chair.

"What's this?" he said on seeing his old jacket resurrected. I was grinning ear-to-ear, prouder than a hen that had laid a goose-sized egg. He wore glasses, and his vision was probably impaired, but he could not find where the hole had been. He was enormously pleased, and for days would smilingly ask me, "How did you do that?" My training in the DP camp had finally found its reward.

My new home consisted of a small, pebbledash duplex with a one-car garage, located in the northwest suburbs of London. It had been constructed before World War II to house the middle class. Tea was served in the front room facing the street. In addition to the table and chairs, the room contained a couple of bookshelves which held, among other attractions, many unbound sections of the Encyclopedia Britannica, dating from the early twentieth century, replete with the most wonderful illustrations of every imaginable thing from horse breeds to medieval catapults. What a delightful way to learn vocabulary!

This room became the place where I sweated over homework, tried to understand my lessons, memorized in their entirety incomprehensible paragraphs so I could write them down verbatim on tests, and labored endlessly, at Auntie Doris's urging, to look everything up in the dictionary. To me, unraveling word definitions was pure futility: unknown words defined by words I did not know. Quite a challenge, but fortunately, nobody had told me it was impossible, and so—I learned.

My arrival at the Bell's coincided with my body's urge to transform into a woman. I was always hungry. I ate just two meals a day with the Bells, as lunch was provided at school. Breakfast consisted of toast with marmalade, and tea with milk and sugar. School lunches were minimal, usually a limp sandwich with mysterious filling, and "fish eyes" for dessert. Tapioca did look unappetizing, but my stomach would be growling so I ate my portion eagerly.

By the time I got back to the house, I was starving again. Food was still rationed and limited, but Auntie Doris took pity on me and always gave me a small snack of bread and cheese before I sequestered myself with my homework. Teatime provided more toast, served with something substantial like baked beans, or fish (canned or fried), and occasionally canned meat—something resembling the Spam we ate in the DP camps. The garden in the back of the house provided vegetables and fruit in season. And always, there was a slice of cake for dessert.

At first, bedtime for me was 8 p.m. The Bells had put me into the back bedroom, which I was to share with Brenda. However, I had it to myself because Brenda preferred to sleep alone in her brother's room while he was at the University. It was quieter there, she said, but I suspect she was not at all pleased to have a roommate. I grew to love the way the evening light shone through the airy curtains in the bedroom, casting a rosy glow over all the furniture and Brenda's knick-knacks.

The back garden ran down to numerous railroad tracks leading north from London. Close by were rail car cleaning yards, coupling and uncoupling wagons for washing late into the night. The first two weeks I could hardly sleep for the noise, but eventually the banging transformed into a percussion lullaby.

In the garage stood Uncle Fred's beloved 1920s-era Model T Ford. He had acquired it after returning home from the Middle East conflicts, where he had served around 1917–1920. He had loved the desert. Most English homes are given names by their owners: Uncle Fred had called his GAZA. He told me to look it up in the Encyclopedia. The article did not mention anything about the years he was there—the Encyclopedia pre-dated the period—but it was my first introduction to a part of the world I knew nothing about. The Bells were always opening new vistas before me. I was a curious child, and looked forward each day to any interesting bit of knowledge I would find.

In truth, I came to love the Bells dearly, even the distant Brenda, who might have resented me but never gave me a moment's pain. I never forgot that Uncle Fred and Auntie Doris did not owe me love and affection, but showed it out of sheer kindness. I was sincerely grateful. Once they had concluded that I was trainable and a quick study, they became my cheering section. I would overhear Auntie Doris on the telephone, boasting to her friends about Dalia's accomplishments: "Imagine, she came in at the top of her class, only eight months after coming to England!"

I focus on the Bells because their support meant everything to me. My start in school was sheer misery. Because I understood so little English, during the first week of school I inadvertently became a pariah. When a group of girls asked me, "Where do you come from?" I thought they meant which country was the one I had departed from to come to England. I made the mistake of answering, "From Germany." Had I known more about the London Blitz and the suffering my schoolmates had experienced during the war years, I might have erased the word "Germany" from my vocabulary.

My response was greeted with jeers and taunts, "Nazi! Kraut! Hun!"—words which at first I did not even understand, other than "Nazi." Teachers, as well as children, tormented me on the sly, by tearing my homework, swiping my pen or my gloves, and tripping me up as I went by.

My worst fears of bullying were coming true, though British rectitude stopped everyone short of inflicting real physical damage. My reaction was to retreat into my shell and focus obsessively on school-work. I lived for the weekends, when I could vent my woes to my parents.

During the first few months with the Bells, every Friday afternoon, as I boarded the train for my weekend visit with Mother and Father, I felt like a bird flying out of a cage. I had the whole weekend to be myself: whiny, untidy—imperfect. Mother might scold, but it did not matter because my parents would not throw me out if I displeased them.

I slept with Mother in the women's barracks; Father lived in a residence for men only. Sometimes both had to work either Saturday or Sunday, but we spent as much time together as we could. Food was plentiful. Special allocations had been made for cancer patients, who needed a better diet, and ample amounts of food were delivered to the wards. However, the sick patients lacked appetites. Rather than waste the food that remained, the staff were allowed to take what they wanted.

Father, whose job as a "porter" meant wheeling non-ambulatory patients to their appointments, was gaining weight rapidly on the left-overs from Mother's ward. There was enough even for my appetite. The two days I had with my parents went by like one minute, and every Sunday night, when I had to return to Hatch End, saw me in tears.

The Bells had enrolled me in the Headstone County Secondary School in Pinner. At first I was placed in the lowest section, Form 1D, the first year of the British secondary school system in effect at that time. Within two weeks, the administration transferred me to section 1C. Even though I still spoke very little English, I did well on all arith-metic problems, I memorized the spellings of words without difficulty, and I excelled in beginners' French, which I found easy.

At the end of the Autumn Term, I was promoted to section 1B. On my report card, the principal, Mr. Manson, wrote, "I hope Dalia will justify her promotion." I was determined, and I was very, very lucky, because in 1B, our Form Master was Maurice Watling. He chose to take an interest in me: as a result, I simply blossomed. My report card at the end of the spring term shows that I was the best student in Form 1B.

Mr. Watling took the time to ask about my background. He had been through the war, and knew all about the history of the Baltic

States, the Nazi occupation, and the 1944 return of the Soviets into those ravaged lands. He kept me talking after school until he had my story in full. By then, my vocabulary had grown.

I confessed to Mr. Watling that many in school thought I was a little German Nazi, and treated me accordingly. He was incensed. Thanks to his efforts, my schoolmates soon viewed me, not as a nasty Nazi, but as one of Hitler's victims—as was everyone else in England. Girls started to invite me to play and be friends.

One of my worst tormentors, Rita Parsons, became my dearest friend. Her baby brother had died because of the bombings during the Blitz, she explained, which is why she had taken revenge on me when she thought I was German. Rita and I were as compatible, and grew as close, as two twelve-year-olds can be. Rita never walked: she rode her bicycle and did so with such expertise I thought she had been born astride it.

After school, we would go to her house, I on foot, she on her bike. Then, if allowed, we would invade Rita's neighbor's house. They had acquired a tiny television set, which to us was a miracle of modern invention. Because the screen was so small, the neighbor had attached a big magnifying glass in front to make the picture look bigger. It also distorted it, but to us, it did not matter. Programming in England was in its infancy; to fill airtime, the BBC sometimes showed imported American cowboy series. Rita adored Hopalong Cassidy, and I—Roy Rogers.

By the spring of 1949, I no longer wanted to spend two entire week-end days with my parents—I no longer had a need to complain and be comforted. And I also had no more need to play with my little doll.

Friday after school, I would come to Rita's home, and leave to see my parents late on Saturday afternoon. Rita and I were never bored. On Saturday mornings, we joined a hundred or more noisy youngsters at a special children's matinee sponsored by the "ABC Cinemas." The program always included cartoons and two cliff-hanging serials. One was invariably a cowboy segment, plus some other such as Tarzan. We each had a blue club card and a special song to sing, identifying us as "The Minors of ABC." It was pure, unadulterated fun.

In fact, I was having too much fun. In the spring of 1949, the Headmaster had promoted me from Form 1B to the top section—1A. At the end of the trimester, my rank was number eighteen out of the nineteen students in class. I was mortified. I could not face my parents. I vowed to never fall so low again.

When school resumed in the autumn, before Rita and I started to play, I insisted on finishing my homework first. Rita's parents welcomed me to their home, because my focus on completing schoolwork resulted in Rita's grades going up as well. She was incredibly smart, but unless motivated, she was not interested in following through on her assignments.

Living immersed in English all my waking hours, six days a week, resulted in rapid competence. By my twelfth birthday, I communicated easily, though my vocabulary still had miles of room to grow. My parents were proud of me, and discussed my future in glowing terms. I would definitely go to the university, they told me.

In fact, it became routine for them to rely on me for translation services, and also for "path finding." If Father wanted to go to the Tate Gallery or the Covent Garden Opera, or Mother to find a market where clothing was sold without coupons, they asked me to do a preliminary test run to map out the route.

After my initial, anxious explorations ended successfully, I developed self-confidence and looked forward to the challenge of asking for directions and traveling alone on the Underground or on swaying double-decker buses. I made notes of the specific lines, numbers, and the exact street locations of the stops where Mother or Father would need to change buses or get off once they reached their desired destination. I even purchased the opera tickets ahead of time.

It was wonderful freedom and heady independence for me, but there were a few times when I was followed by men who seemed very strange to me and spoke incomprehensible stuff, and once a boy on a bicycle almost snatched my purse out of my hands. In 1949, however, it was still considered perfectly normal to let naïve adolescent girls meander alone and unsupervised all over London.

I was thriving, and so was my sister. Milda continued her training to become a "sister" in nursing. She was proud of her uniform. She had a devoted friend, a fellow student, who often invited Milda to stay with her and her widowed mother in a suburb of London. Joyce Dawes was a very good influence, and introduced my sister to the British way of looking at things—which included betting on horses! Because she almost always won something, sometimes more than doubling her student nurse's pay, a bit of gambling became a mild habit for Milda.

In 1949, Milda had two Lithuanian boyfriends, both of whom were "getting serious." Mother rejected one of them as insufficiently cultured and educated, and the other because he was "too short." Milda was upset, but not heartbroken. In any case, she thought, the following year she would turn twenty-one and be able to do as she pleased.

Summer, 1949. Mother reveled in her assignment to the Manor House.

The Matron of Mount Vernon Hospital became quite fond of the Lithuanians on her staff. They were reliable and responsible and worked harder than anyone else. Also, they were Roman Catholic, as was she. In the spring of 1949, she offered Mother an unheard-of promotion for a foreigner: to be the Head Housekeeper for the Manor House, a beautiful Victorian building nestled among two or three acres of lawns, gardens, and fountains.

The hospital used the Manor House as a quiet residence for the night nurses to sleep in during the day. If Mother accepted, she and Father could at long last share private quarters together. Although anxious about her new responsibilities, Mother said "yes." At her request, two other Lithuanians were assigned to join her as cook and assistant: one of these was Milda's best friend Hilda. Mother and Father had a big sunny room, and, for more than a year, thought they had returned to Paradise. Alas, an evil spirit invaded it.

Mother could not bear micromanagement or criticism. During her year as Head Housekeeper, she got used to being the boss. The Manor was a showplace under her management, and everyone was happy.

1950. Father, Mother and I at Jean Bell's wedding reception. Uncle Fred is visible between Mother and me; Auntie Doris enjoys a sip at far right.

Then, in early 1950, there arrived a Senior Staff Sister who decided that her duties included complete control not only of the night nurses, but also of the cooks and the housekeepers. She was a hard-as-nails, redheaded Scot, impossible to understand or to please. Worse yet, she had a spoiled angora cat that shed everywhere and did not confine its messes to the litter box. Mother was miserable and in tears every day. When Mother was upset, Father had no peace.

Also early in 1950, the Bells regretfully told my parents that their son was returning home from the university in June and they would not be able to keep me beyond the end of the school year. Rita's parents, the Parsons, asked me to move in with them. I was thrilled! I loved Rita as a sister. I also loved and admired my sister Milda, but she was much older, and our interests at that age had grown very far apart. Rita and I were same age, as compatible as tea and crumpets. I was looking forward to living with a "twin." But it was not to be.

Mother had fulfilled her two-year work contract and was free to leave the hospital at any time. Father's contract ended in mid-August. Some friends from the Blomberg DP camp had settled in and around Manchester, and wrote that there were plenty of jobs and a large number of other Lithuanians in the area. Mother could not wait to escape from the Staff Sister, that "*prakeikta gyvatė*—accursed snake."

The day after Father's contract ended, we were on a train to Manchester. Milda did not like to be so far from Mother, but also felt somewhat relieved that she would be less strictly supervised. As for me, separation from Rita was so painful that I mourned for weeks.

CHAPTER 20:

We Find Our Permanent Haven

The Matron had written fine recommendations for both my parents. Father immediately found employment as a "hospital orderly" in a Manchester hospital, and a textile factory hired Mother. Their salaries were distressingly small.

We found a place to live in Salford, a drab, sooty neighborhood in the greater Manchester area. We rented one room in a house shared with four other former DP families. So what if "home" was one pitiful room and we had to scrimp? Initially, Mother and Father felt liberated—finally they were free to make their own decisions. Their "indentured servitude" had ended. They were optimistic.

There was, however, an ominous cloud on my horizon. Neither my parents nor I had any understanding of the British system of education, which, during the years we were there, 1948–1952, was unfair and restrictive. There were only two possibilities for children past age eleven: attendance at a secondary school or a grammar school. A secondary school did not prepare its students to pursue a higher level of studies and achieve a profession. The keys to a university education were guarded by grammar schools.

To get into a grammar school, one had to pass a series of tests, which were known among the students as "Scholarship Exams." Apparently, only eleven- and twelve-year-olds were eligible to take them. When these tests were administered to us in Headstone Secondary School in 1949, I had been in England only seven months.

I did not pass. My language skills in English were not sufficiently developed, and worst of all, I—who had been raised on the crystal-clear metric system—was still floundering with farthings, penny-ha'pennies, thruppences, florins, crowns, half crowns, and guineas, not to mention feet, yards, furlongs, and on and on. The school administration made no effort to prepare us for the exam, not even to tell us what areas would be covered. From all those in Headstone School who took the exam, only a handful passed.

In early 1950, when the examinations were administered again, I missed them because I was sick with bronchitis. It never occurred to my parents, or to my foster-parents, to inquire if there was a make-up test.

When school started in September 1950, Mother registered me at the secondary school closest to our residence in Salford. She left me with the Head Master and hurried off to her job. I showed him the reports of my courses and grades from Headstone Secondary. He studied the sheets, frowning, then looked at me with distaste and said, "What were they doing teaching you French in a secondary school? And art? Did they think you could go to the university from a secondary school? Waste of effort. Here, you will take typing and shorthand. We prepare you for a trade and you're done at sixteen. This is not a grammar school," he concluded, almost sneering.

He had someone conduct me to a classroom where a math lesson was in progress. The teacher was covering material I had done years earlier. One puny boy could not seem to get the right answer so the teacher told him to hold out his palm and prepared to whack it with a ruler. When the boy instinctively drew it back, the teacher held his arm in a tight grip and whacked him hard, twice. Others in the class snickered. The child was in tears, blowing on his hand. I was appalled.

After math came English, featuring the spelling of words I had learned long ago. Next, we girls had a double-length class drilling in shorthand. This school taught the "Pitman" system, which uses thick and thin strokes to distinguish related sounds. Because this was the first day for all of us, I found it easy to catch on.

After a tasteless lunch, came typing. The typewriters had seen too much use; many keys were stubbornly sticking, and the ribbons were almost worn out. The noise level in the room drove me to distraction. The last class was British history and geography on topics that I had already covered at Headstone. That made me happy, however, because by then I was exhausted and appreciated a mental rest.

I had lost the habit of confiding in my parents. During the previous year, Auntie Doris had been my main source of information and advice. Mother had not even alerted me to the female monthly periods: it had been Auntie Doris who had reassured me I was not dying and had shown me what to do. Now I dithered.

I knew my parents were determined to send me to university, but the Head Master said it was not possible from a secondary school. Did they understand that? Was the "Scholarship Exam" I had failed in 1949 the only chance I would ever get? I did not want to be a secretary; I daydreamed of studying at Cambridge.

Above all, I feared being punished in public. I could not imagine having to hold out my hand in front of forty prying classmates and have them laugh if I cried out. It made my stomach cramp with anxiety.

And yet I hesitated to dump my fears on Mother and Father. If I told them how awful this school was, what could they do? They had hard, tiring jobs, and so many other worries—like food. Again. Always problems with food! Rationing was still in effect. Now that they were no longer receiving meals as part of their work, they had to obtain food coupons, register with a grocer, and try to figure out how to plan meals from the items and quantities available. Of course, one could buy many things without coupons, like sausages or privately raised poultry, but such items cost too much for us.

I wanted to spare my parents another worry, but my resolve did not last long. My typing instructor had taken an instant dislike to me, and though she did not hit me, she picked on me constantly, and belittled me every chance she got. I became all thumbs. I thought that hell could not be more excruciating. After the second week of school, when the weekend came, I broke down and told Mother and Father the whole, unpleasant tale.

They were in shock. Father later said, "We had to get you out of that school. We could not imagine that the only future for our child was a typing job at sixteen. We had to do something. But whom could we ask for intelligent advice? We did not trust former DP immigrants to have the right information."

Someone suggested that my parents talk to the local Lithuanian priest, who had lived in England since before the war. If he did not know the answers, he would know someone reliable who did. That very Sunday, my parents poured out their worries to him. The priest explained the educational system to them and gave them a glimmer of hope.

Apparently, private and religious schools, which prepared students for university-level studies, could enroll whomever they chose. They were not limited to accepting only those who had passed the

"Scholarship Exams." As it happened, he was the chaplain for an order of nuns, the Sisters of Notre Dame de Nemours, who ran a Catholic high school. He said he would talk to the Headmistress, Sister Mary, and see if she would consider accepting me. Of course, there were costs to consider, and my parents earned very little.

Sister Mary was not about to welcome me with open arms, but to give respectful consideration to the wishes of priests was, for nuns, an ingrained trait. She said she had to interview me first. The student body was composed of native English and Irish girls. How would a Lithuanian refugee fit in? In addition, she had to make sure I could meet the high educational standards of the school. She told the priest to bring me the following Saturday to meet her, and to take some tests which she would prepare.

I spent another terrified week in my miserable school, simmering in a stew of anxiety. If the following Saturday I did not satisfy Sister Mary, I would be condemned to remain for years in my present hell-hole, unable ever to reach my dream of an education.

Friday evening, seeing my distress, my parents took pity on me. They sat me down and told me to relax, that even if I did not please Sister Mary, they would not let me rot in a school I hated. They said I could go back to Headstone Secondary School and live with my dear friend Rita, whose affectionate parents continued to offer me a home with them. What a delightful prospect! Suddenly, all fear left me. Sister Mary was no longer the ultimate judge who would save me or condemn me.

When I met Sister Mary, I was at ease, and the interview went well. For the test, I was placed alone in a warm, sunny classroom. A young nun, Sister Julia, explained how to complete the test, showed me where to find the bathroom, then brought me a glass of milk and some short-bread. She said she would be back to pick up my answers in two hours. I thought the test was quite easy. I finished well ahead of the deadline and had plenty of time to check all my answers.

I was accepted! Mother bought me the school uniform: a dark green jumper and cream-colored blouse, and a green-and-gold striped tie. There were thirty-seven girls in the class, at least half speaking with a definite Irish brogue. In age, we were all about thirteen, but in physical development, we ran the gamut. A few, including me, had already reached our final heights and were developing womanly curves, while others were still skinny and short, as if adolescence had not yet found them.

When I arrived, Sister Mary introduced me as a "foreign refugee from the continent," and with the Form Mistress, selected a seat for me in the back of the room. The other girls were not unfriendly, but neither did they extend an instant welcome. I was in no hurry either because my focus was elsewhere.

I had to catch up on almost three weeks of schoolwork, including Latin and music theory. I did not mind. A happy refrain sang in my mind: *No more typing!* I was so relieved and grateful that I resolved to be the best student they had ever seen, and to show Sister Mary that she need not regret her decision to accept me.

End-of-term tests in all subjects were administered in December. When the grades were tallied, I was declared "first in her class." I thought, *Sister Mary will be so pleased!* The tradition in British schools was for the Head Master or Mistress to honor the top student in each class by hanging a small medal on a chain around the neck, and then to make a little congratulatory speech and to ask the class to applaud. I had been through such a ceremony twice at Headstone Secondary, and—to be honest—was looking forward to a little praise.

The day for recognition came. "Congratulations, Dalia. You did well. Now go sit down," said Sister Mary, hanging the medal around my neck. Was this to be all? I was crestfallen.

"As for you," continued Sister Mary sweeping her eyes and hand around the room at my classmates, "all I can say is that I am thoroughly ashamed of every last one of you. Where is your pride? How could you let a foreigner, a refugee, take the honors from you? You, all born in Great Britain! I will expect a different outcome at the end of the next term." With that, she marched out of the room, slamming the door.

Everyone was silent. I barely dared to lift my eyes. But when I did, I saw many of my classmates grinning at me conspiratorially, as though I had pulled off some splendid trick. It was the first time I experienced disdain for authority. It made up for my wounded pride.

Naturally, I was hurt, and determined I would not be unseated from the top spot. *I'll show them!* I promised myself. I remained number one in my class during the four terms I was there.

It helped that I had an amazing memory during those early teen years. I remember playing a game to test myself: I would listen to my history teacher without taking a note, then write down verbatim what she had said when I returned home. Although I had not inherited Father's photographic memory, I came close to perfect auditory recall.

In the winter of 1950, my father started mentioning the possibility of emigration to the Land of Gold, to America. The United States. The ultimate daydream for the great majority of Displaced Persons. Mother still had her doubts. She could never forget or forgive the way the U.S. soldiers in Germany had treated us immediately at the war's end. Because of the actions of the few, she was convinced the entire nation was composed of robbers and ignorant dolts.

Mother had tried to persuade Father to go to Brazil, or even Australia, but by 1950 stories had reached the Lithuanians in England of the primitive conditions in Brazil and the hardships in the outback of Australia. Maybe the U.S. would not be so bad. She had heard that food, at least, was plentiful, and there was no rationing of any kind. The American films we went to see showed abundance everywhere. She began to soften.

One thing was certain: Mother absolutely did not want to remain in England. What an impoverished country, where you still needed coupons to buy food five years after the war! Besides, she could see no possibility of a better future for herself or Father. Her job at the factory was both stressful and boring, with no hope of advancement.

And Father? Was he to remain an orderly, barely a notch above a janitor, for the rest of his life? No matter that he found the work undemanding, his fellow employees congenial, and was Mr. Popularity at the hospital. He was not full of pride or self-importance, but Mother thought his job demeaned him.

Between them, they earned so little that it took dedicated scrimping to pay for my school and—at last—for rent in a better location. We now had two rooms in a row house on Fraser Street in Crumpsall. We shared the kitchen and bathroom with the bachelor owner of the house and another couple, all DP Lithuanians.

Worst of all, in Mother's mind, was the fate awaiting me, Dalia. The British saw themselves as more deserving than "foreigners." Job applications for better positions required listing not only your own citizenship and place of birth, but also your parents' and grandparents'.

Mother was convinced that even if I managed to complete higher studies, the best I could hope for was a position in a slum. "They are bigots; you will never be equal in their eyes," she told me, "no matter how you try." Remembering how Sister Mary had reacted when I came in at the head of my class at Notre Dame High School, I could not disagree.

The United States had been among the last to open its doors to refugees of the war. Until Congress passed the first Displaced Person Act on June 25, 1948, only a very limited number of immigrants from Eastern Europe were admitted, based on quotas established well before World War II. The Act of 1948 proposed to admit 200,000 persons outside the quota system. Realizing that this number was insufficient, in June of 1950, Congress had increased the number by an additional 200,000. There were conditions. DPs who remained in camps in Germany would receive priority. Refugees who had emigrated from their camps would qualify only if they applied for a U.S. visa within three years after leaving Germany. Mother and Milda had come to England in April of 1947, and were disqualified from applying, but Father could do so until August of 1951.

Another condition in the DP Act mandated that immigrants find an official sponsor of sufficient means to guarantee that they would have support and a place to live. Nobody in the U.S. wanted new immigrants on public assistance.

Mother's nephew, Vytas (the one who gave me the ugly doll in Blomberg), was already in the United States, as was Father's brother Karolis. Neither was as yet earning enough to sponsor us. There were also friends in and around Chicago and Cleveland, all new immigrants themselves. I sensed that my parents did not know which way to turn. They were constantly writing letters and asking around for advice from their Lithuanian friends both in the U.S. and in England.

As long as I did not think too far into the future, I was content. My life bustled with activities both amongst my English classmates and among the Lithuanian immigrants.

By 1951, there were many Lithuanians in the Manchester area. Some wise person had suggested years previously that all of them contribute to a fund to buy property and establish their own club. A marvelous idea! The old Victorian house they had bought needed innumerable repairs, but there were rooms for meetings, a large kitchen, a small private "pub," and extensive grounds for outdoor events such as scout gatherings and weddings.

A great number of young bachelors had come to work in the coal-mines in the greater Manchester area. On weekends, the club formed the hub of their social life. Men and women volunteers also worked on repairs both inside and out.

Soon there were lectures and performances of all kinds. Someone started a newsletter. Father immediately found other adults interested in launching a scouting program for us youngsters who were in danger of losing our Lithuanian culture. I found several girls my age with whom to share teen thoughts and longings. Forget dolls: there were teenage boys to think about. I had a secret crush on one, but his attention was focused on "older" teens, who were less naïve and timid. And prettier.

When Milda came to visit us for a short vacation in February of 1951, she became the instant darling of the bachelor set. One hand-some fellow, Petras Klezas, made up his mind she would be his. Petras had gorgeous blue eyes with long, thick eyelashes and an irresistible dimple in his chin. He had "the gift of gab" and could woo your ears off with sweet talk.

Mother insisted Milda could do better, that she did not see her daughter as the wife of a coal miner. She acknowledged, however, that it was not Petras' fault that he lacked an education: he had been yanked out of high school in Lithuania to work in Hitler's factories, the same as thousands of other young DPs now tunneling underground in England's mines. In any event, Petras was not to be deterred.

Because Milda continued to rely on Mother's opinion, I am sure that eventually she would have prevailed in discouraging the romance, but early in March, 1951, our prospects for reaching America sud-denly changed. Our old friend from Vilnius, the very capable Mrs. Zailskas (whose successful bartering for food during Nazi times had so impressed us), wrote back from Cicero, Illinois, that she had found us a sponsor. If we were serious about coming, Mrs. Zailskas would advance her the money to pay for filing all the paperwork in the U.S. to guarantee our support.

Father wasted no time in applying for immigration on behalf of all four of us. "It did not occur to me," he said, "that Milda would not be considered part of the family just because she was over twenty-one years old. When the staff at the American Consulate in Liverpool in-formed me that she was ineligible to immigrate with us, I was in shock. And Milda went into a complete panic."

My sister had not achieved full independence from Mother. She could not imagine how she would know what to do without asking Mother's opinion or discussing important decisions with Father. If we moved to the States, she would not even be able to talk to us. Telephone calls overseas were exorbitantly expensive.

After much talk, encouragement, and advice from our parents, Milda decided that she would stay to finish her nursing studies, and then immigrate to Canada, where several of her friends from the DP camp in Blomberg had settled. She would be reasonably close to us— on the same continent, at least! But she had a year of schooling and an internship left to complete, and the frightening prospect of remaining in England alone demoralized her.

Milda was insecure. Petras saw his opportunity and swooped in with masculine self-assurance. He spoke glowingly and volubly of the excellent, devoted care he would provide her in our absence. Father had severe reservations about Petras—he thought the man's words did not match his actions. But Petras must have sensed that it was Mother who held the power over Milda. He proceeded to court Mother with effusive letters, compliments, flowers, and candy. A couple of months of assiduous campaigning, and Mother gave up her objections: "Whatever Milda wants," she said.

A point in his favor was that he, too, wanted to move to Canada, and spoke of studying once he could afford it. By May, Petras and Milda were officially engaged. And despite Mother's remaining qualms and Father's reluctance, on August 18, 1951, they were married.

Our parents borrowed from friends and scraped together all they had saved to give Milda a small but "well-watered" wedding reception at the Lithuanian club. I was one of the bridesmaids, and got thoroughly tipsy at the party—the sly bachelors amused themselves spiking my lemonade with vodka.

After the wedding, Milda, with relief, gave up her nursing studies to be a housewife. Shortly before, she had been thoroughly spooked when a patient she had tended died on the operating table during a routine surgery. The surgeon's hand had slipped and the patient bled out. She had never seen a person die in front of her eyes. She had a hard time getting over it.

As mischance would have it, Milda got pregnant on the first night of the honeymoon. Petras, the responsible party, was furious and blamed her. He was not ready for parental responsibilities. Everyone feared her condition would complicate their plans for going to Canada, but their application for a visa was immediately accepted. In late December 1951, they were on a boat heading to Montreal, just ahead of our own departure.

Wedding party and guests at the Lithuanian club in Manchester.

Father worried about Milda, though Mother tried to believe that things would work out. "Promise me you won't rush into marriage," Father said to me. "You must have a way to earn your own living. When you're totally dependent on a man to support you, you give him too much power. He starts to believe he owns you. He's tempted to treat you like a slave. I've seen it happen too often. Promise you'll become independent first." It was easy for me to promise: I was only fourteen, I liked studying, and besides, I was not in love.

It took my parents many months to complete the paperwork to receive immigration visas for the U.S. My father was brilliant in certain endeavors, but obtaining and organizing practical things such as piles of official documentation was not his strong suit. Mother would not get involved at all: this was man's work.

Especially time-consuming were the usual medical tests. Father's need for B12 shots, a newer medication for pernicious anemia, caused concern and delay. Also, we needed official international passports.

My parents still had their Lithuanian *vidaus pasai*—internal identification documents from before World War II—but they were outdated and not acceptable for immigration.

Because Lithuania was off the map, now simply a part of Soviet Union, the only entity which could issue an international passport for its citizens was the leftover pre-World War II "Lithuanian Legation" in London. Both the British and the Americans acknowledged the Legation as the official representative of the defunct Republic of Lithuania. Most Western powers refused, at least officially, to recognize as a legitimate act the Soviet incorporation of Lithuania into its "Union." The Legation, however, was inundated with requests for passports, especially after the passage of the 1950 Displaced Person Act in Washington. Father and Mother's passport application had to wait its turn in line.

Once she had made up her mind to go, Mother resented any delay. She was forty-five; she fretted and fumed. "Who will want to hire me? Everywhere employers prefer young workers they can train more easily. Nobody wants someone my age! And what about Felicius? With his gray hair he looks like an old man!"

Finally, in early September 1951, my parents received an official "Lithuanian Republic" passport. It listed all three of us by name, and a month later, the American vice-consul in Liverpool stamped into it three visas, one for each of us, permitting us to immigrate. While he signed them, he told my father to make haste to book transportation— the medical documents were good for only a few months, and he would have to go through the whole rigmarole of tests and authorizations again if we did not leave by the end of January 1952.

My parents had no money for the trip. Letters flew back and forth to the U.S. seeking a loan. Mother's nephew, Vytas, was getting married that December and had no spare funds to help us, but he promised to borrow enough from his future wife's relatives to pay for the cheapest fares for us across the Atlantic.

Going by ship was our only option. Unfortunately, the demand for economy "third class" tickets was extremely high. By the time my parents consulted a travel agent to make arrangements, the earliest available date for inexpensive accommodations was in March. What now? I thought Mother would have a heart attack. We had been told to leave by the end of January!

The only places still available by the deadline were in the first or the cabin (second) class on the *Queen Mary*. The one-way crossing in cabin class cost over $200 for each person during this "thrifty" winter season (about $2,000 each in 2013 costs). More telegrams to Vytas. Bless his helpful soul: he came through for us despite his own pressing needs. We made the reservation to sail from Southampton on January 15, 1952.

I had such contradictory emotions about leaving England. I had adjusted completely; I had fine friends, both English and Lithuanian; there were many activities that made me happy. For example, in June 1951, Father and I enjoyed a week at a stimulating Lithuanian scout camp in the Lake Country. The nuns at Notre Dame High School, including Sister Mary, had come around to applauding my persistence and abilities. I knew my future in England as a "foreigner" would not be easy, but all that seemed a lifetime away: I was not yet fifteen.

What would I face in the U.S.? Another unfamiliar school system, though I was confident I could handle the work. I spoke the language and had learned how to ignore bullies. I was used to changes.

I knew, from listening to the adults, that United States was a land of immigrants where people judged you on your abilities, not on your lineage. It was, they said, the "land of opportunity." I persuaded myself to be optimistic. I tried to reason like a grown-up, but it was a painful wrench to leave my friends.

On the other hand, going to "America" was like winning the lottery—a badge of honor, a dream achieved. I would be in the land of the cowboys: eat your hearts out, classmates! And we, Father, Mother, and I, could eat our fill, because there was no food rationing to contend with! My head was full of exclamation points.

We did not have much to take with us: one trunk, and a couple of cheap suitcases. In England, since the early days of World War II, clothing had only been available for coupons, and few ordinary people owned more than three or four outfits. Nobody noticed if you wore the same clothes days in a row. I was especially poor in that department, having outgrown almost everything except my school uniform.

I insisted on bringing with me my little English doll and the few books I owned, including the beat-up ones acquired in the DP camp. Mother thought I had lost my mind. "Haven't you outgrown them?

They're old! Throw them out!" But Father approved. He understood nostalgia and my need to cling to the things that had given me joy. Let's face it: we were born pack rats, he and I.

When our train from Manchester arrived in London, there were Auntie Doris and Uncle Fred, Rita and her parents waiting to wish us "Bon Voyage." They helped us find the train to Southampton. All reticence and British reserve flew out the window as we all hugged. Rita and I cried and laughed and promised eternal friendship—which we kept.

And finally, in the early January nightfall, we boarded the enormous liner and were guided to our comfortable cabin. It was quite luxurious. There was a single bed for Father and bunk beds for Mother and me. The beds, chest of drawers, dressing table and chairs were of polished dark wood. The cabin came with our own small bathroom, which contained a shower. I had never experienced one, though I had seen them in some American films. I loved the feeling of warm water falling on my skin, like summer rain, only better.

That same night, January 15, we crossed the English Channel to Cherbourg to pick up more passengers. The swells were huge and the *Queen Mary* had no stabilizers; she pitched and heaved nauseatingly. We succumbed to seasickness. Mother, especially, was in misery. I summoned the steward for help. He had his own unorthodox treatment: chocolate and apples. I was soon cured, but the combination did not help Mother.

Once we were out of the English Channel and into the open Atlantic, the waters calmed down. By noon of the following day, Father and I were able to eat in the elegant, mirrored dining room. By dinnertime, Mother decided that no matter how she felt, she was not going to miss out on all that fancy food for which her nephew Vytas had paid a prince's ransom.

From Cherbourg, the crossing of the Atlantic took only four-and-a-half days. We had a marvelous time, even though we three stood out like the proverbial sore thumbs, wearing the same cheap clothing every day, without jewelry, ignorant of all the unwritten rules of "cabin class" snobbery.

Most of the passengers were well-dressed, affluent Americans, used to finer living and to demanding this-and-that from waiters and stewards at every turn. When we three timid refugees appeared in the gorgeously appointed dining room, I could sense people catching their breaths: *They must be lost! Send them back to third class!*

For the most part, our fellow passengers politely ignored us. Their attitude did not bother us: we had experienced many worse snubs during our flight from Lithuania. On the other hand, the waiters and stewards, whom we thanked for every little thing, treated us like royalty. They appreciated that we had no pretensions to superiority over them.

The interior design of the *Queen Mary* was so opulent, we felt as if we were in a floating castle. She had been refitted and redecorated after the war, during which she had served bravely as a crowded troop ship renamed *The Grey Ghost*. Each of us soon found a favorite spot on the ship for ourselves.

For Father, the quiet, seldom-used library and connecting reading room, with its comfortable couches, created a haven of relaxation. Glass-enclosed bookcases made of walnut burr lined the long side of the entrance. In a recessed corner of the reading room hung an oil painting representing "Our Lady of the Seas." It was usually concealed by sliding doors so as not to annoy the non-Catholics, but it was in view, softly lit, for the daily Mass.

Mother enjoyed sitting in a corner of the main lounge, leafing through magazines and studying the hairstyles and clothing of our elegant fellow passengers. The lounge had a Spanish themed décor featuring awnings, climbing roses and flower boxes. In the evenings, it served as a performance hall, but during the day, its comfortable chairs and tables attracted visitors who found it a cheerful place in which to play cards or just gossip and smoke.

I discovered the enclosed, cabin-class promenade deck that was not in use during this cold-season crossing. No deck chairs were set out, and nobody came to distract my reveries. I adopted it as my special place. It was comfortably warm in the afternoons because it faced south, and we had sun every day beaming in through the glass. Someone had exiled a wobbly table to the area, and it became my private throne.

I sat there for hours, swinging my legs and daydreaming. I reviewed my life, recalling the privations we had endured during the war, our struggles to escape the Red Dragon, the good and the bad of life in the DP camps. I remembered the kindness of strangers and the joys along the way. I smiled to myself about my fixation on dolls. *In America, I'll have a thousand if I want them*, I thought to myself. *Better yet, I'll buy a thousand for my daughter.* I was sure I would marry someday and have at least one daughter.

I wondered about America. I had so much to learn about my future home. Would it be easy or hard to make new friends? Were American high-school students really like those lively teenagers portrayed in Hollywood films? Would I see real cowboys? Were there swallows darting in the skies of America? Would we find, at long last, our own snug nest? *In time, of course we will*, I assured myself, filled with hope.

In the evenings, after dinner, the *Queen Mary* provided its passengers with entertainment. Usually, there was a variety show including dancers and comedians, and once a magician. The night before we were to arrive in New York, after a magnificent "Farewell Dinner," my parents and I experienced Bingo for the very first time.

The three of us, too timid to participate, sat in a back corner and watched, fascinated, as the Master of Ceremonies scooped up the cardboard markers with the numbers, placed them in a bag, and encouraged his assistant to "shake it up." The helper made a dramatic production of it, raising the bag over his head and swinging it around with gusto. Finally, the emcee chose a woman from among the passengers to reach in and pull out the markers, while the people in the audience called on Lady Luck to be their friend and shouted to the woman, "Pick my number!"

We had seldom seen a large group of people so excited, squealing and laughing with no thought of proper decorum. "They're conducting themselves like children," said Mother, unsure if she should approve, but Father was smiling ear-to-ear, and I thought, "*I'll be happy among these happy people.*"

Sunday, January 20, 1952, our journey was coming to an end. "Well, my Sunday Child," said Father to me, "isn't it fitting that our new life here begins on a Sunday?"

The morning had started with a fine mist. As the *Queen Mary* approached New York harbor, our first view was of the tops of skyscrapers, still far off, the rest of the city enveloped in a thin cloud. We three stood at the railing, watching the land of our future coming out to meet us. The mist was dissipating. Suddenly we heard many excited voices calling, "Look! Look, the Statue of Liberty!" And there she was indeed, still rather small and indistinct in the distance, her arm upraised holding—something.

Father grinned, raised his arm, and swung it about. "Shake it up!" he called out to Lady Liberty.

"And pick my number!" I joined in.

Afterword

Lady Luck did not hurry to pick our number. The first few months of life in the United States, living in Cicero, Illinois, were discouraging, but by the summer of 1952, we had found our home. We settled in Stamford, Connecticut, a fine New England town located on the coast facing the Long Island Sound. Father and Mother found jobs that suited them so well they kept them until they retired. Father transferred complicated blueprints to sheet metal, the first step in manufacturing heavy vehicle parts. Mother worked in the laboratory of Stamford Hospital, where she was responsible for sterilizing medical instruments.

My parents saved every penny they could, and within seven years they had their own cozy little house on a quiet cul-de-sac with many maple trees, which blazed brilliantly in the autumn. They lived there happily until retirement took them to Florida, where they enjoyed rewarding years of ease on the Gulf Coast in the company of other Lithuanians, all former "DPs," who often shared memories of the upheavals endured during the years long gone.

My sister Milda's marriage proved to be as unhappy as Father had feared. She left Petras when her little boy, Ray, was two. A few years later, she and the child immigrated to the United States and she obtained a divorce. Then Milda reconnected with Jonas Lietuvninkas, a young man who had been one of her admirers during our years in the DP camp in Blomberg. They married and settled in Darien, about five miles from our parents' home. Jonas adopted Ray, and they had a little girl, also called Milda. Their life was good. Both Ray and little Milda went to college, married, and raised families.

I loved studying. By age twenty-two, thanks to a Woodrow Wilson fellowship, I had a Master's degree in French Language and Literature. Like Father, I enjoyed teaching, first in high school in Connecticut, then in college in California.

In 1969, I finished the course work for a PhD in French literature, passed the exams, and planned out my doctoral thesis—just as all the public universities in the United States abolished their foreign language requirements for graduation. There was no hope of finding a teaching position. I felt bereft. But then I plunged into new studies and became a lawyer.

In 1970, I married Lew Brown. He already had four lovable children whom I quickly learned to cherish. We bought a small house barely a mile from the Mission of San Juan Capistrano and its legendary swallows. I was thrilled when some built their nests under our roof. Two years later we had a son, Algis.

In 1976, we settled in San Jose, California, acquired a comfortable home next to a nature preserve, and stayed there for twenty-six years. As a lawyer, I did not enjoy private practice, but hit my stride working at the Superior Court, supervising the Probate Court Investigations Unit. Our son grew up, finished college, went to teach English in Lithuania, married, had a son, earned a PhD, and stayed on the faculty of Vilnius University campus in Kaunas. Lew and I are waiting for his return to California.

When my father's health started to fail and Mother's hearing declined, they came to live with us in San Jose. Father died of cancer on his seventy-fifth birthday, but Mother stayed active until her death at age ninety-seven. Milda, like Father, died too young of cancer at seventy-five. As I write this, I am seventy-five myself—and try not to worry about every twinge and symptom.

Dolls. Lady Luck gave me a great son, but no daughter. However, I am still hoping for a granddaughter. Over the years, I have collected a legacy for her: a thousand small dolls from every corner of the world, dressed in their colorful native costumes. I hope she will like them.

Made in the USA
Middletown, DE
19 November 2014